INTEGRATING
HUMAN
SERVICE LAW
AND PRACTICE

INTEGRATING
HUMAN
SERVICE LAW
AND | PRACTICE

Rosemary Kennedy

*with **Jenny Richards***

OXFORD

UNIVERSITY PRESS

OXFORD
UNIVERSITY PRESS

253 Normanby Road, South Melbourne, Victoria 3205, Australia

Oxford University Press is a department of the University of Oxford. It furthers the University's objective of excellence in research, scholarship, and education by publishing worldwide in

Oxford New York

Auckland Bangkok Buenos Aires Cape Town Chennai Dar es Salaam Delhi Hong Kong Istanbul Karachi Kolkata Kuala Lumpur Madrid Melbourne Mexico City Mumbai Nairobi São Paulo Shanghai Taipei Tokyo Toronto

OXFORD is a trade mark of Oxford University Press in the UK and in certain other countries

National Library of Australia
Cataloguing-in-Publication data:

Kennedy, Rosemary.
Integrating human service law and practice.

Bibliography.
Includes index.
ISBN 0 19 551781 4.

1. Social legislation—Australia. 2. Public welfare—Law and legislation—Australia. 3. Human services personnel—Australia. I. Richards, Jenny, 1973-. II. Title

344.9403

Typeset by Cannon Typesetting
Printed by Bookpac Production Services, Singapore

Contents

Part I: Relationship between law and human services

Part III: Service delivery— diverse populations and jurisdictions

Figures and Table

Abbreviations

AASW	Australian Association of Social Workers
AAT	Administrative Appeals Tribunal
ADR	alternative dispute resolution
AIWCW	Australian Institute of Welfare and Community Workers
ARO	authorised review officer
ASIC	Australian Securities and Investments Commission
CV	curriculum vitae
HACC	Home and Community Care Program
HREOC	Human Rights and Equal Opportunity Commission
ICAC	Independent Commission Against Corruption
IPPs	Information Privacy Principles
NGO	non-government organisation
NPPs	National Privacy Principles
SAAP	Supported Accommodation Assistance Program
SSAT	Social Security Appeals Tribunal
UN	United Nations

Acknowledgments

We are indebted to colleagues and friends Judy Harvey, Sue King, Gordon Barrett QC, Di Gursansky, and Noel Twohig who made wise and helpful comments on various draft chapters of this book. Their ideas have enriched our thinking and their goodwill has nurtured our spirits. Of course this final product, inclusive of errors and opinions, is entirely our responsibility.

We must also pay tribute to each other. Our cooperative efforts have been mutually encouraging, satisfying, and productive. We believe that our collaboration has enhanced our respective abilities to integrate law and human service perspectives in our own practice and we hope that this book both reflects and demonstrates this integration.

Rosemary Kennedy
Jenny Richards

I am additionally grateful to my mentor Anne Selth, and Adam Richards, my brother and colleague in the law. Through their guidance and their personal and professional example, they have greatly shaped my approach to life and to integrated legal practice in particular; and by extension, my participation in this project also.

Jenny Richards

Part I

RELATIONSHIP
BETWEEN **LAW** AND
HUMAN SERVICES

1

Setting the Scene

Intentions

This book is about law and human service practice. It is not a law book as would be understood by lawyers, nor a human service intervention book. It is not a critical analysis of the law and it certainly does not offer legal advice. It does aim to interpret law to human service readers, to familiarise them with the legal landscape in which they operate, and to promote their 'legal literacy' (Stewart and Knott 2002, p. 9).

No attempt is made here to turn human service readers into pseudo lawyers but they are encouraged to become superior human service practitioners. Such practitioners have, among other things, an appreciation of the architecture of the law, and the ways in which it does and does not constrain and shape human service activity. They may not be able to name a piece of legislation from memory, or cite a particular section of an Act, or know how a particular case has established a legal principle, or perform proficiently as an expert witness. However, they will have a better than average knowledge of the types of legislation that impact on their fields of practice, of relevant jurisdictional issues, and of the outline of pertinent common law. They will be familiar with the structures and personnel through which justice is administered in their jurisdictions. They will be confident enough to engage with the legal system and in partnerships with lawyers and other justice personnel as needed. They will have knowledge of courts and basic skills as a witness. If some of them become, as they will, extremely conversant with specific Acts and questions of justice administration, or adroit expert witnesses, these are bonuses, rather than universal expectations.

While there is diversity in the legal knowledge and expertise of effective human service workers, all require basic competence in the following areas (adapted from Albert 2000, p. 340); these are elaborated throughout this book:

- identifying and assessing the legal rights of clients and referring them appropriately
- identifying and assessing the legal dimensions of all human service work situations
- looking for and finding human service related law
- accessing legal resources
- interacting confidently and collaboratively with legal structures and justice personnel
- writing court reports and knowing what is involved in testifying in court
- educating lawyers and other justice personnel about human service work, its aims, values, and mandates
- influencing social policy which underpins, explains, implements, or complements law
- lobbying for changes in law.

Audience

This book is targeted at mid- to later-stage human service students and to human service practitioners in Australia. It attempts to speak directly to those who are working or about to work in the field. For those students who have limited practical knowledge and/or experience of the human services and perhaps even for experienced people, the material in the book is potentially dense and daunting. The law is not simple—nor is human service work—and the interaction between the two is complex. But with some patience and an open mind this complexity is navigable, even exciting. The authors hope that the practice questions and answers throughout the book will engage readers by putting flesh simultaneously on both human service work and on the related law. However it is unlikely that any reader, experienced or otherwise, will find this book fully digestible in one go. It is potentially of most use when dipped into, re-read, and consulted as and when personal and professional practical questions arise. Teachers of human service law subjects have in this book a text and a reference that addresses their students directly. Teachers thus have a base from which to extend and shape their conversation with their students on the relationship between the law and human service practice.

So what and who are the human services? The human services, sometimes also known as the community services, can be defined as both profit and non-profit 'social services designed to meet human needs that are required for maintaining or promoting the overall quality of life of the prospective service populations' (Zins 2001, p. 7). There are debates about the scope of the human services but commonly encompassed are juvenile and adult corrections, child and family welfare, social services, mental health services, disability services, rehabilitation services, community health, and general crisis services. Not surprisingly, the miscellany here is represented by an almost infinite array of job titles, which depending on how one defines things, include generic and target group descriptors, and occupational and professional designations (Kennedy and Harvey 2001). For example, generic titles include project, support, community, outreach, liaison, residential care, and welfare workers to name only a few. There are also youth, aged, family, child, domestic violence, and refugee workers. Additionally there are the more familiar human service titles like counsellor, case manager, rehabilitation counsellor, psychologist, and social worker. It is hoped that this book will speak directly to all of these workers, students in related courses, and to any others in the fields of practice listed above.

The inclusive approach taken here is justified by the changing nature of the human service work world. Competition in the labour market has opened up new positions with wider eligibility criteria, private rather than state employers are increasingly prominent, and 'permeable professional boundaries' prevail (O'Connor, Smyth et al. 2000, p. 8). For better or worse, increasingly volunteers, non-university qualified, and diversely qualified people are taking up jobs based on competency rather than qualifications (O'Connor, Smyth et al. 2000; Shapiro 2000; Kennedy and Harvey 2001). Simultaneously, new Technical and Further Education (TAFE) and university human service courses are being developed to attract and graduate students for this wider market (Kennedy and Harvey 2001).

The big debates about professional territory, expertise, and consumer protection provoked by these changes are tangential to this book. The book recognises that education, work, and service delivery boundaries are spongy and it addresses the whole sector because the law has similar application across most human service work and all professional and occupational groups. So the inclusive approach is pragmatic but it is accompanied by two particular aspirations. It is hoped that this book *does* connect with practitioners regardless of their formal or higher level professional education backgrounds. Practitioners need all the professional development assistance that they can get and yet those with limited formal training are often invisible in professional writing, conferencing, and other discourses. At the same time it is hoped that the book *does not* disaffect practitioners and students in the professions (social work in particular) who are struggling to forge a more robust separate identity in the contemporary human services. Social work has an all-pervasive presence in this book and social work readers will find many places where social work leadership is evident, called for, or possible. The human services provide social workers with a very big stage on which to perform and it is hoped that the inclusive approach taken in this book might remind them of the potential for their profession on that stage.

In summary the book is geared to a wide spectrum of readers, all with an interest in the human services, but there are two caveats. First, the position of psychology is different from that of the other occupational and/or professional groups mentioned above. It has a more homogeneous theoretical underpinning, recognition as a discipline, arguably a more identifiable public profile, and as will be explained in chapter 4, it is a registered profession in Australia. It also tends, like most professions, to be insular. For all these reasons psychologists may find this book insufficiently attentive to their internal professional preoccupations and it does not pretend to address them specifically. However psychology too is affected by the workforce changes just outlined (Franklin, Gibson et al. 1996; King, Yellowlees et al. 2002) and most of the law addressed herein is also applicable to psychologists in practice. In fact, as will be seen, many of the references used in the book are from psychology. Second, while the book is not pitched at lawyers or other justice workers, those whose work intersects with the human services may find it instructive, if only to help interpret their experiences of an unfamiliar world and its ethos.

Genesis

There are three things to declare about the origins of this book and its underpinnings. First, it has grown out of the authors' years of independent and joint tertiary teaching in law subjects in social work, human service, and rehabilitation courses. The first author has also been teaching in counselling, psychology, and case management courses, in many human service practice and service delivery subjects and in work-based training for human service agencies. The second author also has significant experience teaching various subjects in law schools. There are echoes of human service student questions, concerns, and views from many of these courses throughout the book. The authors' joint human service teaching has always been accompanied by an unsatisfactory search for an integrated, inclusive, contemporary, comprehensive, and Australian textbook that focuses on workers as much as on fields of practice and client concerns. There is some excellent material available, but at any time for the authors' needs it has been out of date, jurisdictionally limited, too elementary, too legal, too profession specific, too issue specific, not applied to human service practice, or lacking a unifying theme. So this project has come about.

The second declaration is that the authors both have qualifications in law, and the first author also in clinical psychology. Both have worked a little in legal practice, a lot in universities, and quite extensively and diversely as volunteers and consultants in the human services. The first author has also worked as a psychologist, human service manager, and investigator. This hybrid experience and background will reveal itself throughout the book and a reticence about singular professional allegiances may have already been noted. More will be said about this very shortly.

The third declaration follows from the first two. This book attempts to integrate and build on what is already available in a number of areas. Previous human service or social work law books from Australia, the United Kingdom and the USA are drawn on frequently throughout this one. But social work, generic human service, case management, and psychology professional and practice literature will also be much in evidence. Australian law texts and a wider range of legal articles appear regularly too.

Terminology

A few points about the use of language are necessary. There is the term 'human service worker'. Given the explanations above, this is the inclusive label used when workers across the human services are being referred to. At times a specific occupational or professional designation, particularly 'social work', will be used. This is because that particular group is being discussed, and/or because the sources cited are referring to it. Generally, others' commentaries about social work and other human service subgroups are herein assumed to have applicability throughout the human services, unless qualified by the primary or the current authors.

'The law' is referred to frequently throughout the book. When used as an umbrella term signifying the 'other' from a human service perspective, it includes substantive law, the legal system, and lawyers. Sometimes it denotes substantive common law and/or legislation. Whenever the term is used it is hoped that its meaning is made clear by the contextual discussion.

The word 'agency' is used to describe the organisations that employ workers and deliver human services. However 'agent' and 'agency' have particular legal meanings concerned with the power to act on behalf of others. Workers in fact will often be legal 'agents' for their agencies. If the legal meaning of the term is being intended, this will be made clear in the text; otherwise, it is used in the human service sense.

Last, the vexed term 'client' must be mentioned. There are many debates about which terms are appropriate to describe users of services. 'Service users', 'consumers', and now 'customers' are sometimes referred to. In that part of the human services which overlaps with health, the word 'patient' may be used, and in the education sphere, 'student' is the norm. The term client is used here without any significant judgment about its merit, because it is in relatively common usage in both law and the human services. In the contemporary human services characterised by privatisation and contractualism, organisations procuring services or being serviced are also referred to as clients. So for instance the agency commissioning a policy paper from a consultant or the court requesting a bail report can be seen as clients. However, for the purposes of this book, the word client will generally refer to human service users unless it is otherwise stated.

Assumptions about legal knowledge

It will be assumed that readers have, through general knowledge and/or their introductory studies, a basic understanding of the political and legal institutions of Australia, including the structure of the Federation and its component jurisdictions, and the hierarchy of Australian courts. A basic understanding of how both federal, and state and territory parliaments make laws, the place of bills and delegated legislation, and how courts interpret law, will also be assumed, as will the differences and interaction between common law and legislation and between private and public law.

A legal dictionary is always a useful thing to have on hand, as unfamiliar legal words can be checked as they appear while reading, or at work. If this checking process is entrenched in human service practice it becomes a simple but powerful form of professional development. Some readers may have legal studies texts that will be useful complements to this book. Others may refer to accessible introductory texts such as Carvan's *Understanding the Australian Legal System* (2002) and *Laying Down the Law* by Cook and Creyke et al. (2001).

In all jurisdictions there are legal aid bodies and community legal centres with public education mandates, which provide legal advice and comprehensive educative material. In most jurisdictions, a law handbook is produced regularly. These are all essential legal resources for workers seeking to expand their general legal knowledge and to service and refer clients. Web sites for some of these main legal services and for law information are provided at the end of this chapter. Appendix I of this book also provides some very basic assistance in accessing and reading a piece of legislation and a legal case. It is not intended to replace the resources mentioned above. Rather it is offered as an immediate refresher for those who have some experience with the law and human service practice and as an encouraging prompt for those who do not.

The law is a work in progress. It is always changing, generally slowly and sometimes rapidly. During the writing of this book there were quite dramatic changes afoot or mooted in many relevant areas of law, for example in industrial relations, child protection, family law, privacy, and negligence. It should not be a problem if legislation mentioned hereafter is amended, or repealed, or if significant new High Court judgments appear. The nature of the beast is that these things will happen. What this book hopes to do is familiarise readers with the origins and shape of law relevant to the human services so that they know what sorts of things to look for and where, when they need accurate, current information about the law. As the scope of the book is wide and the intended audience and its jurisdictional interests diverse, all relevant legislation or common law on any matter is never fully cited. The result would be encyclopaedic and it has already been said that attempts to produce accurate and comprehensive records may be out of date as soon as they are written. So examples of specific law from different jurisdictions are selected to illustrate the varied and similar ways in which law approaches and responds to professional work and social problems.

One final point on the law concerns the few human service precedent cases in Australia. Thus it is necessary to extrapolate, often cautiously, from cases, for example in education or psychotherapy or medicine. There are two corollaries to this. The first is that some legal details about human service practice will remain uncertain until courts clarify them in future cases. The second is that the dearth of cases does not mean that there is no legal risk to human service agencies and workers. Legal cases are waiting to happen, and it is an aim of this book to reduce the likelihood of them happening to, or impacting too negatively on, readers.

Structure and approach

The book is divided into three Parts. The first conceptualises the relationship between law and human services. The second covers the general legal obligations, rights, duties, and regulation of human service workers. The third considers a number of areas of substantive law relevant to service delivery with different populations and jurisdictions. However the three Parts are not discrete. The general rights and duties of workers are elaborated on and qualified by the matters raised in relation to specific service delivery areas in Part III. There are echoes and illustrations of the Part I material throughout the other two Parts. There is an almost infinite array of substantive law topics that are relevant to human service delivery, but only some of the more general and common ones are covered here in Part III. Again it is believed that workers who are generally conversant with the law and its place in their work, will be able themselves to pursue other law pertinent to particular jobs and fields of practice. In the first and second Parts there is an attempt to address topics in reasonable depth because they are not commonly fully explored elsewhere. Conversely, Part III is characterised instead by breadth, partly because the areas are large and partly because many of them are canvassed very well elsewhere.

Practice questions and responses appear in each chapter where it is expected that a point may require clarification, or provoke disputation. These questions attempt to second-guess some of the thoughts that could be going through a reader's head and to encourage engagement with the material presented. As explained earlier many of these questions come from student and worker reactions during the authors' education and training experiences. Readers will no doubt have additional questions. These may be explored in the classroom, in professional development sessions through work, or perhaps through private research. This book may provide the answers to these additional questions or at least suggest where answers might be sought.

The groupings of material in chapters and chapter headings have meanings in their own right. The intention in these groupings is to demonstrate the multiplicity of legal factors that bear upon practice, along with patterns and themes, and to challenge segmented thinking about both law and practice. There are efforts made in many chapters to entice human service workers into the world of law through practice scenarios and examples. Each chapter concludes with a collection of key practice points that attempt to encapsulate the practice implications of the material and ideas just covered. The web sites at the end of chapters include some pertinent and authoritative legal and related sources for additional information.

Positions and themes

While the authors are wary of pigeonholing themselves professionally, they are neither detached from nor cynical about professional work in general. A call for improved 'professional' practice in the human services reverberates throughout this book. This practice is informed, objective, disciplined, competent, open-minded, and always with client interests uppermost, regardless of worker qualifications or identification as a member of a particular profession or occupation. Moreover, workers who function 'professionally' consciously exercise discretion, and decision-making is one of the organising themes of the book.

A number of other positions or themes will be evident. Given the aims of this book, the law is presented relatively normatively. This does not deny the importance of a critical analysis of law. For a start, the fact that the law described herein reflects almost nothing of the wisdom of Indigenous customary laws and cultures raises a fundamental question. However, these critiques are for other places. At various points in this book, where potentially contentious material is raised, other sources that critique a legal approach or the law in question are cited for follow-up. And often at these points, a warning about the difference between an emotional reaction to the law and an objective assessment of it will appear. All too commonly human service students and workers react very negatively to the character and operation of legal systems and the law. Their objections may be well founded but unless they are able to translate these into informed and strategic responses they are likely to lack credibility and to waste energy. So a plea for understanding fully, thinking carefully, and acting strategically, becomes a motif of the book.

Despite the limitations of the law and the legal system, both can actually be very powerful in sanctioning and supporting effective human service practice. Throughout the book, the potential for positive interaction between legal imperatives and quality practice will be reiterated. There is a last but critical point—while the law and the human services are recognised as different on many counts all through this book neither realm is accorded priority here. Each system is flawed and there are better and worse practitioners and practices in both realms. It is argued that capable human service workers can and should be equal partners and contributors in their necessary interactions with lawyers and the legal system.

Some useful web sites

Legal aid and community legal centres

www.lawlink.nsw.gov.au/lac.nsf/pages/index
www.lawlink.nsw.gov.au/
www.legalaid.tas.gov.au
www.legalaid.canberra.net.au/
www.legalaid.qld.gov.au/
www.legalaid.vic.gov.au
www.lsc.sa.gov.au/
www.legalaid.wa.gov.au
www.nt.gov.au/ntlac
www.austlii.edu.au/au/other/clc/
www.austlii.edu.au/au/other/clc/clc_tocs.html

Other general law information links

www.aph.gov.au/library/intguide/law/welfarelaw.htm#links
www.lexscripta.com/legal/authorities/legalaid.html
www.law4u.com.au/
www.lawstuff.org.au/

Case law and legislation

www.austlii.edu.au/
www.scaleplus.law.gov.au

Some Indigenous law links

www.worldlii.org/catalog/2540.html
www.nwjc.org.au/atisla.html
www.geocities.com/Athens/Acropolis/7001/alrm.htm
www.naalas.org.au/
www.anao.gov.au/WebSite.nsf/0/ea1872d915d751b6ca256dd70004e737?OpenD
ocument&Click=

2

Law and Human Service Nexus

Client problems and beyond

It is readily accepted that human service workers come into contact with the law through the lives of clients. Workers may experience criminal law, discrimination law, social security law, or child protection law for instance, with and through their clients. Certainly many human service clients have significant legal problems, but this is only a part of the landscape of the relationship between law and human services. To begin with, much human service work does not involve direct contact with clients. For example, in policy, project, research, administrative, consultancy, and management jobs, workers may not be directly servicing clients. Thus it is reasonable to think of human service work as a direct and indirect service continuum. On this continuum, identifiable human clients are serviced at the direct service end, while at the indirect service end the focus is more on service policy, organisations, and systems. Of course many human service roles involve a mixture of these things and thus fall around the centre of the continuum. However, law is relevant, with varying degrees of visibility, along the continuum.

Preston-Shoot and his colleagues (1998a; 1998b) propose yet another continuum in their explanation of the interface between law and social work practice. At one end of their continuum legal language, procedures, and culture dominate, while at the other end, social work understandings and interventions prevail. In the middle, a mixture of legal and social work analyses and processes apply. This continuum also highlights the pervasive presence of law in social work, and it is argued here in all human service practice, even though the balance between the legal and human service ethos shifts from job to job and function to function.

When the service continuum and the law/social work continuum are linked orthogonally as in figure 2.1, the presence of law, to greater or lesser degrees, in all types of human service work can be demonstrated. A number of fictional human service jobs are placed in the figure to illustrate this. Their positioning relative to the axes and each other may be arguable, depending on the criteria used to assess ethos and the directness or otherwise of service delivery. The specific location of each job is not so much the point as is the significance of law, across the spectrum of human service work.

So, for example, in the upper area of the law/direct service quadrant, child protection and probation jobs could be situated. Individual clients are being processed here within apparent legal parameters. Human service language and understandings will be significant in this work but the ethos of law might prevail through extensive statutory regulation and court scrutiny of work. In the lower and more legal part of this quadrant, the vocational rehabilitation claims assessor could attend in part to specific injured workers. However, their work might be characterised by a business and legal perspective through its location in an insurance and workers compensation system.

In the outer part of the law/indirect service quadrant may be a member of a tribunal or a director of a company. In these, activity will be dominated by legal language, culture, and constraints even if carried out by human service workers. In contrast the drug policy officer may be relatively removed from direct service delivery to clients and engaged in drafting legislation. This work may be done by a lawyer but within a professional context which is attuned to human service needs and interests; thus it retreats from the legal end of the continuum. The employment consultant may be a human service worker, but the job may require the development of business networks within a heavily legislated and contractualised private employment market. Thus the language of law and legal interests might prevail in it.

In the outer part of the human service/direct service quadrant might be a counsellor whose experience is almost entirely comprised of relatively unregulated human service intervention through relationship development with clients. The community house coordinator may have a strong community development orientation and do some direct work with community members. But they also have legal responsibilities to house staff, to service users, and for financial accountability. Thus this job is placed on the human services side of the continuum but moving towards the law end. The aged care worker in this quadrant may attend mostly to individual clients but within a legally permeated context because of adult guardianship and nursing home accreditation issues.

In the extreme outer part of the human service/indirect service work quadrant might be a training consultant who develops policy and training packages, for instance, on group work skills. This job may be removed from immediate clients and it might be carried out in an entirely human service milieu. The housing project officer on the other hand may have closer connections to direct service delivery and their work may also be more pervaded by a legal world view, say through the project's concern with residential tenancy legislation.

The legal centre officer is placed at the centre of the human service/law continuum because the work may be carried out in an agency environment that reflects the mixed ethos referred to by Preston-Shoot and his colleagues (1998a; 1998b). This worker is also placed at the centre of the direct/indirect service continuum because the job may involve a mixture of case and research work.

Figure 2.1 The relationship between law and human service work

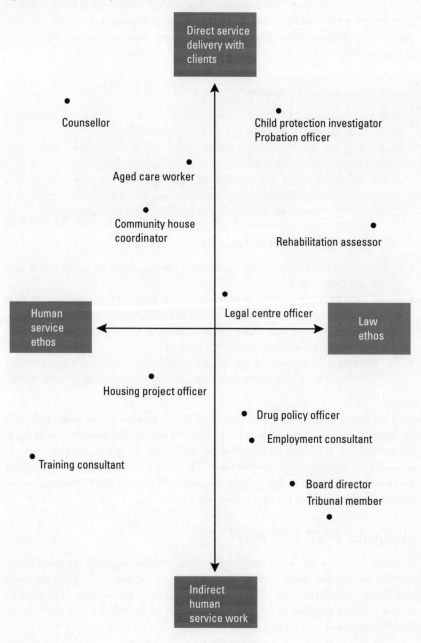

For most human service agencies and workers, different jobs and tasks at different times will move them up and down the continuums and between quadrants. For example, the counsellor may also be on the board of a counselling training and consultancy company. The vocational rehabilitation claims assessor may also do some private counselling. When the aged care worker makes guardianship applications before a tribunal they may adopt a quasi-legal approach in their work. The education consultant may assume a slightly more legal orientation when they develop packages on the chairing of meetings, for instance.

Practice question and response

Question: I am already a bit overwhelmed and I do not follow the positions of some of the jobs in this figure. How can I move on?

Response: At various points in the book questions such as this will be posed and attempts made to help progress in reading. In relation to figure 2.1 you might find it interesting to come up with your own jobs and their positions relative to the axes. The main point of this personalised exercise and of the figure in general is to demonstrate that the law has a place throughout human service work even though that place may not always be obvious.

Three points are drawn from figure 2.1:

- Law is not just a matter of client difficulties. The law impacts on human service work beyond direct service concerns.
- In many areas of human service work, for example those in the right-hand quadrants, a legal ethos is evident, and it is accepted to greater or lesser degrees that law is integral to the work. However in other areas of human service endeavour where a legal ethos does not exist, the law is no less significant to the work.
- While figure 2.1 declares the importance and variable visibility of law in human service work it reveals nothing about the nature and quality of the relationships between the two realms.

This chapter explores the significance of law in human service work, addresses the character of the relationship between the two arenas, and promotes an integrative perspective in human service thinking. However, the law and human services do not come together naturally and easily. There are profound differences between the two, discussed later in this chapter, which must be appreciated before genuinely integrative thinking and practice is possible.

Integrate what and why?

So what is meant by integration? Integration implies weaving separate things together so that the result is more than the sum of the parts. The position taken here is that the effectiveness of human services agencies and workers is dependent on the knitting together of legal and human service knowledge and skills into a seamless approach to service delivery.

This integration requires more than the superimposition of legal information on human service activity. It implies more than mere interaction with the law (Preston-Shoot, Roberts et al. 1998a). It involves changing the form of human service thinking, decision-making, and practice and 'requires the capacity to conceptualise legal and social systems and their inter-relationships' (Breckenridge 2002, p. 84). This is not to promote legalism, nor to imply that human service practitioners should become pseudo lawyers. Rather it posits that they should consciously locate and analyse their practice within interacting layers of contextual and often contradictory factors, inclusive of legal ones. In addition, it demands that they welcome new learning from law so as to extend the repertoire and sophistication of their thinking, actions, and influence across their practice.

Why is integration important to effective service delivery? Three reasons are outlined here and then explored more fully.

- First, the issues and problems faced by agencies, workers, and their clients are characterised by social, legal, psychological, organisational, service delivery, and other elements that are fused. Uni-dimensional appreciation of and responses to these problems are dangerously incomplete. Integrated problems demand integrated responses.
- Second, legal and human services increasingly intersect and overlap. Workers who have embraced legal perspectives in their thinking will be more competitive and functional in these new work and service environments. That is, the central area representing a mixed law/social work ethos in figure 2.1 is expanding.
- Third, there is much that the human services can learn from law, quite apart from substantive law, which it can use to strengthen its own procedures and practices generally, and its impact in the legal system more specifically.

Human service client, worker, and agency concerns

Clients

It has been acknowledged that many human service clients have legal problems. For example a prisoner, a juvenile offender, and an incarcerated mental health patient may only have human service client 'status' as a result of legal action. Other clients may also have quite evident legal issues in the entangled set of circumstances that brings them into the human service sphere. Workers who have a good understanding of legal issues will, with their clients, make assessments and develop service plans more complete and substantive than they would otherwise be. For example:

- Imagine the family in which there is substance abuse, neglect of children, and domestic violence. The family support worker here will be assessing needs, and developing and monitoring service plans that have legal, medical, and human service components. For instance, on the domestic violence question, they may be referring a parent to community legal and medical centres, advocating for immediate police and legal assistance, briefing and influencing a lawyer, counselling both parents, collaborating with a children's worker, and supporting a parent seeking a restraining order. The legal and other parts of this work are indivisible. The worker is not giving legal advice but ensuring that it is available, and just as importantly, that it is given in accordance with family member needs. A worker who is intimidated by or ignorant of the relevant law and legal processes will be offering a truncated service to this family.

- Imagine the culturally divided rural community in which youth offending is prevalent and some business and community leaders are demanding more severe police and court responses. Others are claiming that unemployment, discrimination, and police harassment of young people are to blame. The community workers here may be mediating community conflict, promoting mutual understanding, developing youth programs, and collaborating with and advocating in youth court and police services. They are not lawyers, but to function well they must weave knowledge about discrimination law and the juvenile justice system, at least, into their practice analyses and responses. Their influence and impact will be diminished if they cannot engage with others confidently and above all, correctly, on questions of legal rights and procedures. This legal expertise, then, is an integral part of their general human service expertise.

Other clients present with difficulties in which legal possibilities are less obvious. For example:

- Imagine the client with an intellectual disability who cannot manage interpersonal relationships at work, who gets into fights, who loses jobs, and who then self-harms. Here human service workers may be thinking about interpersonal skills training, and/or job preparation and anger management programs, and/or additional job supports, and/or different medication. But perhaps workplace discrimination and/or unfair dismissal are also involved, in which case legal options can be incorporated into the package of human service response strategies.
- Imagine the frail aged person with incipient dementia, who lives alone, resists any form of alternative accommodation, and refuses essential medication. There is some obvious human service work to be done here around risk assessment, and exploration of client and family resources and preferences. But there is a possible set of legal questions that are part of both a full understanding of and response to the situation. For example, should legal substitute decision-making procedures be activated? What licensing or other quality assurance regimes apply in relevant alternative accommodation? There may also be financial and asset considerations under aged care, banking, administration, and perhaps social security law.

Workers

The experiences of human service workers, inclusive of and beyond client concerns, are similarly imbued with legal possibilities, both obvious and not so obvious. Workers themselves may be injured at work, sacked, not promoted, impugned by colleagues, or make mistakes; they may be members of professional and other bodies, they may be self-employed and/or self-insured, they may chair meetings and enter contracts with others; they will handle sensitive information; they may work in tribunals and courts and they may develop policy and draft legislation. In all these and many other matters, legal and human service elements are entwined.

The competent human service worker is attuned to the personal and professional legal risks and potential in all work experiences, and knows the source, authority, and full scope of their duties and powers. For example:

- Imagine the human service worker held to be ineligible for a job. On the face of it this is a simple personal disappointment. But who set the eligibility criteria, what is their status, and how were they promulgated and applied? There are legal elements to each of these questions and while a legal quest may not solve this particular situation it may help clarify it and reduce the chance of repeat upsets.

- Imagine the human service worker who as a result of family pressures forgets to warn a colleague about a client suicide threat. There are matters of supervision, teamwork, and agency procedure here but there are also connected legal questions. Could the client's family sue and if so, whom? Could the worker be dismissed? How can the tangle of risks and obligations be unpicked?

- Imagine the worker who establishes an influential advocacy group. What risks might this achievement incur? Is the worker personally liable for group debts? How can the continuity of the group be ensured? The answers lie in strategic planning combining political, legal, and interpersonal factors.

Agencies

Human service agencies similarly function within a context of interconnected imperatives. They are employers; they have a range of legal duties to their workers, service users, and funders; they have contractual obligations and rights; they have liabilities; they may have accreditation and/or licensing requirements; they are accountable in various ways to various bodies and the community; the list is endless. For example:

- Imagine the unit that runs foster care and family support programs. It seeks to service families well, but may be preoccupied with ensuring its continued government funding, with staff selection, supervision and appraisal processes, with fundraising, and with its relationship with its host organisation. Legal dimensions loom large in all of these preoccupations. Balancing administrative and service delivery activities so that legal obligations in both areas are met is not easy.

- Imagine the agency that supports minors caring for parents with substance abuse problems. It may share the concerns of the foster care agency. It also faces questions about reporting possible child abuse and neglect and drug-related offences. What does the law require of it and how will it develop helpful human service support processes while also accommodating legal imperatives?

- Imagine the agency in which a worker who was assaulted at work some time ago is now making mistakes and requiring both support and patience from clients and co-workers. The agency may be concerned about the state of this worker and keen to promote their recovery. But it faces issues of public accountability and it also has legal responsibilities to clients and other workers. What are these competing imperatives, which are legal, and how might they be balanced?

Intersection and overlap

Commonalities of interests

The human services and the law have always had interests and ideals in common even though they may function in parallel, or even antagonistically. At a number of levels, they are both concerned with rights and advocacy, even though they may not mean quite the same things (Preston-Shoot, Roberts et al. 1998b). Human service workers and lawyers both commonly 'function in the context of individual cases' (Staller and Kirk 1998, p. 93), even though the human service role in relation to clients may be characterised by greater ambiguity and a 'multiplicity of account-ability' compared with that of a private practice lawyer (Preston-Shoot, Roberts et al. 1998b, p. 145). It is not uncommon to see lawyers taking on what might be seen as human service work with clients. For example, legal aid solicitors in local courts may organise emergency accommodation before they apply for bail for clients. Or they may seek community support resources for asylum seekers released from detention centres. Similarly, human service workers often interact closely with the law. For instance, some workers accompany young people being questioned by the police and while not lawyers, they may be very adept at monitoring the legal rights of their clients in these situations. Clients can be cross-referred. For example, drug rehabilitation and legal aid workers in a region may have formed a relationship where they refer clients to the others' services for legal advice on the one side and say, health advice on the other.

Both human service and legal workers interpret and apply law in their work. See how the Legal Policy Officer job in figure 2.2 places a lawyer in a team of people ensuring that supported residential facilities for people with mental health and other disabilities are complying with the Victorian regulatory regime. Here a lawyer is entering the heart of traditional human service territory, in the interests of the rights of disadvantaged residents to have safe and reasonable quality accom-modation. In some fields, human service and legal workers may both contribute to the drafting and amending of laws in the interests of those whose legal rights or protections are inadequate. Their expertise, methods, and roles may differ, but their aspirations may be similar.

Human service workers and lawyers do sometimes actively cooperate on projects of mutual interest. For example a number of Australian refugee advocacy groups concurrently mount legal challenges and seek social services through the combined work of legal and human service workers. Even in the absence of immediate shared interests, workers can, and some do, see the rich potential in each other's expertise. Enterprising human service workers cultivate resources and contacts, including legal ones, wherever possible. They nurture mutually beneficial relationships with lawyers and others in the legal system such as court sheriffs and police prosecutors, so as to smooth work pathways and extend their own productive capacity. They see legal connections as part of their total stock of resources, not optional extras. Alliances and networks of these kinds are more likely to flourish where the human service workers, at least, understand that law is integral to their work, and are attuned and open to legal possibilities in situations.

Practice question and response

Question: Isn't it false to try and develop a friendship with someone just because they happen to be a lawyer?
Response: Yes, it probably is, and that is not what is being proposed here. Rather it is suggested that human service workers become alert to and develop professional legal contacts in the same way that they nurture good relationships with any other staff and services who can contribute to their work effectiveness.

New developments and possibilities

There are now emerging in the legal and human services, interdisciplinary approaches such as therapeutic jurisprudence which attends to the impact of legal activity on emotional and psychological well-being (Wexler and Winick 1996; Winick 2003; Winick and Wexler 2003). Therapeutic jurisprudence can found changes in justice and court systems so that they are psychologically constructive for the participants as well as serving the social imperatives of law, and it is being applied in some Australian court pilot programs (King 2003). Similarly, there is an increasing range of policies and programs that blur traditional boundaries or at least stipulate joint action between legal and other services. Two major examples of this merging are new court systems, and ways of resolving disputes beyond the traditional legal adversarial approach. In both of these developments, which reappear in chapter 7, the legal system has been opened up to what might be called the human dimensions of legal problems and sometimes to human service interventions and practitioners.

Alternative dispute resolution (ADR) approaches such as negotiation, mediation, conciliation, facilitation, and arbitration have been incorporated into a number of court systems. For instance mediation, now central in Family Court activity, may be done by lawyers and/or human service workers. In other changes to the administration of justice, diversionary programs attempt to both keep people out of formal court processes while attending to their particular life circumstances, and special courts integrate more flexible legal, and therapeutic or social interventions and sanctions. Family or group conferencing is now a common feature in juvenile justice systems (Alder and Wundersitz 1994; Daly and Hayes 2001), and special drug, domestic violence, and Indigenous courts are also on the increase.

These new developments can be controversial. For example doubts are voiced about mediation in the Family Court (e.g. Alexander 1999) and family conferencing (e.g. Blagg 1997; Daly and Hayes 2001). Moreover the associated integrated team approach is often fraught, as Cull and Roche, for example, show in relation to family conferencing in the United Kingdom (2001), and Freiberg says of Australian drug court teamwork (2002). However these developments are a fact of life and in some universities they are reflected in new double degree programs in law and social work. These developments offer employment possibilities for both legal and human service workers, and they do provide opportunities for the latter to directly enter and influence the world of law. For the ACT Court Manager job advertisement in figure 2.2, social workers, psychologists, and lawyers are eligible. The Queensland social worker position illustrates employment possibilities for social workers in the heart of legal aid and Family Court territory. Competitive and credible human service applicants for these jobs will no doubt be legally literate and personify integrated thinking and practice.

Figure 2.2 Law and human services job intersections

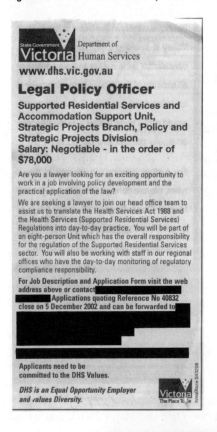

Manager Court and Facilitation Services
Senior Professional Officer Grade B
$67,576 - $76,073
Position Number: 11297

Seeking an experienced manager to lead the court unit, family group conferencing and the assessment unit. The successful applicant will be a highly respected professional with high level skills in interpreting legislation, developing policy and practice guidelines and assisting regional staff in high quality child protection practice. They will be a key member of the Child Protection Management Team and participate in other senior management forums.

The successful applicant will have a tertiary qualification that makes them eligible for membership of the Australian Association of Social Workers; or full registration with the ACT Psychology Registration Board or other state equivalent; or law with eligibility to be admitted as a legal practitioner in the ACT.

SOCIAL WORKER

Salary: $57,245 to $61,672 per annum
Attractive Salary Packaging arrangements
Vacancy Number: 03/03

Applications are sought for a Social Worker in the Family Law Team in the Brisbane office of Legal Aid Queensland. Job share arrangements will be considered.

Major duties include:
* Prepare complex court reports of use in the Family Court, child protection and criminal jurisdictions.
* Chair Family Law Mediation Conferences.
* Liaison and consultation on case management matters with lawyers.

Applications must address the selection criteria which are contained within the Position Description obtained by accessing our site www.legalaid.qld.gov.au/about_us/pd

Please quote the Vacancy No of the position you are interested in.

Applications close on Monday, 3 February 2003 and should be marked "Confidential" and addressed to the Human Resources Manager,

Legal Aid
QUEENSLAND

We encourage EEO target group members, particularly Aboriginal & Torres Strait Islander people, to apply.

Learning from and utilising a legal orientation

The third reason for seeing law as an integral component of human service practice is, like the second one, largely utilitarian. There are a number of things that can be appropriated from the law to significantly improve the quality of human service practice.

Proper process and procedure

Preoccupation with proper process and procedure is a fundamental feature of the law. This is particularly reflected in administrative law, an area most relevant to the human services. Administrative law's 'role is [in] redressing power imbalances between the citizen and the state' (Downey 2001, p. 28).

Human service workers are not as alert to the significance of formal processes and procedures in decision-making as they might be, and are commonly confused or frustrated by what they see as unnecessary attention to detail. For example:

- A client may have been refused further service by a human service agency on solid grounds, so why does it really matter how this decision was made or how the client was informed about it?
- A community development worker may be angry when the local authority refuses permission for an exciting community event to be mounted because the appropriate forms were not completed and signed properly.
- A supervisor may have received convincing complaints from workers of bullying by a co-worker. How could that culpable worker then have grounds for complaint about a transfer to another section of the organisation?
- Why is it that a worthy grant application is rejected because it did not reach the funding body by the advertised deadline, while another less impressive application is successful?

In all of these instances the process or procedural issues have legal implications. Human service workers can save themselves angst, time, and effort if they have a better appreciation of these implications. But there are other more important reasons for understanding the significance of process and procedure and adopting a legal sensitivity about them:

- Workers can improve their effectiveness as client advocates. For example, a worker acting on behalf of a client with Centrelink is more likely to succeed if they use data about departmental decisions based on wrong criteria, than if they rely on evidence about the client's parlous financial state, even though it is the latter matter which may be of most concern to them.
- Workers alert to procedural issues are in a better position to constantly review and improve their own work practices. They are also more likely to have the confidence to challenge their co-workers and organisations, in their own and their clients' interests, when processes are compromised.
- Human service workers themselves exercise power and make decisions about others, and Swain (2002a, p. 51) rightly stresses the 'relative powerlessness of the service user vis-a-vis' the worker. He goes on to argue that most of these decisions will be private and

unchallenged, and for this reason they, more than most, should be made in accordance with principles of procedural fairness.

Perhaps the most important reason of all for appreciating some basic elements of administrative law is that they are entirely consistent with and affirm good human service practice principles. It can be empowering for human service workers to realise that good practice is not in conflict with the law and that in fact the law can be utilised by them to support and sustain their own positions in the face of poor processes elsewhere.

The question of proper process and procedure, particularly as it relates to the work of individual human service workers, will be elaborated on in chapter 3.

Normality of disagreement and debate

The Australian legal system is an adversarial one in which parties do battle through their advocate lawyers. So dispute and debate are normal phenomena in the legal culture, as is mental preparedness to defend or attack either side of a case or argument, and a desire to win. These things are not the norm in the human services. If anything they are feared (Staller and Kirk 1998) or taken as indicative of failure with relationships. But human service workers who are willing to entertain open and regulated conflict management, and to value mental agility, can benefit enormously. Their intellectual resourcefulness in their own work can be extended, their work outcomes accentuated, and they are less likely to reject or be injured by different perspectives and opinions.

Practice question and response

Question: Everyone knows about lawyers who savage each other in court and then go out to lunch together. How could you suggest that human service workers emulate such hypocritical behaviour?

Response: From within a lawyer's frame of reference this behaviour is not hypocritical but most appropriate. Effective court advocacy requires lawyers to separate how they see their case from how they see the opposing counsel. Human service workers who develop this capacity, spend less energy protecting themselves from conflict and have more freedom to move within and beyond their familiar professional spaces.

Approach to evidence

Both human service and legal practice is founded on evidence, albeit with different slants. In courts at least, the accuracy, reliability, and precision of evidence (along with its curtailment) become paramount. Later chapters will show that the human services are not as sharp with information management as they might be, and valuable lessons can be learned from some aspects of the law's exactitude. More attention to detail in the human services will assist in improved practice, as well as being useful if evidence is to be given in court.

Normality of appeal/review

The right of appeal is fundamental in law. It is an accepted part of the legal system that decisions made by a legal adjudicator may be appealed to a superior one, and legal work is always done with an eye to this possibility. McMillan and Williams (1998, pp. 64–6) explain that 'administrative justice', so relevant to human service work, may be protected or sought through judicial review, merit review of certain administrative decisions, Ombudsman review, and human rights bodies review. These avenues are part of the 'normal' functioning of law. Also accepted in law is the right of claimants to investigate all review possibilities and pursue the one that is most likely to produce the desired result.

The notions of formal appeal or review or even complaint have come relatively recently to the health and human services, but these processes are now widespread and will be examined elsewhere in this book (see, in particular, chapter 11). Ombudsmen, commissioners, and other investigatory and review bodies are an increasingly prominent part of the human service experience, and most agencies are now expected to have grievance procedures in place for staff and clients. Nonetheless, complaint and review processes do not sit easily in the culture of human services where interpersonal relationships are so significant and complaints or appeals are often taken, if not intended, personally.

Complaint or grievance processes are often specific to an agency. They may be informal or formal, may or may not have the force of law, and may or may not result in a decision being reviewed. Appeal processes are generally more formalised in law, can review action in some way, and cannot progress unless legislative grounds are satisfied, including that the matter is within jurisdiction. For example, a Commonwealth government public servant has some rights of review about actions related to their employment, under s 33 of the *Public Service Act 1999* (Cth). But termination of employment is not reviewable under this section; other legal courses must be pursued for that action.

The very complex cultural issue of response to dissatisfaction cannot be explored in detail here. But assimilation of a legal orientation by human service agencies and workers can help ameliorate the traditional trauma caused by complaint or appeal. Four points of adoption are suggested:

- The first is to function with the idea of appeal always consciously in mind and to know what bodies may review the various decisions made. If decisions are made, procedures applied and documents maintained by agencies and workers in the knowledge that they may be scrutinised later by a review body, a mental inspectorate screens and adjusts action. This approach can both improve practice and reduce risk of legal or other negative reactions.
- The second is to genuinely accept that people always have rights, inclusive of the right to appeal human service decisions and/or intervention. Despite the rhetoric of self-determination, many human service workers find it hard in practice to admit that their clients may seek satisfaction beyond, or even in opposition to, their own efforts.
- The third is to strive for less subjective responses to complaints and appeals. This is always difficult when the professional medium, as is so often the case in the human

services, involves personal, private, and perhaps intense relationships. Complaints should always prompt introspection, but workers who cannot put some emotional distance between themselves and the action may suffer significant personal distress.

- The fourth is to understand the differences between grievance and/or appeal processes in different realms and at law, and how they work. Human service workers assisting others to appeal or complain, or who themselves are aggrieved, may be passionate about the situation, but vehemence alone does not persuade, or carry legal weight. A dispassionate and informed head is useful in thinking through desired outcomes, the review options available, the procedural requirements and limitations of each, and strategic choices of action.

  For example, is a new decision being sought or is the complainant mainly interested in voicing discontent with some aspect of an agency or its service? Once these sorts of basic aims are clarified, the most appropriate choice of complaint/appeal process can be made. It may well be that in many situations the best results can be obtained by skirting formal grievance and appeal processes and making informal approaches to the original decision-maker (Douglas and Jones 1999). Whichever type of process is chosen, the grievance itself needs to be formed convincingly and the desired outcomes articulated clearly. There is an empowering benefit to human service workers in being confident and strategic about their use of complaint/appeal mechanisms. This is an important area also to be revisited in the following and later chapters.

Law and human services: an uneasy co-existence

Much has been said so far about connections between the law and human services. But this is not to deny that there are very significant differences and tensions between the two that test and challenge individuals who attempt to straddle professional boundaries. For closed or less confident human service workers, these differences may present an impenetrable barrier between themselves and the law. Many lawyers in turn do not seek to penetrate the differences and simply ignore or are unaware of the human services. Some lawyers may be reflecting 'law's tendency to make claims to truth and thus to discount the validity of knowledges outside of law's frame of reference' (Graycar and Morgan 2002, p. 422).

The histories, cultures, and rituals of law and human services are dissimilar, as are many of the roles and functions of lawyers and human service workers. Van Wormer (1992, p. 123) surveys what she calls the contradictory professional attitudes of law and social work. In her comparison, law's historical origins lie in professional combat, and it values attack, 'tricks of the trade', and winning through battle; it is concerned with clients' civil rights; it aims to shift responsibility for client behaviour to others; its knowledge base is precedent; lawyers are largely private practitioners; and it has been male-dominated, privileged, and elitist. In contrast, the origins of social work lie in charitable work, and it emphasises means and outcomes, resolution through negotiation, individual responsibility, and client rehabilitation; its knowledge base is social science research, workers have been largely public employees; and it is female-dominated with attendant low social status. While superficial stereotyping about both law and social work is arguably evident here, as is an element of social work righteousness, the general point about degree and extent of difference between the realms is nonetheless instructive.

Other commentators have pursued the question of divergence more critically in relation to things such as values, knowledge, training, and methodologies. It is beyond the scope of this book to explore them fully but a few salient points are raised. While Staller and Kirk (1998) would challenge van Wormer's (1992) claims about the extent to which social work knowledge develops systematically from a social science research base, they agree that it is dissimilar in many respects to that of law. It derives, they say, from a scattered and uneven mix of things such as practice wisdom, research findings, and policy and is not aggregated anywhere into an integrated or accessible whole. It has been lamented elsewhere that social work's areas of expertise remain ill-defined and easily trivialised (Abbott and Wallace 1998; Lymbery 1998). Its ambivalent attitude to knowledge and the 'conceptual muddle' of its value base have also been noted (Preston-Shoot, Roberts et al. 1998a, p. 73). Stoesz (2002) argues that human service education, grounded in this uncertain knowledge base, is generic, inferior, and underwhelming, and sets low expectations about performance.

The knowledge of legal practitioners on the other hand, evolves though analysis of precedent and is compiled into a comprehensive universal case classification and retrieval system, known as case law. Legal education according to Staller and Kirk (1998, p. 97) utilises the Socratic method to prepare lawyers to face critical questioning and 'equate[s] preparation and performance with professionalism'. That is, challenging questioning techniques that test cognitive skills are the norm, and clever verbal manoeuvring is prized. So in summary, at the extremes, there is a confident group in lawyers, honed to perform in public, to win and impress; and in contrast, a human service group unsure about its social mandate, status, and methods.

Another line of commentary focuses on differences in reasoning and approaches to practice. Hacker (1999) contrasts thinking and practice in medicine and law, but some of her conclusions resonate for human services and the law. In her analysis of adversarial legal thinking, everything is open and anything can be relevant or irrelevant, depending on its value in a particular argument in a particular case. So any bit of information might be utilised to reify or dichotomise or disparage a position, and ultimately to persuade. The particularity of facts in any one case and the interests of the individual litigant will dominate legal thinking and drive action. Conversely inquisitorial medical thinking seeks the correct answer and is bound by the current state of research knowledge in an area. Medical and other similar non-legal thinking is subject to shades of grey and qualified assertions. Competing duties and interests may have to be prioritised and individual client need may not be the sole determinant of action. In medical thinking according to Hacker (1999), and it is added in human service thinking, mistakes will happen and are normal. In legal thinking, mistake means that someone is potentially to blame and thus liable. In summary, law deconstructs, seizes weaknesses, explodes arguments, while medicine and arguably the human services attempt to construct, to 'put things back together' (Hacker 1999, p. 7), to fix what is damaged, or explain what is experienced.

While the social stereotypes of both lawyers and human service workers are, fairly or unfairly, generally negative, again they are dissimilar, and each group imports and elaborates on the poor image of the other. The arrogant lawyer image is common in society. When the authors ask human service students about lawyers, predictable words such as greedy, smart, untrustworthy, rich, be-suited, amoral, and conceited constantly appear. The human service worker title is less well known than that of social worker so it is the public image of the latter that prevails. Social workers carry a public image of passivity and insecurity (Hawkins, Veeder et al. 1998, p. 55), and/or as unreliable, immature, gullible, and unrealistic (Bar-On 1995, p. 70) and/or as professional victims (Stoesz 2002). When law students are asked by the authors about social workers, they offer comments like: vague, woolly, look and act like clients, ineffective, undisciplined, and sorting out their own problems.

Where does all this lead? It confirms that there are both real and perceived obstacles to mutual understanding and cooperation between the human services and the law; and for many human service workers the result is entrenched feelings of inferiority, intimidation, and hostility in relation to law. It is argued here that the differences must be both accepted and understood but not allowed to block or stall engagement. Functional human service workers do confront their own negative stereotypes of the legal system and lawyers, and challenge the latter's stereotypes of them. They are also open to the positive images of lawyers, for example as fighters for justice. In turn they present themselves to the law as practical managers and clarifiers of complex human need situations. As Zifcak (2002) writes, some form of reconciliation between the two realms must be sought at the individual human service worker level. Those who achieve a degree of mental equilibrium about these two arenas are commonly excited by their interactions with the law and see how it can extend and improve their own practice. Hacker (1999, p. 6) says that 'medicine needs the law to help define its boundaries' and the same can be argued for the human services. The very differences that may cause distress to human service workers can also be perceived as invigorating, challenging, and, in the longer term, confirming.

Practice question and response

Question: Surely the implication here is that human service workers should accept law and the legal system uncritically and just adapt to them?

Response: This is a profound question and not simply answered. In summary, adaptation is being promoted, but not uncritical acceptance. Human service workers (and ideally lawyers) must maintain an analytical and informed perspective about both the human service and legal systems. Without this they will not be motivated or able to engage in effective systemic advocacy and change. But on a practical daily basis differences and frustrations will be faced, and have to be managed without too much energy being dissipated. Thus it is proposed that human service workers develop a serviceable mental set that helps them to both cope and develop. If this message were to be directed primarily at lawyers rather than human service workers, it would challenge them to do likewise in relation to the human services.

Practical ways in which integrated thinking might be enhanced and some form of personal reconciliation achieved by human service workers, will be turned to in the next chapter.

Key points for practice

- An appreciation of law needs to be integrated into analysis, decision-making, and practice in the human services because the context and the nature of human service work are suffused with legal and other entwined elements.
- Client problems often have legal dimensions, but even beyond these, all aspects of agency and worker functioning also have legal components.
- Human service workers are wise to engage with the law as they share interests with lawyers, may be in competition with them for jobs or working with them in new developments, and can learn very useful things from a legal orientation to appeal, process, debate, and evidence.
- This engagement will not be without its challenges as the cultures, traditions, approaches, and styles of law and the human services are quite different. Difference must be understood and accepted before personal reconciliation and integrated practice are possible.

Some useful web sites

Ombudsmen

www.nt.gov.au/omb_hcscc/splash.htm
www.ombudsman.gov.au/
www.ombudsman.vic.gov.au/

Law societies and bodies

www.lawcouncil.asn.au/
www.liv.asn.au/
www.lawsociety.com.au/page.asp?partid=66
www.lawsocnt.asn.au/
www.lssa.asn.au/
www.taslawsociety.asn.au/
www.lawsocietywa.asn.au/
www.qls.com.au/

3

Incorporating Law into Human Service Work

Integrating law in thinking and decision-making

How might human service workers find their bearings amid the numerous claims that have been made in chapter 2 about law and human service work? Any number of approaches might be used but here the focus is on decision-making as both a product of thinking and a tool for organising it. Figure 3.1 presents a decision-making framework in which legal imperatives are imbedded among others that impinge on workers in their daily practice. There are some general introductory points to be made about this framework. Each of the concentric circles within it is then discussed, followed by a commentary on the interactive effects of the influences. The chapter concludes with comments on the application of the framework in practice.

Why an emphasis on decision-making?

Even if it is not recognised, the mechanism for most human service work is decision-making, about issues both large and small. Lipsky's (1980) notion of the street level bureaucrat is relevant here, as is the quote from Swain (2002a, p. 51) in the previous chapter about the 'relative powerlessness' of clients in relation to workers. Decision-making is particularly pertinent in the balancing of legal and human services imperatives (Braye and Preston-Shoot 1997; Brammer 2003). Each time an adult guardianship order is sought, a child protection notification made, or an employment contract entered into, very significant decisions are being made. But workers also decide whether or not to carry work files home on the bus, return phone calls, pass on titbits of gossip, delay writing case notes, and make private use of the Internet at work. And organisations through the legal agency of their managers and through their polices and procedures, decide whether or not to affirm comprehensive record keeping, take staff and client safety seriously, respect worker privacy, and so on. In other words, the minutiae of human service daily lives also depend on decisions.

Practice question and response

Question: But as a human service professional I am most interested in evolving relationships with people and your emphasis on decision-making implies that I am some sort of contriving authority figure, doesn't it?
Response: Well you are someone with authority; you would not be doing human service work if you did not have it. The authority may vary in form and it may be exercised in different ways, but it exists. Your relationships are likely to be more accountable and more honest if the authority, and the purposes and types of decisions that necessarily accompany it, are declared.

Why an emphasis on imperatives?

Decisions are not made independently of their context. Every decision, no matter how tiny, is a product of a cognitive processing of influences or imperatives, even if it seems spontaneous. The decision-maker may be unaware of the basis or even identity of the forces that are, or should be, impacting on them. The intention here is to expose and articulate major imperatives and the sources of their authority.

Why look at imperatives other than law?

Legal forces are only one set among many. Throughout this book it will be shown that law is a 'defining mandate ... but it is an insufficient mandate to reflect the complexity both of practice and service user's lives' (Preston-Shoot, Roberts et al. 1998a, p. 77). When major imperatives, for example legal, value, ethical, or political, are considered separately, their interactive effects, the conflicts between them, and the relative priorities given them, may be overlooked.

Influences on human service worker decision-making

The worker as decision-maker or exerciser of discretion

At the centre of figure 3.1 is the worker with a unique profile of values, skills, knowledge, and a belief system, which together mediate all external forces. There are arrows impacting on this sphere to reflect the external forces on the worker, but there are equally important arrows facing outwards that represent the worker's efforts to resist or change external forces. No matter how externally constrained a worker may feel or be, there is always a process of sorting, balancing, and deciding going on, even if unconsciously. The worker exercises discretion or 'decide[s], discern[s] or determine[s] to make a judgement, choice or decision, about alternative courses of action or inaction' (Gelsthorpe and Padfield 2003, p. 3). Sometimes workers will be making decisions about themselves and sometimes about others,

Figure 3.1 Influences on human service worker decision-making

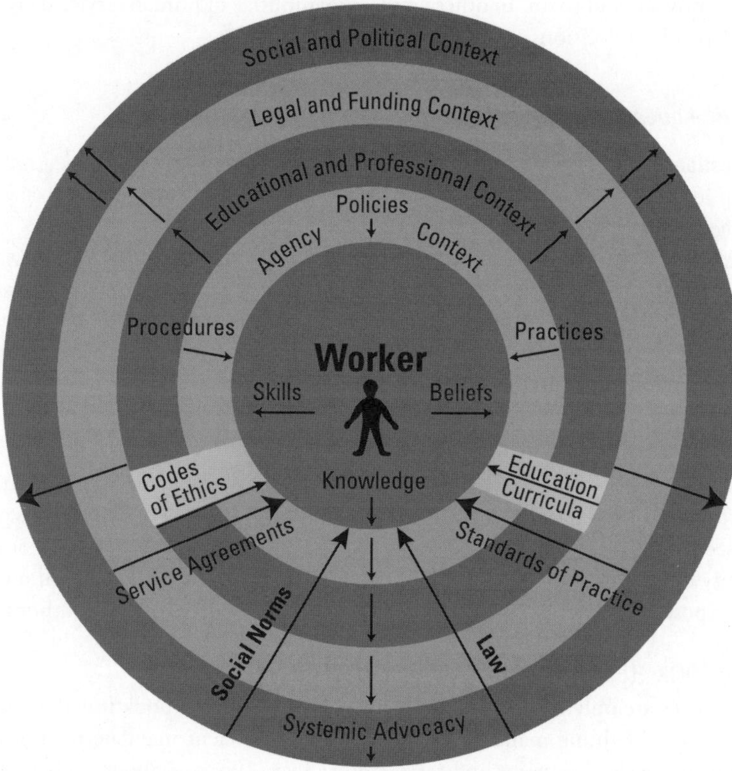

Social and Political Context

Legal and Funding Context

Educational and Professional Context

Policies

Agency   Context

Procedures   Practices

Skills   Beliefs

Worker

Codes of Ethics   Knowledge   Education Curricula

Service Agreements   Standards of Practice

Social Norms   Law

Systemic Advocacy

(Developed from Gursansky, Harvey et al. (2003, p. 179))

and it is these latter decisions that demand most careful attention. This raises the question of what guides, if any, there are about making fair and just decisions which impact on others, and the law can be very helpful here.

Administrative law principles

At this point quite a long detour is made into the principles of administrative law introduced in the previous chapter. It is helpful for human service workers to have an understanding of these principles because they often work in agencies and with bodies that are bound to apply the principles in their decision-making. Moreover human service workers are themselves decision-makers, and often 'primary decision-makers' (Cole 1996, p. xiii) obliged to comply with the principles. The principles are a useful general guide to good practice in decision-making even if not formally required by law on all occasions. When used by workers they build acknowledgment of the exercise of power into decision-making, and in turn they can help make decisions legally and professionally more robust. If they are not utilised by the worker, decision-making is more likely to be capricious and indefensible. What are the bare bones of these administrative law principles?

Making decisions—the power and the process

The proper exercise of power is one of the central concerns of administrative law and there are two parts to it. One part is about whether or not the body, authority, or person who made the decision had the power to make it, and the second is about the manner in which it was made. If one or other of these is compromised the decision is 'ultra vires', that is, outside power, and it may be open to legal challenge.

Legislation or other relevant instruments invest decision-makers with power to make certain decisions and if they decide on matters outside this mandate they are said to be beyond power. The Federal Privacy Commissioner, for example, does not have power to investigate allegations made about breaches of Information Privacy Principle 7 if the claimant is not an Australian citizen or permanent resident (Jackson 2001). Think about legislation that gives a body power to 'regulate' residential facilities. Does that mean that it has the power to make a decision, for example, about the amount of bedroom space per resident, which could effectively close a facility? A facility affected by such a decision might well, in challenging the decision, argue that 'regulate' does not include this type of decision. Perhaps a worker has legislative power to 'investigate' allegations of some sort. Does this mean that the worker who finds allegations proved can make determinations about a penalty? It will depend on the scope of their power and if they go beyond it their decisions may be challenged as ultra vires.

Sometimes there is no question that a power exists but the manner in which it has been exercised is in question. A decision may be procedurally ultra vires if it was made improperly. For example, notice might have to be given before some action is taken, or warnings given in writing or public advertisements placed. Or there may be other substantive or procedural defects in the exercise. For example, a decision may be substantively challengeable if it is against the law, dictated by a third party, too harsh or rigid, improperly discriminatory, motivated by an improper purpose, based on irrelevant considerations or not on relevant ones, or based on inadequate or mistaken evidence (Allars 1990). The worker who is investigating allegations may be operating within power but if they, for example, have made their decision without knowledge of critical information, or they have been influenced by their boss's opinion, their decision may be legally flawed. This leads into procedural fairness.

Procedural fairness

Procedural fairness is a principle of administrative law establishing how decisions are to be made. If it is breached the decision may be legally challengeable. However, it does not apply to every decision that is made by anyone. Procedural fairness essentially applies to decisions made in the public sphere where a person's rights may be adversely affected. This covers the decisions of government departments, local councils, government ministers or officials, and other administrators exercising public power (Ardagh 1999). The fact that so much government power now is delegated elsewhere through privatisation raises a set of legal challenges beyond the scope of this book (e.g. O'Brien 1991; Downey 2001). However procedural fairness also applies to private bodies that have the power to make decisions affecting large numbers of people, such as trade unions and clubs (Allars 1990). There are several fundamental principles of procedural fairness.

Hearing rule

This rule focuses on the claimant. In brief, they have a right to know that a decision affecting them is to be made and to put their position on it. They have the right to present any information that is relevant to the decision but not necessarily in person (Ardagh 1999), to have reasonable time to collect it, and also to know the full extent of the case against them. They must be made aware particularly of any adverse information about them that the decision-maker will be taking into account so that they have the opportunity to rebut it. In addition, the decision-maker must genuinely consider the information put by the claimant. So, for instance, consider a situation where clients have complained about a worker's behaviour and the employer is considering penalties. This rule requires that the worker know exactly what has been said about them, have an opportunity to present their side of the story, and be genuinely listened to before the penalty decision is made. The hearing rule is one of the reasons why workers might not be able to ensure the confidentiality of information that is given to them if it is relevant to a case against someone else. This matter will be returned to in chapter 6, on information management.

Practice question and response

Question: So must I always tell a client or co-worker if I come across or form any negative views about them?

Response: Not necessarily. You may not be making a decision that could affect their interests. Even if you are, your decisions may not be immediately subject to procedural fairness requirements for some reason. For example, there may be forensic reasons to delay informing them while more information is collected. The point is that principles of procedural fairness are general guides to good and lawful practice but they do not apply to every decision and they may sometimes be mediated by other imperatives.

Rule against bias

This rule seeks to ensure that decisions are made solely on the basis of material presented and without bias for or against anyone whose interests are involved. A reasonable suspicion of bias on the part of the decision-maker may be enough to make a decision challengeable. Perhaps the management committee of an association is deciding on which private consultant it will choose to conduct a research project. The chairperson of the committee may also be a job applicant for work with one of the consultants being considered. The chairperson may believe that they are able to be quite objective in the current decision-making process. However if the committee decision is subject to the rules of administrative justice it may still be flawed at law on the basis of the bias rule. In this case positive bias for one consultant might be suspected.

Evidence rule

This rule does not mean that the technical rules of evidence that apply in courts must be satisfied. The essence of this imperative is that decisions must be based on probative evidence, not on speculation, rumour, or gossip.

Duty to enquire

This imperative requires the decision-maker to seek relevant information and to clarify matters so that they have a complete understanding of the situation before they make a decision. This duty does not impose an obligation to seek all information; rather questions about what was reasonable in the circumstances will be asked (Allars 1990).

So procedural fairness is not about the substantive decision but the process by which the decision is reached. Its principles pervade many work environments as they are incorporated into organisational codes of conduct, grievance procedures, and so on. It is also mediated in many situations by an overlay of specific legislative provisions and other contextual factors. It used to be called 'natural justice' but this term is less widely used now as it could be seen to promise a favourable outcome to the complainant. In fact this may not happen, even where procedural fairness has been accorded. All that is guaranteed by the principle is that applications are heard and processed in a fair manner. One practical result of this is evident in review and appeal processes, mentioned in the previous chapter. Many internal reviewers or tribunals do not have the power to substitute their own decision for one that is appealed. Even if it is found that procedural fairness was breached in the original decision, the reviewer will not automatically change the actual decision. Instead it will often be sent back to the original decision-maker for reconsideration, with adherence to procedural fairness principles. The outcome of the second decision may thus ultimately remain the same as long as proper procedure is followed.

Human service workers are commonly ignorant of or impatient in the face of these procedural demands of law. Their frustration is somewhat ironic given the importance of process in their own professional methods. It is common knowledge in the human services that the quality of information elicited in an interview will depend largely on the way the interview process is managed. It is known that the attention paid to group process and maintenance is critical to group productivity. It is also accepted that client satisfaction is largely determined by the quality of relationships with workers. The place of process in human services and law is in fact very similar despite human service frustration with what is seen as 'legal nitpicking'.

It is assumed in law that sound decisions are more likely to result from sound decision-making processes and this could hardly be disputed in the human services. Human service codes of ethics and professional ideologies too are entirely consistent with the philosophical underpinnings of administrative law. Slightly different language might be used but the same notions of what is good are being applied: transparent and non-discriminatory processes, the right to know about adverse assertions, direct approaches to individuals, a chance to be heard, use of best evidence, objectivity and consistency, and fair and thoughtful exercise of discretion. This is one of many occasions throughout this book where the similarity between legal requirements and good human service practices stands out.

Procedural fairness at law has been translated by Brayne and Carr (2003, p. 58) into a social work checklist. In their words, the bases of lawful social work decision-making are that:

- comprehensive factual information is available to all parties
- comprehensive legal information is used
- the principle of proportionality is applied
- the decision is '[r]easonable and fair'
- the decision is comprehensively documented
- the decision is made without delay.

Practice question and response

Question: But I am only an ordinary worker who has little power. Surely you are not equating the decisions that I make with those of someone like a government minister or agency director?

Response: Your exercises of power may seem insignificant to you but their impact on others can be profound. Lipsky's (1980) notion of the street level bureaucrat, or front-line worker who makes policy in daily decisions when for instance filling in forms a certain way, referring or not referring someone on, providing a service or not, being helpful or not and so on, is very relevant here. In addition your 'small' and perhaps relatively private work decisions can contribute to the return of someone to jail, the removal of their children, their death through suicide, or their successful bid for funding. Surely these decisions must be made with principles of procedural fairness in mind?

It is hoped that this book might encourage workers to exercise power in their decision-making more consciously and carefully, even if they are not subject to administrative law review. If they do this they are already integrating law into their practice and improving the quality of their professional work at the same time. At this point the detour into administrative law comes to an end and the journey through the contextual imperatives shown in figure 3.1 continues.

The agency or employment context

The immediate context for most workers is their employing agency that has policies, procedures, and practices, both formal and informal, that impact on their decision-making. Some of these requirements will have the force of law if they are also enshrined in legislation or if they are express or implied terms of the worker employment contracts. These legal dimensions of the employer context will reappear in later chapters. Other employment expectations may be more a question of subtle cultural expectations. Again there are arrows facing in and out from this circle. Obviously agencies are meant to comply with laws and funding body requirements and be sensitive to social expectations, but they too will attempt to influence and resist or mediate these external imperatives. The worker in turn will comply with, filter, and defy agency expectations in daily work decisions.

For self-employed workers or subcontractors there is still an employment context in the form of the written contract, and the contracting agency expectations and norms. Insurer requirements may also apply if the worker holds professional indemnity insurance.

Educational and professional context

Both the worker and agency are in turn impinged upon by human service educational, professional, and cultural forces. This is the human service ethos of figure 2.1. This ethos influences thinking about appropriate values and behaviour and perpetuates professional myths, symbols, and language. Professional codes of ethics, and the content and philosophical orientation of human service course curricula in any period, acculturate workers and permeate the rhetoric of the human services. Again the arrows are two-way. In some agencies, particularly those where there is homogeneity in the professional backgrounds and identity of workers, the two-way impact of professional education and association views might be quite strong. So, for example, in an agency that employs only social work graduates, the common language of social work educational experiences and of the Australian Association of Social Workers (AASW) Code of ethics may be evident. The extent to which this language impacts in behaviour is another matter which will be retuned to soon but it does influence perspectives and understandings at least. In other workplaces the influences of this contextual circle may be more diverse or less evident.

Legal and funding context

The legal and funding context in which the worker, relevant professions and agencies exist includes general law (e.g. administrative and industrial law), law specifically relevant to the human services, and funder imperatives, generally with the force of contractual if not other law. It was argued in the previous chapter that all human service situations contain legal elements, obvious or otherwise, which impose duties, powers, and perhaps protections, and present risks. Of course agencies and workers often struggle to comply with all aspects of the law and sometimes they fail to do so. For example, workers may find themselves breaking the speed limit when driving to a work crisis. Agencies may at times breach occupational health and safety requirements or deny service on policy/funding grounds where they are legally obliged to provide service. The main thing is that they are informed about the risks of non-compliance and able to balance these intelligently against other imperatives.

Social and political context

All of the above forces are in turn initiated or shaped by their social and political context. Social norms change as do political responses, and parliaments make or amend laws accordingly. The behaviour of a worker at any point in history is impacted by current social expectations and sensitivities and thus there are arrows directed from this area right into the central circle. Some workers are not as attuned to this communal environment as they might be and unwisely see it as irrelevant to their daily work lives. Yet others are alert to the risks and possibilities presented by shifting social norms. Some understand that certain political environments threaten their particular work interests while at other times a sympathetic environment can be capitalised on. Some workers and agencies engage actively in systemic advocacy at this level.

These influences in interaction

Describing these imperatives separately is one thing, but explaining their relationship is another and much more difficult matter. Three points about their relationships are particularly salient.

Prioritising imperatives

These imperatives are not prioritised by workers and influence their practice, as might be imagined. For example, professional codes of ethics are often accorded priority in agency and worker discourses when in fact they may have limited and uneven effects on daily actions (Coady 2002). The law is often similarly invoked. Phrases like 'duty of care' are bandied about as if they both identify and command good practice. As will be seen later in this book (see chapter 5), this may not be the case. It is speculated that employer imperatives may be more powerful than others because the employer has the power to terminate employment. Sinclair (1996) certainly argues that organisational codes are eclipsing professional ones in significance for and impact on workers. It is also often the most informal, least public, and most personal forces that compel and determine action in any practice situation (e.g. Sinclair 1996; Holloway and Grounds 2003; Weber 2003). Neither law nor ethics should be given uncritical pre-eminence when it comes to an analysis of forces that actually do influence how agencies and workers act. The aspirational roles that both law and ethics can play in the evaluation and improvement of human service practice is especially critical. Both may also become central when something goes wrong and investigations result, but on a daily basis they probably determine fewer decisions than they should.

Practice question and response

Question: You seem to be suggesting quite wrongly that my professional code of ethics is unimportant?

Response: Not at all. Codes are very important but they are seldom specific enough to compel particular decisions and their enforcement provisions are often limited. They should guide behaviour but they cannot prescribe it and to claim otherwise may be less than truthful.

Legal and other imperatives are sometimes internally and interactively contradictory

As explained in the previous chapter few human service situations have prescribed solutions. A process of investigation, sorting, and weighing is generally necessary before a considered decision is possible, and this requires both prioritising and reconciling competing forces. For example, it is possible to break the law but this does not necessarily mean that an employment contract has also been broken. A theft committed by a worker outside of work may be one such example. It is possible to breach an ethical and employer rule, but not the law. For instance a sexual relationship with a consenting adult client, and some whistleblowing behaviour may both contravene professional and employer requirements, but not the law. Social norms may conflict with professional ones, personal imperatives may compete with employer ones, and the list could go on. Examples of competing or contradictory imperatives will appear throughout this book.

Legal and other imperatives are commonly confused

Sometimes the law is wrongly invoked when another force such as a social norm or an employer culture is evident. Compliance or not with the employment expectation may have legal implications but the procedure itself may not be 'the law'. Sometimes non-legal imperatives in a situation may be emphasised while the equally significant legal ones are ignored. For example, a derogatory comment about a colleague may be seen as merely unprofessional, when it may also be defamatory in law. Sometimes personal values and law are poorly distinguished. It is not uncommon to hear workers assert that they have a legal duty of care when in fact the operating imperative is their own belief system. They may or may not actually have a legal duty in the circumstances.

The law is sometimes invoked when in fact government and/or employer policy is the driving force behind a decision. A striking illustration of this is provided in the case of *Presland v Hunter Area Health Service & Anor* [2003] NSWSC 754 (Unreported, Adams J, 19 August 2003) which reappears in later chapters. There the plaintiff killed someone after he was released from hospital while still subject to acute psychotic episodes. He later sued the hospital for negligence in not detaining him. The point of interest here is that a psychiatric expert witness giving evidence in the case emphasised the importance legally and in other ways of keeping people out of mental hospitals. This is familiar territory for health and human service people who understand and implement policies of deinstitutionalisation. However the New South Wales Supreme Court commented that the psychiatrist was mistakenly talking about policy rather than applying the *Mental Health Act 1990* (NSW). The actual provisions of the Act required assessment of that plaintiff's mental state at the point of admission and genuine consideration of his detention. The court said 'persons who need to be detained should be detained' (para. 119).

It is hoped that this book will help improve accurate identification and prioritising of different imperatives.

Making integrated decisions in practice

Following is a human service decision-making checklist evolved from the figure 3.1 framework. It does not provide a formula for reaching a decision. That is an exercise of sophisticated professional judgment and practice. Nor should it imply a linear and mechanistic approach to decision-making. But it does encourage consideration of the range of imperatives in any situation and places the legal demands and solutions in context. It also reinforces the diverse effects of law, which may constrain, authorise, sanction, and/or protect action. The sort of cognitive checking that is proposed will not be undertaken consciously for all decisions in professional life, but if it is embedded in thinking so as to be almost intuitive it will broaden mental horizons, encourage honest reflection, and reduce the stressful surprise factor in much human service work.

- Keep an open mind about the 'facts' in a situation at all times and keep questioning their accuracy.
- Identify additional information or 'facts' which are required for an informed decision to be made.
- Identify prevailing social expectations, public interest arguments, and current political sensitivities.
- Identify any funding body requirements or expectations.
- Seek information about legal mandates, duties, powers, and protections, and less obvious legal dimensions of the agency and worker role.
- Seek advice about matters or questions outside of personal expertise.
- Consider professional expectations—codes and education experience.
- Check, enquire about, or request agency policies, procedures, and practice rules.
- Examine own values and concerns.
- Weigh competing forces within and between imperatives and determine which ones are most compelling, to whom, and why. Consider:
    - urgency
    - levels of risk to public, agency, self, client and others
    - costs of legal and other actions
    - resources available
    - timelines.
- Always make decisions with principles of procedural fairness in mind.

If human service workers understand the extent, source, and type of constraints and stimulants on their work, they have wider scope for independent action following assessment of the risks of compliance and non-compliance. This is not a call for risky behaviour in practice. Rather it recognises that many decisions are made in situations where there is no clear direction from any source and where every alternative course of action has advantages and disadvantages. Being able to assess and weigh up legal, personal, professional, employment, and political risks for each alternative is an essential characteristic of good practice.

All that said, this book is about human service law and it will focus on the legal context and dimensions of practice. But in light of the above commentary it will frequently acknowledge issues other than just legal ones, and will conclude that a legal answer or strategy may not be discernable, or may not offer the best way forward in any particular situation.

Key points for practice

- One way of integrating legal awareness into human service work is to think of practice as comprised of decision-making influenced by a range of personal, employer, professional, legal, and socio-political imperatives.
- The human service decision-maker works at identifying and prioritising these imperatives in any situation and at reconciling contradictions within and between them.
- Human service workers who apply basic principles of procedural fairness in their own decision-making are likely to make better and less legally changeable decisions.
- Human service workers who acknowledge that they do exercise power, and often legal power, in their decision-making are more able to exercise it with care and caution.

Some useful web sites

Administrative law

www.austlii.edu.au/au/cases/cth/aat/
www.austlii.edu.au/au/cases/cth/rrt/
www.austlii.edu.au/au/cases/nsw/NSWADT/
www.law.unsw.edu.au/subjhome/adminlaw/

Professional associations

www.aasw.asn.au/index.htm
www.aiwcw.org.au/
www.aps.psychsociety.com.au/
www.pacfa.org.au/scripts/default.asp

Part II

LEGAL OBLIGATIONS,
RIGHTS, AND REGULATION
OF | HUMAN SERVICE WORKERS

4

Professional, Business, and Employment Matters

Behind the scenes of service delivery

Consider the following situations:

- A refugee support agency appoints someone without a degree as a social worker.
- A mental health worker worries about personal safety.
- A youth agency subcontracts its outreach services to a staffing agency.
- A community house coordinator is outvoted in management committee meetings.
- The treasurer of a disability self-help association frets about its finances.
- A local government office requires its project officers to take on front desk duty.

What are the unifying elements in these situations and why are they important in human service work? The situations fit within a loose conglomeration of professional, industrial, and 'business' matters. They are the machinery behind service delivery. They concern professional classification and identity, employment rights and obligations, and responsibilities that flow from the increasingly common management functions of human service workers. In canvassing the contemporary context of the human services, O'Connor, Smyth et al. (2000, pp. 6–8) underscore the contraction of state activity and the marketisation of services with headings like 'changing occupational structures', 'changing sites of employment', and 'permeable professional boundaries'. In Rosenman's words (2000, p. 193) '[w]orkers in the human services, who may have initially entered the field from a desire to help people, find themselves confronted by a world of competitive tendering, budgetary, financial, and staff management concerns; and outcomes evaluation …'. As Weinbach (2003, p. 12) says, '[m]anagement is everyone's work' and it is increasingly being shared in human service organisations.

No longer are workers only employees with one-dimensional professional trajectories and primary interests in direct service. To survive in this new world and to be effective workers, they must be conversant with and make more use of entrepreneurial attitudes and the prevailing language of business and management.

Thus this chapter addresses legal factors that impinge on human service jobs and titles, employment rights and obligations, and on worker management responsibilities. It is not comprehensive and there are many other areas that could have been included if space permitted. For example, duties of directors, insurance, fundraising, taxation, and financial management are not covered, although a few of these areas, for example indemnity insurance, are touched on briefly in other chapters. The aim here is to outline the broad shape of legal rights and responsibilities that are thrown up by the fluid employment context. The chapter begins with an overview of the regulation of professional titles, practices, and affiliation issues. It then moves into the 'business' world of contracts, management functions, and meetings, and from there to a limited commentary on employment law.

Professional profile

No licence to practice

To the amazement of many, the state does not regulate the titles or intervention methods of human service workers in general, or social workers or counsellors in particular. There is currently no legislation in any Australian jurisdiction specifically directed at social work, counselling, or similar professional identities. The Northern Territory has been the only jurisdiction to attempt regulation of social workers—under the *Health Practitioners and Allied Professionals Registration Act 1985*, people claiming the social work title were required to have qualifications and experience acceptable to the AASW. However, the social work relevant sections of that legislation were repealed in 1993.

It will be evident throughout this book that human service activity is actually regulated and constrained in many ways, but not through worker titles, and not through particular methods or functions being defined as exclusive to particular practitioners. Anyone, regardless of qualifications, can with impunity call themselves a social worker and/or engage in what might be thought of as social work or human service approaches or modalities, for example, counselling, case management, or psychotherapy. The state will neither act nor impose sanctions about their claim to the title or their engagement in the practices. Of course, university-qualified social workers who want an identifiable professional profile in society, may take a dim view of the situation. Likewise members of professional associations such as the AASW and Psychotherapy and Counselling Federation of Australia (PCFA) may fret. Yet other individuals view the diversity of practice opportunities as liberating for both workers and service users. Clients are generally ignorant of the qualifications of their workers and may have other more immediate preoccupations. Employers tend to set their own rules about titles and expertise, as will soon be explained.

Practice question and response

Question: Are you really saying that nothing will be done when someone who lacks a social work degree calls themselves a social worker in Australia?

Response: Yes. Assuming that they are not acting fraudulently or breaching some other general legal provision, the mere fact of them using the social work title will not invoke any state action.

Human service workers are not licensed in New Zealand either (Connolly 2001). In contrast, in the USA social workers at least are subject to some form of licensing regime, and in the United Kingdom all social care workers are in the process of being state registered (General Social Care Council 2003). Many other professional groups in Australia such as psychologists, medical doctors, lawyers, physiotherapists, and occupational therapists do have their titles and sometimes practices (e.g. the administration of psychological tests) regulated by the state.

For example in Victoria and Western Australia, psychologists are regulated by the *Psychological Registration Act (2000)* and *(1976)* respectively, and in the Northern Territory by the *Health Practitioners and Allied Professionals Registration Act 1985*. This Northern Territory legislation also applies to occupational therapists, osteopaths, and physiotherapists, and its omnibus form of regulation for groups of health professionals is also being considered in South Australia (Department of Human Services 2003). Nurses in Western Australia are subject to the *Nurses Act 1992* and in Queensland the *Nursing Act 1992*. Individuals calling themselves lawyers in Tasmania and the Australian Capital Territory are covered by the *Legal Profession Act 1993* and the *Legal Practitioners Act 1970* respectively. Traditional Chinese medicine has been recently brought under some level of state control in Victoria with the *Chinese Medicine Registration Act 2000* because of perceived inadequacies in self-regulation and resultant potential dangers to the public (Carlton 2002).

Intending members of the above professional groups cannot practice unless they are registered by the state. This generally means that they satisfy some minimum qualifications, good character and perhaps experience requirements, and that they pay annual registration fees. Also, complaints about their practice are processed by specific registration boards, and if proved, may result in deregistration. This is a very powerful sanction as it prevents continued practice as a lawyer, nurse, or whatever. Thus the force of the state is brought to bear on individuals who falsely make claims to some professional titles and techniques or those who breach professional conduct provisions. Why the human services are excluded from these regulatory regimes, and whether or not the regimes actually serve the purposes that they are designed for, are contentious topics for another time and place. Suffice to say that some of the reasons for exclusion are inherent in the pluralism of human service aims, qualifications, and practices (e.g. Barker and Branson 2000), and some concern broader issues of professional social legitimacy, status, gender, and risk (e.g. Allsop and Saks 2003).

Human service workers in some fields need to be specifically accredited, as opposed to registered for general professional practice. For example workers who provide contracted return to work services under the *Workers Rehabilitation and Compensation Act 1986* (SA) must be accredited by the state WorkCover Corporation. But more commonly it is employer agencies which need to be accredited to provide services (Saltzman and Furman 1999; Barker and Branson 2000). For instance, Australian aged residential and child-care facilities must be accredited under various federal or state and territory Acts.

The absence of licensing in the human services is both a cause and result of the deregulated employment market where employer preferences as to backgrounds and qualifications prevail (Kennedy and Harvey 2001). Some employers seek people who have a social work degree and are eligible for membership of the AASW. This is a form of professional self-regulation but it is less formal than state regulation. Some employers, often for very similar jobs, will ask only for 'relevant qualifications'. Some are silent as to qualifications. There are no specific legislative requirements to either complicate or assist their decision-making about which sorts of experience and qualifications are necessary for the work being advertised, although big employers such as public services generally set eligibility criteria under their workforce management mandates. In summary, the interests of particularly qualified groups of human service workers are not protected by legislation and all must compete on a relatively open market for jobs.

Employment in the human services

The real job advertisements in figures 4.1, 4.2, and 4.3 illustrate the kaleidoscopic character of the human service employment scene. The NSW Mid West Area Health Service Senior Social Work positions in figure 4.3 require a qualification in social work and eligibility for membership of the AASW. Here the employer is relying on AASW criteria for recognition as a social worker. The ACT Family Services Worker jobs in figure 4.2 demonstrate how qualification differentials, while not precluding eligibility for applicants, may impact on salary progression levels. The advertisement invites tertiary qualified applicants—a wide pool—but specifies that progression past a certain level is dependent on AASW eligibility or registration as a psychologist. The SA Domiciliary Care social worker job in figure 4.1 shows how employers, in this case the Commissioner for Public Employment, may apply their own criteria for what constitutes a social work or equivalent qualification.

The Tasmanian Senior Intake Workers advertisement in figure 4.2 does not mention

Figure 4.1 Newspaper job advertisements

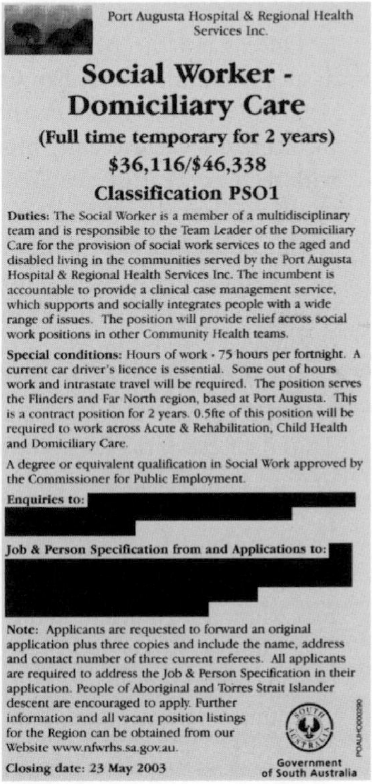

Port Augusta Hospital & Regional Health Services Inc.

Social Worker - Domiciliary Care

(Full time temporary for 2 years)

$36,116/$46,338

Classification PSO1

Duties: The Social Worker is a member of a multidisciplinary team and is responsible to the Team Leader of the Domiciliary Care for the provision of social work services to the aged and disabled living in the communities served by the Port Augusta Hospital & Regional Health Services Inc. The incumbent is accountable to provide a clinical case management service, which supports and socially integrates people with a wide range of issues. The position will provide relief across social work positions in other Community Health teams.

Special conditions: Hours of work - 75 hours per fortnight. A current car driver's licence is essential. Some out of hours work and intrastate travel will be required. The position serves the Flinders and Far North region, based at Port Augusta. This is a contract position for 2 years. 0.5fte of this position will be required to work across Acute & Rehabilitation, Child Health and Domiciliary Care.

A degree or equivalent qualification in Social Work approved by the Commissioner for Public Employment.

Enquiries to:

Job & Person Specification from and Applications to:

Note: Applicants are requested to forward an original application plus three copies and include the name, address and contact number of three current referees. All applicants are required to address the Job & Person Specification in their application. People of Aboriginal and Torres Strait Islander descent are encouraged to apply. Further information and all vacant position listings for the Region can be obtained from our Website www.nfwrhs.sa.gov.au.

Closing date: 23 May 2003

Government of South Australia

qualifications. They may be required, but because the titles and/or modalities of child protection work, like most in the human services, are not directly regulated by the state, it is inessential to declare the qualifications and professional identity of applicants at the point of advertisement. The two counsellor jobs in figure 4.3 also illustrate diversity. The WA Vietnam Veterans Counselling Service advertisement invites only AASW eligible social workers or registered psychologists. However the Queensland job casts its net more widely. It is theoretically possible that it might accept social work qualifications that are not acceptable to the AASW, or psychology ones not adequate for state registration. In contrast, the Manager Advocacy job in figure 4.2, which on the face of it would seem to be of interest to a wide range of human service workers, requires higher qualifications and traditional human service ones are not mentioned in the list provided.

Figure 4.2 Newspaper job advertisements

"Yvonne draws water from a well drilled by World Vision in her village in Bolivia. Missing from this picture are her six brothers and sisters who died from diseases carried in the dirty water her community used to drink. Do you share our vision for a world where children need not die for the want of a drink of clean water."

World Vision

Manager, Advocacy Network Australia

This is a unique opportunity to provide leadership and strategic direction to the work of Advocacy Network Australia (ANA); whilst contributing to the wider World Vision Australia, NGO and partnership networks. You will play a key role in achieving the team's objective to influence and mobilise citizens and key institutions in order to achieve attitudes, policies and practices that reflect a community that no longer tolerates poverty.
Key priorities of ANA may include research and dissemination of information relating to issues such as peace and conflict, trade and debt, child rights and HIV/AIDS.
You will have the following qualities:
* strong networking skills;
* significant experience of international development and policy work;
* ability to persuade and influence with diplomacy;
* higher qualifications in a relevant field such as development studies, politics, economics, law, sociology or international relations;
* demonstrated strategic planning skills;
* exceptional knowledge of the human rights, aid & development sector; and
* ability to prepare major reports, submissions and discussion papers.
Further information is available on our website, www.worldvision.org.au
If you believe you will reflect a passion and commitment to our vision, mission and Christian values, then please send a detailed resume with covering letter to ▮▮▮▮▮▮

Applications close: 28th January 2003 and will be acknowledged by 10th February 2003.

World Vision Australia is a Christian overseas aid agency that pursues freedom, opportunity, justice and peace for everyone in the world.

Family Services Workers Level 1
$37,499 - $44,349
Position Number: Several (expected vacancies)

Seeking motivated professionals for temporary and permanent expected vacancies. These positions provide direct statutory child protection service delivery in a regional setting.
The successful applicants will have a tertiary qualification and progression past the fourth increment will require eligibility for membership of the Australian Association of Social Workers or full registration with the ACT Psychology Registration Board or other state equivalent.
Contact officer: ▮▮▮▮▮▮
Selection documentation: ▮▮▮▮▮▮
Selection documentation is available on the Internet at the following address: **http://www.decs.act.gov.au/department/vacancies.htm**
Applications for the above positions should be forwarded to: Workforce Management, ACT Department of Education and Community Services.

APPLICATIONS CLOSE 4 JULY 2002

The ACT Public Service is a unified and professional service built on the principles of public interest, community values and a culture of service.
Successful applicants will become permanent officers (unless noted otherwise) of the ACT Public Service on attractive terms and conditions.
Women, and Australians from culturally and linguistically diverse background, Aboriginal and Torres Strait Islanders and people with a disability have an equal opportunity for appointment to the ACTPS. An appropriate selection panel will be formed, or special needs addressed, if requested by a member of one of those groups.
Applicants must be either an Australian citizen or have permanent residence status.

ACT Public Service is an equal opportunity employer

Senior Intake Workers, Child Protection Advice and Referral Service
Child and Family Services, Hobart

$50,804 - $55,287 per annum
* As a senior and experienced member of this vital service respond to reports regarding the safety and wellbeing of children and young people and provide initial assessment, advice and referral services.
Contact: ▮▮▮▮▮▮

Vacancy No's: 501678 & 501674
Tasmania offers a relaxed lifestyle, incredible scenery, exciting recreation options, affordable real estate, and no traffic hassles. Visit Tasmania at http://www.discovertasmania.com.au
For position and application information - visit http://www.jobs.tas.gov.au or call ▮▮▮▮▮▮ Forward your application by Thursday 17 April 2002 to: The Recruitment Unit, ▮▮▮▮▮▮

Figure 4.3 Newspaper job advertisements

Counsellors
2 positions
Children and Family Service
Kids Intervention Prevention Programme (KIPP)
Funded by Department of Families

1. **COUNSELLOR** - (Maryborough/Hervey Bay & Cherbourg - Part-time 32 hours. The position is based in Maryborough and covers Hervey Bay and the Cherbourg Community as well.

2. **COUNSELLOR - Outreach.** Part-time - 20 hours per week. This position will provide an outreach counselling service in the shires of Tiaro and Woocoo.

Wide Bay Sexual Assault Association Inc is a community organisation providing excellent conditions for employees in a rural region area of South East Queensland.

Tertiary qualifications in Psychology, Social Work, Counselling or other suitable behavioural science degree, required.

For position description and selection criteria ▬▬

Closing date for applications addressing the selection criteria is 5pm Tuesday 28 January 2003. Applications should be addressed to:

**The Management Committee
Wide Bay Sexual Assault Association Inc**

MARYBOROUGH QLD 4650

MID WESTERN AREA *HEALTH* SERVICE
Senior Social Worker
Grade 2
Permanent Full Time
Bathurst Base Hospital
Recruitment No: 022002/123
Essential:
• A tertiary qualification in Social Work
• Eligible for membership of the Australian Association of Social Workers
• Experience in staff management and administration
• Minimum of three years' hospital social work experience
• Current NSW Driver's Licence
Salary: $1052.37 per week.
Enquiries: ▬▬
Closing: Friday, 26 July 2002.
Visit us on the web @ www.mwahs.nsw.gov.au
Application Packages (including position description and all essential/desirable criteria) must be obtained by telephoning
▬▬ Applications must be received by close of business on the specified date.
We are committed to Equal Employment Opportunity, Ethical Practices, the principles of Cultural Diversity and promote a smoke-free work environment. Appropriate criminal record and child protection checks conducted for all positions.   Mid Western Area HEALTH SERVICE

---

*Vietnam Veterans
Counselling Service, WA*

Counsellor

APS 6, VVCS, WA
Salary: $50,689 – $56,790
Perth
Position Number: 667 (full time, ongoing)

A Counsellor, who is an experienced therapist, can coordinate contracted counselling services, and build professional partnerships, is required to contribute to the VVCS, WA team.

The VVCS, WA provides counselling, group programs, contracted outreach, community education, development, liaison, and referral services for all eligible veterans, who have military service, and their family members.

The successful candidate will work within a skilled, professional team, and have a strong commitment to high quality, outcome focussed clinical services. In addition this person will have well-developed skills in a range of therapeutic interventions with individuals, couples, families, and support group interventions. This person will have a commitment to the process of quality assurance. The person will need values that support an understanding of the psychological and social needs of the veteran community.

Tertiary qualifications in psychology or social work are required. Registration as a psychologist or eligibility for membership of the AASW is mandatory. Two years supervised counselling experience is essential.

Conditions of service are those applying to permanent officers of the Australian Public Service.

Enquiries to: ▬▬

Selection Documentation: ▬▬

Applications addressing selection criteria and enclosing details of relevant qualifications and experience should be forwarded by close of business Friday, 28 March 2003.

Practice question and response

Question: This is all very confusing. What do I call myself and what work can I do?

Response: In summary, employers rather than the state will determine job titles and your eligibility for their work. Beyond the employment designation, you can label yourself pretty well as you wish, and engage in any sort of human service practice provided you are not contravening the regulatory regime of a licensed professional group (e.g. psychology), or opening yourself up to accusations by clients and/or employers of misrepresentation about your qualifications and experience.

Professional and industrial affiliations

Human service workers, like others, engage in mutual support and collective action through membership of professional and industrial bodies. There are two main relevant professional bodies, the previously mentioned AASW, and the Australian Institute of Welfare and Community Workers (AIWCW). There are others more concerned with arenas of practice than professional designation, for example the Case Management Society of Australia, and the Australian Professional Society on Alcohol and Other Drugs. Membership of these bodies confers rights such as access to professional development activities, professional literature, and professional indemnity insurance. It also brings legal obligations in the form of such things as payment of fees, and compliance with codes of ethics and/or standards of practice promulgated by the association. Many more human service workers are members of trade unions than are members of professional associations. The diversity of employment is reflected in the range of trade unions relevant to human services work, the Australian Services Union and public service unions being only two examples. Through union membership, workers seek support in their disputes with employers and in their work conditions. Again, membership brings with it legal rights and obligations.

Workers do need to be attuned to the legal nature of membership rights and obligations for these bodies and to understand their basis. This means being conversant with the constitution, articles of association or whatever legal document founds the body, and its rules. It is not only important that workers can do this in pursuit of their own interests and questions, but that they can alert their clients and other work contacts to the existence of such documents and their power. Legally literate and confident workers know how to find and read fundamental documents when they consider that their own or others' rights have been compromised or need to be protected. This point reappears throughout this chapter and the book.

Taking care of business

Management responsibilities

More and more, human service workers are assuming management functions. Their helping roles are being reconceptualised, as for example in case management (Gursansky, Harvey et al. 2003), and in addition they are increasingly taking on traditional management tasks such as human resource and budget management and organisational governance. Two pertinent topics that recur in the lives of most human service workers and which are underpinned by law are briefly canvassed here. These concern the governance of bodies and meeting procedure.

Governance of bodies

Many human service workers sit on or chair management committees or boards of community groups, help create or advise such bodies, contract with such bodies to perform work, are employees of such bodies, or set up their own consultancy or subcontracting businesses. Thus it is important that they have some familiarity with the form of these bodies and their own legal responsibilities in relation to them. As to status, these bodies may have individual legal form separate from their individual members and this is achieved through a process of incorporation. If a body is not incorporated in some way, individual members can be sued and held liable for its debts and activities. An incorporated body can sue or be sued, own assets, enter into contracts in its own right, protect its members from some liabilities (Roberts 1991) and be eligible for some grants. There are a number of ways in which legal bodies can be created, some under specific state and territory acts covering particular areas of human service activity, for example health and children's services. As well, there are other general forms of creation and structure quite relevant to the human services, as outlined below.

Incorporated associations

Most nonprofit community organisations now incorporate under the relevant state or territory *Association Incorporation Acts* (Gibson and Kelsen 1993). Associations must have aims consistent with the legislation, a set of rules which detail administration and management mechanisms, and must apply and be registered in the jurisdiction. The association rather than the members owns any property and carries any rights and liabilities. Members cannot take profits. Annual general meetings must generally be held, and there are legislated duties of officers and committee members, such as disclosure of interests, proper use of information, keeping accounting records, and so on.

Cooperatives

Entities engaged in cooperative activity may be formed as cooperatives under relevant state and territory legislation, for instance the *Co-operatives Act 1997* (SA) (e.g. Legal Services Commission of South Australia 1999). Housing associations, familiar to many human service workers, commonly take this legal form. They must be registered, have boards of directors and officers, with specified duties, and they may allow profit-sharing among members.

Sole traders

Here an individual conducts a business, for example a human service worker may operate as a training consultant. This requires little more than registration of a business name if desired, registration with the Australian Taxation Office for a business number and for GST, and attention to relevant state or local government licences or approvals. With this form of entity the individual and the business are indivisible as are the debts, liabilities, and assets of each (Gibson and Kelsen 1993).

Partnerships

Here less than twenty individuals (limited by the *Corporations Act 2001* (Cth) (CCH Australia Limited 2002)) can work together with a view to sharing profit. For instance, a group of human service workers may set up a counselling and psychotherapy centre. Partnerships are not actually separate legal entities but they have legal form and obligations, largely covered by the Partnership Acts of each state or territory and there are few formalities for their creation. Generally partners share losses and liabilities for partnership debts and actions. All partners, unless it is otherwise agreed, have control and management of the partnership.

Companies

Registered companies formed for the purpose of making profits are variously classified, and covered in each jurisdiction by the complex *Corporations Act 2001* (Cth). These bodies must be registered, keep specific and extensive financial records, make disclosures and hold meetings as required, and file annual returns with the Australian Securities and Investments Commission (ASIC). They are generally controlled by a board of directors (CCH Australia Limited 2002), the duties of these directors are highly regulated, and breaches of the Act can result in both civil and criminal penalties. While these bodies have not been the norm in human service work in Australia they are likely to become more prominent, as employers at least, if not as creations of human service workers themselves.

Details of all these entities and the practical responsibilities of members, officer holders, and committee members are outlined much more comprehensively elsewhere (e.g. Roberts 1991). Information is also available from the Councils of Social Service, law handbooks, Legal Aid Commissions, Community Legal Centres, and the corporate affairs departments of the states and territories, and from ASIC. However a number of general points are highlighted here. Many people, including human service workers involved with both profit and nonprofit bodies experience difficulties with things commonly intensified by collective activity, for example conflicts about processes and procedures, resources, power, and control. The interpersonal and group skills focus in much human service training provides a sound platform from which these workers can approach the difficulties, but it needs to be supplemented by a sense of legal confidence. That necessitates some idea about the following things (derived from CCH Australia Limited 2002, p. 312), many of which have been referred to in the descriptions of the bodies above:

- the structure of the body
- the law that governs it
- its establishment formalities
- its legal lifespan
- the extent of liability for those involved
- how it is meant to be controlled
- the formalities for its operation
- how new parties can be involved or old ones excluded
- how it may be disposed of
- how it can be wound up.

Familiarity with these points and confidence in seeking out relevant information is essential for any worker looking to understand the parameters of their own responsibilities and to protect their own and others' interests. Too seldom do human service workers show acumen with formal rules and governing law when facing conflict in these bodies, despite the fact that it is extraordinarily empowering. The same theme emerges in the next section.

Practice question and response

Question: We just want to do what is best for our mutual support group members and all this information seems pretty unimportant, to say nothing of tedious. How does it help us care for each other better?

Response: If you and your group work perfectly you can ignore these points. But groups are seldom perfect. What if someone in the group buys equipment and does not pay, or is injured on an outing, or harasses others, or objects to decisions made, or disrupts group activity? A little early consideration about formal group structure and conduct will minimise the negative impact of such events on the group.

Meetings, meetings, meetings

Meetings are an all-pervasive fact of human service work life. There are staff meetings, interagency meetings, team meetings, community meetings, union meetings, case meetings, board meetings, annual general meetings; the list is endless. Workers act as members, chairs, secretaries, executive officers, and this list could go on too. Yet many human service workers curse meetings as ineffective and/or unnerving and/or difficult events. Most of these workers have a solid grounding in group work theory and practice. They often know more than they realise about group development, dynamics, and productivity, and perhaps do not make the link between this knowledge and meetings. However this group work knowledge and skill foundation, overlaid with confident use of meeting rules and procedures, can make human service workers formidable meeting managers. It is the procedural dimension of meetings that is pursued here.

What are these meeting rules and procedures? They are based in history and common law and they cover notifications of meetings, content and structures of agendas, quorum requirements, debate, motion, voting and adjournment conduct, minute taking, and the management of correspondence. Formal procedures may not always be appropriate, but they are useful aids to help structure and focus thinking in even informal meetings. They are an essential addition to any person's arsenal of meeting management techniques and they have considerable empowerment potential for human service workers. Workers who are familiar with the rules are less easily intimidated by others who employ them, and can themselves use them to help control and direct meeting behaviour. This may require an attitudinal shift on the part of many human service workers who intuitively resist any hint of formal prescription in their interpersonal relationships.

It is not suggested that meeting rules be memorised, rather that their potential be recognised and their easy accessibility ensured. There are many straightforward 'how to' resources available on meeting procedure, for example Walsh (1995), Roberts (1991), and Puregger (1998). There are also legal authorities in *Joske's Law and Procedure at Meetings in Australia* (Chappenden 1982), *Horsley's Meetings* (Lang 1998), and the *Guide for Meetings and Organisations* (Renton 2001). These are invaluable resources when in-depth information and practical guidance about any aspect of meeting conduct is needed.

Practice question and response

Question: This is all very well, but how does it help me to cope with the dominant people on my board of management who neither listen to us human service workers, nor understand about our work and our clients' needs?

Response: Well, your difficulty is a complex one, but a little legal thinking may help you develop one component of your response strategy. The problem is currently described as one of interpersonal relationships and power. It can be reframed partly as one of law in which procedures are complied with or not by members. Formal procedures might then be adopted or used more tactically to contain, uphold, or sanction individual member behaviour and expression.

Contract law

Contract is a familiar and increasingly important term in the human services and fundamental to:

- outsourcing of services
- many of the problems which beset clients
- relationships between workers/agencies and clients
- relationships between employers and employees.

These points will be revisited after an outline of the most basic elements of contract law. Contracts are largely a matter of common law and private or civil law, mediated by more recent legislation at state and federal level, for example the *Trade Practices Act 1974* (Cth) and the Sale of Goods Acts in each state and territory. These Acts will reappear in chapter 11, on finance. Contract law has a long history in which the rights of parties to make their own legal bargains, with their own idiosyncratic rights and obligations, have been firmly established. There are several essential components of a contract, regardless of its subject matter, as outlined below:

Intention to create legal relations

There is no valid contract without an intention by the parties involved to create legally binding arrangements. Often this intention will be expressly written but sometimes the intention is not declared. If a contractual dispute then occurs the courts may have to construe intention. They start from a presumption that business and commercial dealings are intended to be legally binding and that family and social ones are not, but these presumptions can be rebutted by the particular facts of a case. It is more likely that legal intention will be implied where one or both parties have significantly exposed or committed themselves, for example financially or through foregoing an opportunity.

Agreement

In a valid contract the fundamental terms have been agreed to. This requires an offer and an acceptance. That is, a party makes an offer that includes terms, and indicates a willingness to be bound by them. Offers can be withdrawn before acceptance. Acceptance occurs when another party does or says something that indicates acceptance of the terms and a willingness to be bound by them too. A legally binding contract is created at this point and both parties must fulfil their obligations under it. The terms of the contract can be explicit or implied. In many commercial contracts some terms may be expressed, and also implied by legislation, for example the *Trade Practices Act 1974* (Cth). Other terms may have to be interpreted by courts as implied, when a dispute arises. Courts will look to what the parties said and did in an effort to determine what they really intended.

Consideration
In general each party to a contract must provide what is known as consideration and a familiar example is when a party provides a service and another pays for it. But money is not always involved and if it is, it does not have to be full value but rather to be seen by the law as sufficient. People are allowed to make what others might see as bad bargains. 'Consideration can be:

*   an act for a promise
*   a promise for an act; and
*   a promise for a promise' (Carvan 2002, p. 125).

The performance of an existing duty, or of a duty imposed by law is insufficient consideration.

If the parties to a contract fulfil their contractual obligations, the contract has been discharged. However if any of the parties allege breach, that is, failure to perform duties under the contract, the dispute may be taken to court by one or other of them in a civil action. The court may require parties to specifically perform their contractual obligations, it may impose an injunction which requires parties to stop doing something, and/or it may award damages, often financial.

Contracts, with some technical exceptions, do not have to be written and if they are, they do not have to be presented in any particular form. Written ones may be easier to enforce or prove but oral ones are no less legally valid. In addition the existence or otherwise of a valid contract is something that only a court can conclusively determine. Most contracts of course never go to court because they are discharged or the parties give up on them and their legal validity is never tested.

Contracts and the human services
The law of contract is extensive and technical. Human service workers are not expected to have a detailed knowledge of it despite the specialist skills developed by some of them, for example in consumer protection or consumer credit work. However a number of general comments are offered around the bullet points that introduced this section.

Outsourcing of services
Increasingly human services are being delivered under contractual relationships between funder and provider bodies. The Job Network is an example of government contracting with private providers on a national scale (e.g. Downey 2001). Human service agencies and workers are accustomed to the idea that they may owe their clients or service users legal duties, but are less attuned to the legal dimensions

of these funding contracts. Contract drafting and contract management are growth areas in the human services, and skill and experience in these areas lag. For both service purchasers and providers, traditional human service thinking must be supplemented by an awareness of the legal requirements for and implications of contractual discharge and non-performance. Purchasers may not be sufficiently alert to the power potential which flows from well-drafted and monitored contractual rights. They are increasingly in a position to demand better service delivery through the exercise of these rights. Providers may not be sufficiently attentive to the legal obligations that underpin their performance, and the desirability of becoming firmer and clearer in their contextual negotiations. This is not a plea for increased litigation in the human services as much as a call for the use of legal thinking to help improve service contracts and their performance.

Client problems

Many human service clients face both life and service problems with contractual bases and/or possible solutions. Poor or inadequate human service experienced by clients may be challengeable in contractual terms, a bargaining point to be kept in mind by their worker advocates. Wise workers are alert to these possibilities and refer on appropriately for legal advice. Contracts made by clients under duress of, say, violence or economic threat may be voidable, as may contracts formed through undue influence and where the terms have been forced and are very unfair to one side. This is particularly pertinent in the aged care arena where family members may pressure aged relatives about money or assets. Contracts made by individuals whose mental capacity was in doubt at the time through illness or intoxication may be voidable too, if they did not understand what they were agreeing to and if the other party was aware of their state. This is particularly relevant in areas of disability, substance abuse, mental health, and aged care.

Contracts made by minors may not be enforceable although there are a number of qualifications under state and territory legislation that are not uniform across Australia. For instance, under the New South Wales *Minors (Property and Contracts) Act 1970* in general a contract is binding if it benefits the minor and they understood that they were making a legal arrangement. In South Australia under the *Minors Contracts (Miscellaneous Provisions) Act 1979* contracts may be unenforceable unless ratified in writing by the minor after they reach 18 years.

A contract may be illegal at law, which means that a client may be either released from it or lose rights that they would have had under it. For example, illegal migrants and sex industry workers are often employed in circumstances that breach immigration and criminal laws and their dismissal and injury compensation rights have traditionally been compromised accordingly (Guthrie 2002).

Relationships between workers/agencies and clients

The word contract is often used colloquially in the human services to signify an agreement between workers/agencies and clients even though legal intention may not even be considered. Cordon and Preston-Shoot (1987) argue that legal thinking can improve these agreements, whether or not a legally binding contract is intended. They explain how legal processes of offer and acceptance can be used to promote full discussion and exploration of issues between workers/agencies and clients about intention and consideration before agreement is reached and recorded. In other words, a 'contractual attitude' prompts comprehensive and mutual assessment before a service plan is written and when it is drafted it should include all of the elements of a good legal contract, that is, the terms and mutual responsibilities are expressly detailed, along with time and review lines, and penalties for non-performance.

Cordon and Preston-Shoot claim that many service agreements do not satisfy legal consideration requirements in that the worker offers nothing, or that the client promises to do only what they are already obliged by law to do (e.g. comply with bond conditions). In addition they stress the need to safeguard clients' interests in the context of power differentials between staff and clients in service planning, and concerns about duress, undue influence, and mental capacity. In relation to service planning with clients, they suggest (Cordon and Preston-Shoot 1987, pp. 37–8): a cooling-off period; involvement of an independent friend or advocate; inclusion of escape clauses.

Relationships between employers and employees
Perhaps the most important contracts in the lives of human service workers are those that they have with their employers. They are now considered.

Employment law

Employment law is a complex area in which common law principles, for example contract law, are overlaid with interactive state and federal legislative regimes that are currently in flux. The *Workplace Relations Act 1996* (Cth) is the principle Act in Australia and it is commonly paralleled by state and territory equivalents. These industrial laws govern things such as wage rates, leave entitlements, work conditions, and termination of employment. It is not possible or necessary to fully canvass these areas of law here, and only a number of key features are highlighted. These concern basic duties, employee status, and occupational health and safety.

Duties of employers and employees
Both employers and employees have fundamental rights and duties underpinned by contract law among other bases. All employees, whether casual or ongoing, and employers are in contractual relationships and their contracts, like any others, may or may not be in writing. Many are partly in writing and partly oral (Creighton and Stewart 2000). Some workers have limited documentation about their job agreements, for example a letter of offer, and may not realise that there is actually a legal contract, even if in the final analysis its details have to be deduced by a court. Even if some employment terms are express, others may be implied through law, and others by fact, such as agency conventions, or the specific conduct of the parties involved. It is vital for both employers and employees to have an appreciation of these fundamentals and their sources because, as will be evident in later chapters, they underpin all work practices and are vital in questions of misconduct and liability.

The bases of employment rights and duties are (CCH Australia Limited 2002, p. 584):

- express terms of the employment contract
- implied terms of the contract, deduced from things such as work manuals, accepted customs and practices in the agency and from policy
- enterprise agreements and awards
- specific entitlement or other governing legislation
- work rules, procedures, and so on detailed in agency manuals.

General duties of employers and employees have been established over time under common law. They are implied, if not express, terms of employment contracts, superimposed with legislated requirements, for example occupational health and safety law. In bare outline, the employer is obliged to (adapted from Gibson and Fraser 1999, pp. 582–5):

- provide work
- pay wages as agreed (these must not be less than those set out in the applicable award or enterprise agreement)
- take reasonable care to ensure worker safety.

The employee is obliged to:

- comply and cooperate with lawful, safe, and reasonable commands
- exercise care and competence in carrying out duties
- provide trustworthy service and not 'act in a manner hostile to the employer's interests' (CCH Australia Limited 2002, p. 590)
- maintain employer confidentiality
- make available to the employer inventions made during employment
- disclose information relevant to the employer's interests
- account for money and property received through work.

If a worker breaches employment obligations, disciplinary responses may span reprimand through to dismissal, depending on the nature and severity of the breach. If an employer breaches employment obligations, workers can take action, often collectively with union support, under various legislative provisions. For instance, contractors can seek review of unfair contracts, by the Federal Court under the *Workplace Relations Act 1996* (Cth) (Creighton and Stewart 2000), and there is legislation in all jurisdictions relevant to discrimination in the workplace.

Practice question and response

Question: My clients were sacked because they were said to have bad attitudes. Surely this is unfair dismissal and can they be reinstated?

Response: It is improper for this sort of question to be answered by anyone but an employment law advocate with access to all the relevant details. There are probably several perspectives on the human side of this story. At law, a matrix of common law and statutory provisions will have to be interpreted and applied. Your clients need to consult their union, lawyer, and/or the relevant state or territory legal aid commission or industrial relations unit or employee advocate. If it is found that they were unfairly dismissed, reinstatement is one of a number of possible legal outcomes.

Employee or contractor status?

In a human service world increasingly characterised by privatisation and out-sourcing, the distinction between employee and contractor status sometimes blurs. But it is a critical distinction for a number of reasons. These include determination of minimum benefits under employment law, tax, attribution of liability (e.g. when wrongs have been committed), and attribution of responsibility (e.g. in workers compensation). Contractors generally carry their own insurance responsibilities and liabilities. Despite legislation in a number of jurisdictions containing some provisions about employee status, the distinction continues to evolve as courts determine difficult cases. Whether or not someone is an employee or contractor is not dependent on what they are called but on how courts construe the whole relationship between them and the putative employer. In deciding this question courts consider things such as:

- who controls the way work is done and monitored
- if payment is made regularly or in a lump sum
- if PAYE tax is taken out of pay and holiday and sick leave paid for
- the exclusivity of the work relationship
- whether the parties have different work addresses and advertising operations
- who provides and maintains equipment
- if the putative employer has dismissal rights over the worker
- how subcontractible the type of work is
- who covers workers compensation insurance.

The main message for workers and employers is the need for clarity about what is intended, and what protections, rights, and obligations they each plan to bear. With the trend towards work arrangements traditionally known as 'atypical' (Creighton and Stewart 2000, p. 13), for example casual, agency or home work, or subcontract, it is particularly important that legal help is sought in drafting agreements so that intentions are realised in legal form.

Safe work?

In every Australian jurisdiction there is a raft of legislation covering occupational health and safety obligations of workers and businesses/employers, and workers compensation for work injury (see Johnstone 1997). For example, in Victoria the *Occupational Health and Safety Act 1985* and the *Accident Compensation Act 1985* and its amending Acts largely cover the ground, while in Queensland the *Workplace Health and Safety Act 1995* and the *Workcover Queensland Act 1996* apply. Safety law is particularly relevant in human service work where stressful if not dangerous activity is common. The legislation, regulations, and codes of practice in each jurisdiction need to be fleshed out by agencies' rules, policies, and procedures covering their own special circumstances.

For instance how many staff are specified for a shift team in a correctional facility; what lifting procedures are used in an aged care facility; what personal safety mechanisms apply for staff making home visits in a domestic violence program; how is workplace stress dealt with; and how is verbal abuse at the front desk managed? These agency provisions commonly overlap and intersect with others from relevant industrial agreements. It is unlikely that most workers will know the details of these agreements and legislation, unless they sit on employee representative health and safety committees, or union committees, or work with injured employees. But as shown, all workers have a general legal duty to comply with safety instructions, and their employers to support and instruct them in safe work practices. Whether or not these legal regimes are effective is a debate for other places but it is clear that stress, at least, is an endemic problem in the human services, and 'workers must become more proactive at a managerial, political, legal, and economic level to ensure that their needs are adequately addressed' (Buys and Kendall 1998, p. 9).

Key points for practice

- Receptiveness to business, commercial, and management viewpoints is not inconsistent with care for people; it is in fact intrinsic to effective practice in the contemporary human services.
- Willingness to entertain and learn from business, commercial, and management perspectives is largely a matter of an open mind. Receptive workers can develop more comprehensive repertoires of strategies for use in their own interests and those of their service delivery.
- In Australia human service worker titles and practice modalities are not licensed by the state. Workers have considerable latitude in how they describe and profile themselves. They cannot assume that the presence or absence of a particular qualification will automatically exclude them from or include them in consideration for employment.
- Workers join many types of professional and industrial bodies. Membership confers both rights and obligations that are generally unquestioned until something goes amiss. Wise members are informed about the location and content of these rules.
- Much human service work activity is located in and conducted by collectives or bodies of various legal forms. The legal shape of these bodies will have a major bearing on the liabilities and responsibilities of those involved and they are well advised to know what these are.
- Meetings are both the mainstay and bane of much human service work. Meeting conduct and procedure has a legal base, which if understood better and used by human service workers can be very empowering.
- Contract law underpins a considerable amount of human service work activity and all relationships between employers and employees. Wise workers are familiar with the

elements of a contract in law and the express and implied terms of their personal employment contracts.

- The status of a worker as an employee or a contractor is vital in the determination of a range of liabilities and responsibilities. Prudent workers and service purchasers seek clarity about their own status and cover risks accordingly.

Some useful web sites

Corporate issues

www.ato.gov.au/
www.asic.gov.au/asic/asic.nsf
www.acoss.org.au/links.htm
www.dtrft.qld.gov.au/
www.managingwell.net/

Employment and work safety

www.employeeombudsman.sa.gov.au/
www.careerconnections.com.au/information/wage_employee.htm
www.dewr.gov.au/
www.oea.gov.au/graphics.asp?showdoc=/Default.asp
www.industrialrelations.nsw.gov.au
www.ir.qld.gov.au/
www.eric.sa.gov.au/home.jsp
www.irv.vic.gov.au
www.workcover.nsw.gov.au
www.workcover.qld.gov.au/
www.deet.nt.gov.au/wha/index.html
www.wst.tas.gov.au/node/WST.htm
www.comcare.gov.au/
www.qwws.org.au/

Professional bodies

www.aasw.asn.au/index.htm
www.aiwcw.org.au/
www.aps.psychsociety.com.au/
www.pacfa.org.au/
www.austprofessions.com.au/

Unions

www.asu.asn.au/
www.actu.asn.au/
www.labor.net.au/unions_labornet/
http://cpsu-spsf.socialchange.net.au/

5

Getting it Wrong

More than a legal duty of care

Human service agencies and workers commonly proclaim their 'duty of care'. What they understand by this is uncertain. They do, properly, seem to be accepting obligations. But what exactly are these obligations and when are they fulfilled or not? For example, are the following things violations of a duty of care:

- failure to pick up suicidal signs in a client
- tiredness at work
- lax staff supervision practices
- incorrect assessment of child abuse
- absence of agency email protocols
- chronic inability to meet report deadlines
- failure to prevent a client escape
- poor interviewing skills?

Once violations of duties are somehow determined, what sanctions might then apply and to whom? More specifically what are the legal aspects of these questions? These are the focus of this chapter. However, the legal points that follow form only one part of a broader consideration of social accountability in the human services. A comprehensive analysis would involve all of the contextual circles shown in figure 3.1 and is beyond the scope of this book.

Incompetence, mishaps, breaking the rules, and more

So is this chapter about professional negligence, malpractice, and liability? Yes, but in a wide rather than a precise legal definitional sense. Here the interest is in agency and/or worker performance, intentional or not, which might or does cause harm. Thus anything from inadvertent mistake and/or general ineptitude through to criminal behaviour is relevant. Unprofessional, unethical, incompetent, inadequate, unsatisfactory, and illegal are some of the terms used loosely in the discussion of professional conduct in this chapter. Professional negligence in its traditional legal sense is only one of a number of topics to be addressed. It will be shown that the phrase 'duty of care', in its strict legal sense, represents only one component of one form of legal risk to agencies and workers. There is much more to accountable and legally responsive practice than acknowledgment or satisfaction of a legal duty of care.

There are four reasons for taking an inclusive approach here:

- The term 'professional negligence' suggests malpractice suits against agencies and workers. These have not been integral to Australian human services as they have in the USA, where there are stronger traditions of both litigation and private practice. The Australian history is more akin to that of the United Kingdom in which human service workers have traditionally been public employees. These differences are reflected in human service and law textbooks. US textbooks routinely include sections on professional malpractice and civil processes (e.g. Saltzman and Furman 1999; Albert 2000; Barker and Branson 2000). British texts seldom do this (e.g. Braye and Preston-Shoot 1997; Cull and Roche 2001; Ball and McDonald 2002; Brammer 2003). Australian texts seldom do either (e.g. Thompson 1989; Bates, Blackwood et al. 1996; Carvan 1996; Swain 2002c).
- The term 'malpractice' invokes images of major scandal. Dramatic examples of professional misbehaviour such as fraud, rape, or murder are familiar because of the publicity that attends them but they are not the norm (Smith 2002). They are in fact the 'tip of an iceberg' (Sampford and Blencowe 2002, p. 255). According to United Kingdom writers Hunt and Campbell (1998), there are high levels of misconduct of a less spectacular nature among social service professionals, for example, verbal abuse, non-responsiveness, failure to consult clients, and affronts to service user privacy/dignity. The inconspicuous and routine character of much of the inadequate practice in the human services must be emphasised.
- Wrong conduct may not have legal consequences. There may be no discernible reaction from those who are impinged upon, especially if they are disempowered. However wrong behaviour and its effects are of no less concern even if attended by legal silence.
- Wrong conduct may not have direct legal consequences but there may be other effects. Ethical, professional, and employment responsibilities still hold, even when legal ones do not apply or are not invoked.

Performance is not sanctionable unless a rule is breached. Thus the chapter begins with a cursory discussion of rules of conduct, their sources, and relevant standards of performance. This is followed by a summary of ways in which unsatisfactory conduct may attract the attention of the law. The chapter ends with a commentary on the variable outcomes of transgressions because of the co-existence and interaction of legal and other factors.

Rules and standards of conduct in the human services

The general rules or principles of conduct in the human services originate within the various contextual circles shown in figure 3.1. But standard setting and assessment of performance, which are the mechanisms for determining if general principles have been complied with in specific circumstances, are notoriously vexed matters in the human services. This is largely because of the absence of social and professional consensus about what constitutes adequate human service provision and practice, and partly because standards shift over time. Sometimes general rules or principles are not accompanied by any standards at all. Where standards do exist, they have different levels of authority, scope, and detail. They may be standards of service or standards of conduct (Braye and Preston-Shoot 2001, p. 46). They may be directed at agencies and/or workers.

Formal societal rules are articulated in legislation or common law. Often the statement of the law is brief and blunt, and its application in each case involves a search for criteria or standards to determine if there has been a breach. For example, sexual assault is unlawful. The relevant pieces of criminal legislation specify this. But determining whether particular behaviour constitutes a sexual assault may require a complex legal interpretative activity. Much of the legislation relevant to human services work involves words like 'need', 'harm', 'hardship', 'reasonable', and 'safe-guard', which are notoriously ambiguous and cause Braye and Preston-Shoot to refer to the 'myth of clarity' about the law (1997, p. 51). Some legislation is accompanied by a comprehensive regulatory framework that includes guidelines, at least, if not standards, but this level of interpretative detail is uncommon.

Funding sources may establish or adopt rules or standards, which are often underpinned by and have legal authority. For instance the Australian Supported Accommodation Assistance Program (SAAP) service agreements with agencies require the latter to offer case management services that reflect SAAP principles and guidelines (Gursansky and Kennedy 1998). But determining whether a case management service is adequate or whether a particular worker is conducting themselves appropriately is another matter. In other examples, funded agencies may be required to have staff qualified in specified ways and to have policies that maximise contact between clients and family members. But who determines whether a family contact policy, its related procedures, and its execution are satisfactory and how do they do it?

Then there are aspirational and ideological codes of ethics, commonly promulgated by professional associations like AASW and AIWCW. They include broad, static statements that are very often ambiguous in the face of specific fact situations. For instance, is the AASW code infringed when a social worker forgets an important appointment because of family pressures? Probably yes in a number of ways but this will require some interpretation. Is a human service worker who has difficulty understanding research reports, or who has been found guilty of a road traffic offence, potentially in breach of the AIWCW code of ethics? It is unclear. Some overseas professional associations are now developing more detailed standards of service, if not practice. For example, the Case Management Society of America has authored a set of standards covering things like case manager qualifications, client focus, case load sizes, and care plan content (Smith 1995). Increasingly organisations too have broad codes of conduct for employees. In the case of the Commonwealth Public Service the code is enshrined in legislation and regulations (s 13 of the

Public Service Act 1999 (Cth) and Regulation 2.1) and this pattern is common now too with state and territory governments.

There are also agency or employer policies from which rules and standards are derived. These may be called standard procedures, operating regulations, practice manuals, standing orders, and so on. They are generally in written form. But there are also unwritten accepted practices in most agencies, which may constitute express or implied terms of contracts of employment. Agency policies and procedures may or may not have specific legislation underpinning them (e.g. occupational health and safety). They cover work practices more specifically than do codes of ethics or conduct even though they may owe an aspirational debt to both, and it is against them that worker performance can be most readily assessed. They may detail, for instance, how drugs are to be administered, or when and how physical constraint can be used, or how client assessments are to be conducted, or who can access records and when, and so on.

These sets of rules and standards often overlap, for instance sexual assault is proscribed by all of them. But in relation to other more common phenomena there may be discrepancies and perhaps even conflict between them. The cardinal point for agencies and workers is to be aware of the rules and standards, inclusive of the discrepancies and ambiguities, which apply or might be applied to them. This awareness not only encourages more thoughtful and informed practice; it also helps reduce the element of surprise, if and when the mechanisms of the law are applied. This leads into how the law works when rules are allegedly infringed or standards not met.

Infringements and the law

Errant agencies and workers are subject to a myriad of possible legal responses or actions that interact and overlap. These actions are grouped loosely and discussed here under the categories of public law, private law, and public/private law. Public law is most relevant to the public interest, and when rules of the state are infringed. Private law operates when wronged parties who can prove that they have been damaged take action. Some circumstances might activate both public and private law. The grouping in this section is used only as a vehicle for highlighting who might take action when something goes wrong, against whom the action might be taken, with what authority, and with which sanctions.

Public law

Breach of statute of general application

There are many statutes that command the behaviour of all citizens. For example, road traffic, food handling, and fund raising legislation apply to agencies and workers in and beyond their work. If the provisions of these and other statutes of general application are infringed the state may take action and apply penalties, even if no specific harm has resulted from the conduct.

Human service workers, again like all citizens who commit crimes, are subject to criminal law. Criminal conduct may or may not happen in the course of work. For instance, a worker could assault a person at work, or during a social occasion unrelated to work. Legislated sanctions apply if the individual is found guilty. Sanctions, as will be seen in chapter 8, include jail sentences, suspended or otherwise, fines, or a range of other community service options. Serious criminal behaviour by public officials may also activate other legislation in some jurisdictions, designed to combat corruption and provide for confiscation of assets, for example the *Crime and Misconduct Act 2001* (Qld).

Practice question and response

Question: So what will happen with a worker's employment if they are found guilty on a criminal charge?

Response: There is no simple answer. The outcome will depend on the severity of the offence, the nature of the offence and its relevance to the work, whether it occurred in the course of work or not, the sanction and its effect on carrying out work duties, and the terms of the employment contract.

Breach of statute or statutory duty inherent to human service work

Human service agencies and workers are often required under a legislative regime integral to the work, to do or not do certain things. That is, many have statutory duties and powers and the state can take action against them for non-compliance. For instance, legally mandated notifiers must report suspicions of child abuse or neglect. This familiar example of a particular duty of workers is elaborated in chapter 9. Statutory duties may be relatively specific as just seen, or more general, and many of them are part of a complex arrangement of interlocking and perhaps overlapping legislative provisions, regulations, and employer procedures. Privacy legislation is one such integrated example. Sometimes a whole body of workers may be subject to a statutory provision and sometimes a particular subgroup of workers is named. Sometimes the legislation is directed more at the agency.

Corrections work is a rich source of examples of legislated duties binding agencies and/or workers. Take a named group of workers and general duty requirements: under the *Criminal Law (Sentencing) Act 1988* (SA) s 49 (3), probation and community service officers have a duty to ensure that persons assigned to them comply with bond conditions. In the Northern Territory, the *Parole of Prisoners Act (2002)* s 3R outlines the duties of parole officers, including case record and report preparation. Obviously these broad legal duties have to be fleshed out by regulations and employer operating procedures.

Corrections work also offers illustrations of specific requirements of individual officers. A person performing functions under the *Corrective Services Act 2000* (Qld) who discloses confidential information risks a maximum penalty of a fine or two years imprisonment under s 243. In New South Wales under the *Crimes*

(Administration of Sentences) Regulations (2001) departmental officers must notify the Commissioner of their relationship to, or association with, prisoners (s 236). In addition, correctional officers must report allegations of misconduct, which they believe to be true, in other correctional officers (s 247). The same New South Wales Regulations provide an example of agency legislated duty, as under s 12 all inmates in correctional centres must have case plans. What this might mean for the duties of individual officers will depend on departmental procedures and terms of employment. Likewise, what constitutes a case plan is likely to be a matter of agency policy and procedure.

An interesting example of a broad statutory duty of a general group of workers is seen in the *Public Service Act 1999* (Cth). Under s 13 and Regulation 2.1, Commonwealth employees must behave while on duty overseas in a way that upholds the good reputation of Australia. Again, what this actually means for alleged breaches by individual workers will depend on departmental or section procedures and on the details of the particular case. Legislated imperatives on workers and agencies, particularly those in the public sector, are many and varied.

If a breach of a statute by a worker occurs through work, their employer may be vicariously liable if the worker was acting as an agent and the employer had not taken reasonable precautions to prevent a contravention of a statute. Two Victorian examples of this vicarious liability are provided by the *Racial and Religious Tolerance Act 2001* s 17 and the *Equal Opportunity Act 1995* ss 102 and 103. Inappropriate use of email and the Internet by employees is a particular area of vulnerability for employers who may be vicariously liable for, say, sexual harassment or defamation via these mediums (Jebb 2003). Of course, whether or not an employer is found vicariously liable for an employee's breach, they are likely to take a dim view of the employee's behaviour, and may take their own action against the worker under the contract of employment and industrial law.

Practice question and response

Question: But how can any worker be expected to know all these legal requirements?
Response: A worker is not expected to know all legislated duties across the human services. However they should be informed about the legal obligations applicable in their specific area of work. Both they and their employer have a responsibility to ensure that they know what their obligations are and to be up to date about them. Their employer is expected to have in place procedures that flesh out the legal imperatives, keep staff aware of them, and monitor staff compliance.

Some of these legislative imperatives will be expanded upon in later chapters. The main point here is that failure to perform as required by law can result in penalties including prison sentences and more commonly fines. Some human service workers label every imperative as legal. Yet others are cavalier about the legal nature of their obligations and assume wider discretionary power than the law permits. This may be due to ignorance or perhaps it reflects a pattern of unchallenged disregard here, which Braye and Preston-Shoot (2001) see in Britain. They argue that United Kingdom local authorities commonly ignore their statutory duties and that courts have been reluctant to intervene. In a similar vein, Swain (1998) finds very few prosecutions in Australia of mandated child abuse notifiers who failed to report. Given this context, agencies and workers could be forgiven for thinking that they do not face a real legal risk if they breach statutes. However, they are not released from their moral and ethical duties and times may be changing in relation to their legal duties and private law actions.

Breach of practice licence?

As explained in the previous chapter, human service workers are not licensed to practice by the state. Thus errant workers cannot be reported to registration boards, they will not face disciplinary proceedings through such boards (e.g. Daniel 1998; Wilson 2002), their names will not be placed on open negligence lists (e.g. Committee on the Health Care Complaints Commission 2002), and they will not be prevented from further practice through licence suspension (Smith 2002). However ethical, employment, and other legal obligations still apply if they misbehave.

Practice question and response

Question: A counsellor at my work was sacked for behaving very badly. Surely they cannot continue to function as a counsellor?

Response: They can. There may be practical impediments, for example, negative referee reports, incarceration in jail and/or convictions that must be declared to prospective employers. But the worker will not be legally deregistered as there is no licence to withhold. They can seek and may get work as a counsellor in another agency or operate in private practice.

In summary, if statutory provisions are breached, the force and authority of the state apply. However it is likely that there are many fewer human service breaches pursued in law than occur. They may be hard to detect and to prove, especially if they are sins of omission rather than commission.

Public and private law

Breach of funder requirements

If an agency or workers do not perform satisfactorily, usually to specified service standards, funding may be withdrawn, not renewed, or its recovery sought. This action is generally underpinned by legal mechanisms, for example legislation and/or contract law. Its impact can be devastating for both agencies and workers.

Breach of employment requirements

For human service employees who 'get it wrong' in some way, the employer is the most likely responder, and their ultimate sanction is job termination. Employer action is by far the most common way in which human service workers who err or make mistakes in many of the less obvious ways mentioned earlier in this chapter are disciplined or sanctioned. Employers have a responsibility to supervise and monitor all workers. Employers have particular responsibilities to confront poor performance and to take action if improvements are not forthcoming. Employer action, underpinned by contract and industrial law, and in the case of public servants also often statute as instanced by the Australian Public Service misconduct process (Public Service and Merit Protection Commission 2000), may result in anything from mild rebuke, through to formal reprimand and finally termination. This action may or may not be accompanied by other forms of action, say by professional associations, or under public or civil law.

Employer agencies themselves are also subject to a barrage of legal imperatives, some mentioned earlier. Their employees may take private contractual action against them if they fail to perform contractually. Also both they and their employees are covered by industrial, and occupational health and safety legislation to name two examples.

Private law

Contract law

This topic has been covered in the previous chapter and mentioned again above. In summary both agencies and workers who do not fulfil their legal contractual obligations can face breach of contract and damages claims. Among other things they could be required to perform contractual obligations and/or to pay compensatory money.

Negligence law in flux

The whole area of legal duty, fault and damage between citizens is controversial and fluid. There are long-standing legal and social policy debates about the necessity for findings of fault when someone suffers injury, and who should carry the risks or costs of damage (e.g. Mann 2003). Much human service work is in the public sector that lies at the centre of one such debate. The position of public authorities, and the '[questionable] deterrent value of civil actions' (Reynolds 1995, p. 145) on them are particularly contentious. For example, Rodger (1995) argues that legal findings in favour of wronged individuals against child protection authorities in the United Kingdom can reduce services for the majority. If these authorities experience substantial damages claims, or excessive regulation, they may minimise their creative and innovative activities in future and/or engage in 'defensive or procedural practice' (Braye and Preston-Shoot 2001, p. 48). In addition legal claims tie up already constrained human service staff and financial resources for long periods of time, to the detriment of new and future clients. But in the United Kingdom, the protection of public welfare authorities from legal scrutiny is waning (Braye and Preston-Shoot 2001; Brayne and Broadbent 2002; Brammer 2003; Brayne and Carr 2003; Dyer 2003). It would seem that Australia too is becoming a more litigious society (Katter 1999), a trend to be noted by human service agencies and workers.

But there is a countervailing trend to be factored into human service thinking. In Australia in recent years, there has been considerable government and public disquiet about negligence cases, especially in the health field, resulting in large damages awards. There is now a 'liability insurance crisis' (Walmsley, Abadee et al. 2002, p. 141). Medical indemnity insurance costs are of particular and continuing concern. Some charitable groups and churches too have faced high-profile suits by individuals damaged while in their care. The Federal Government warns of potential floods of claims from Indigenous people removed from their families and otherwise injured in social welfare systems. These phenomena have resulted in much government legislative activity and the law is consequently in flux in this area. Negligence, traditionally an area of common law, is increasingly being codified in legislation. The recent Ipp report (Commonwealth Treasury (Ipp Report) 2002) recommends the enactment of civil liability legislation for each jurisdiction in Australia and most are moving in this direction. States and territories have legislation or bills which codify things like standards of professional conduct, protection for volunteers, exclusion of dangerous activities, limits on damages awards, limits on time within which claims must be made, and so on. Considerable change can be expected over the next few years with significance for professional liability in particular.

Negligence defined

Negligence is a tort, 'a wrong' involving fault, traditionally necessitating a civil action mounted by the wronged party or plaintiff. The general principles of negligence have been extended incrementally, clarified, and argued about in significant common law cases. As explained above, they are increasingly being codified. To establish negligence under common law it is necessary for the plaintiff to prove all of these elements:

- that they were owed a duty of care by the defendant
- that the duty was breached
- that the breach caused them damage.

Professional negligence claims also require establishment of these elements. There are few human service precedents in Australia (Bates, Blackwood et al. 1996) and much that is said about how the law of negligence applies is speculation. Thus education and medical cases are used to predict the legal obligations of human service agencies and workers. Nonetheless some points about the three elements of negligence in relation to human service practice are offered.

Duty of care

This is where the chapter started. It is both ethically and professionally proper for human service agencies and workers to assume that they do owe a duty of care to clients and to deliver services accordingly. It is also legally prudent, as the character of the relationship between client and worker is often likely to impose a legal duty of care. Acceptance of this legal duty encourages consideration of who the client is in each situation. Such a question is not easily answered in much human service work where complex combinations of family members, peers, other service providers, the community, and so on are common.

This struggle to identify the existence and scope of duty is mirrored in law too. For example, in the relatively recent Australian High Court case of *Sullivan v Moody & Ors* (2001) 207 CLR 562, it was concluded that the South Australian Department of Community Welfare in investigating child sexual abuse allegations, owed a duty to the children but not the accused fathers. The court was concerned here, among other things, that duty to the fathers could lead to unlimited liability, and that it would be incompatible with other duties of the department. However the High Court recently found that the employer of a parent negligently killed at work does owe a duty to that person's children in *Gifford v Strang Patrick Stevedoring Pty Ltd* (2003) 198 ALR 100. Similarly the New South Wales Court of Appeal has held that the state owes a duty to those who might be harmed by a prisoner who makes a foreseeable escape from custody in *Godfrey v New South Wales [No 2]* (2003) Aust Torts Reports 81-700.

New South Wales has already codified some aspects of general duty of care and duty to third parties in the *Civil Liability (Personal Responsibility) Act 2002* ss 5B and 5C (Walmsley, Abadee et al. 2002), and other jurisdictions are moving in a similar direction. Despite new legislation, much about the position of human service agencies and workers with respect to duty of care will remain uncertain until relevant precedent cases are determined.

Yet other law limits rights under negligence law. For example, a private law cause of action for breach of statutory duty does not arise under the *Social Security Act 1991* (Cth) (Sutherland and Anforth 2001, p. 701). This does not mean that social security workers do not have any ethical, or other extensive legal and agency duties to the public. It is more about citizens having access to other rights of redress through relevant tribunals that can review agency and worker actions. This is an illustration of the problem of using a legal duty of care to define the scope of human service obligations.

Practice question and response

Question: But how do I know that I owe a legal duty to someone in my work?

Response: Unless there is a clear legal precedent, or specific legislation covering the relationship that you are concerned about, you may not know, because it is a legal duty ultimately only determinable by a court. However, if you behave in your work as if you owe a duty to people for whom you have some responsibility then you reduce your legal risk. At the same time you are more likely to be operating as an aware and accountable professional.

Breach of duty

A breach is premised on action not being acceptable in some way and this brings the discussion back to the issue of standards. The law is particularly volatile in this area as governments are in the process of deciding how to codify tests of breach of duty, for which types of professional activity, and for which professional groups. Common law and statutory duties may also overlap or on occasions conflict.

Courts however have established that professional standards of care are higher than those expected of ordinary people. A professional person may breach a duty of care by doing or failing to do something that would not be classed as a breach for a layperson. Under common law, where many of the cases have concerned doctors, peer review tests have been applied to professional conduct. For example, in the lead medical case of *Rogers v Whitaker* (1992) 175 CLR 479 at 483 it was said 'The standard of reasonable care and skill required is that of the ordinary skilled person exercising and professing to have that special skill'. The recent case of *Presland v Hunter Area Health Service & Anor* [2003] NSWSC 754 (Unreported, Adams J, 19 August 2003) concerned a mentally ill man who killed someone after leaving hospital. The New South Wales Supreme Court applied the standards of an 'ordinary skilled psychiatrist' (para. 158). It was found that a psychiatric registrar negligently failed to detain the man in hospital by not meeting this standard of care, when there was foreseeability of damage to the plaintiff or others. The court also pointed out that professional standards do not demand perfection. Errors may happen as long as professional judgments are made with reasonable skill and care.

The Ipp Report (2002, p. 1) recommends that a peer review test for medical practitioners be enshrined in Australian legislation and left open for extension to other professional groups. The report also recommends that the basic rule about standard of care for professionals be restated in legislation referring to persons 'professing that skill' (2002, p. 2). This wider phrase may be quite relevant to human service workers who without state licensing often subjectively categorise themselves as having particular skills. The test or standard for the provision of a professional service in the *Civil Liability (Personal Responsibility) Act 2002* (NSW) s 50 includes the following points:

- Liability is not incurred if the professional acted in a manner widely accepted by peer professional opinion as competent professional practice.
- Widely accepted does not mean universally accepted.
- Differing professional opinions can be relied on in court.
- Professional opinion that the court considers irrational cannot be relied on.

The Queensland *Civil Liability Act 2003* includes very similar provisions for establishing standards of care for professionals.

But how do the courts decide what practice is widely accepted by peer professional opinion in an area? It is very difficult, particularly in the human services where there is limited consensus about intervention approaches and where so much of the work is dependent on confidential relationships. Again the analysis comes full circle to the earlier discussion in this chapter on rules and standards. Courts are likely to consult, but not necessarily rely on, the following guides when attempting to decide if something is professionally acceptable:

- professional associations codes and standards
- funding body requirements
- relevant research and practice literature
- professional education curriculum
- agency procedures.

At common law, and it would seem now in emerging legislation despite technical variations in wording, courts have the final say about determination of standards, particularly if they think that standards are lax in an area of practice (Jackson, Powell et al. 1992). This may be quite relevant to the human services and it is worth noting that a respondent agency or professional will not be able to rely on subjective or parochial opinions that the court finds unconvincing.

Practice question and response

Question: As an aged care worker, I know that I work as well if not better than my colleagues so surely, legally, my standards of performance are fine?

Response: Perhaps not. A court may decide that the standards in the agency are lower than those accepted more widely in the field. If this is happens, your conduct, although better than that of your colleagues, may still be considered inadequate.

In relation to deciding whether there has been a breach of duty in schools, Stewart and Knott (2002, p. 18) list useful legal indicators. These are also helpful when thinking about duty and risk in the human services:

- 'The foreseeability of harm (Walmsley, Abadee et al. (2002) would now suggest reasonable foreseeability);
- The magnitude of the risk of that harm occurring;
- The gravity of the harm that may take place;
- The cost and practicability of preventing it;
- The justifications for running the risk'.

Damage caused by the breach and liability

It must be proved by the plaintiff that the damage suffered has been caused by the respondent's breach of duty. This is the element of causation. Damage can include physical injury, psychological injury, or financial loss. In the human service world of complex human interactions where single causal relationships are hard to establish and their consequences even harder to quantify, causation is not an easy thing to establish, but neither is it impossible.

As with the first two elements of negligence, governments, for example in New South Wales under the *Civil Liability (Personal Responsibility) Act 2002*, are codifying and perhaps limiting the common law tests of causation and scope of liability. In the Australian Capital Territory, New South Wales, and Western Australia, new civil legislation is placing controls on injuries claims, as is personal injuries legislation in the Northern Territory and Queensland and wrongs legislation in South Australia and Victoria (Walmsley, Abadee et al. 2002). There are Professional Standards Acts in Western Australia and New South Wales to limit the liability of members of certain professional associations (Walmsley, Abadee et al. 2002), but human service workers are not included.

If a negligence claim succeeds, damages are awarded against the defendant. How are they paid? Insurance and employment status are the major factors here.

Self-employed workers and/or contractors are reliant on professional indemnity insurance. Traditionally, human service workers have not attended to this issue, partly because private practice has not been the norm in this area, and partly because they, unlike some registered professional groups (e.g. lawyers), have not been required legally to carry it. But as Partlett (1985, p. 368) said a while ago 'insurance is the incoming tide' and some private employers now even require their employees to carry personal professional indemnity insurance. The AASW provides indemnity insurance, but it like most, does not give unlimited protection. It covers injury caused inadvertently only in the 'course of acting as a social worker' (Australian Association of Social Workers 2003). 'Intentional wrongdoing' will generally not be covered by any indemnity insurance (Saltzman and Furman 1999, p. 482).

If the person found liable is an employee going about their work, the general legal rule is that their employer will be vicariously liable for their actions and the damages. Legislation now enshrines this rule and mediates it. For example, the *Wrongs Act 1936* (SA) s 27c(1) and the *Law Reform (Miscellaneous Provisions) Act 1984* (NT) s 22A declare employer liability unless the behaviour of the employee is serious and wilful or gross misconduct respectively. In New South Wales under the *Employees Liability Act 1991* (NSW) ss 3 and 5, the employee is indemnified if the employer is also liable, again unless the employee's conduct is serious and wilful misconduct. For this reason, and the fact that employers may have more resources ('deeper pockets'), agencies are often sued directly when their workers cause damage. But again there are limits on the protection. Employers will not be liable for employee conduct outside the parameters of their work role. Employers may also escape liability if they can show that they took all reasonable steps to prevent the likelihood of the damage ever happening, for example staff had been appropriately and adequately trained. It is always very wise to have clarification of individuals' employment status, and qualification of the scope of work roles and standards of conduct in place, but particularly so when legal action threatens.

Negligent misstatement

This is a subcategory of negligence, involving wrong advice, which also has three elements:

- existence of a special relationship between the advisor and the advisee
- competency on the part of the advisor to give advice
- the advisee's reasonable reliance on the advice and resultant loss.

This is an area of legal risk not adequately recognised in the human services. Despite the lack of precedents, it seems to have considerable latent legal potential. As service access becomes more complex, service information more overwhelming, and service availability more scarce, wrong advice may be very costly for those who rely on it. Legal action may become more common. Human service agencies and workers do need to be mindful of advice which, although honestly given, is careless. Workers in particular should be very careful about giving gratuitous advice, in their work capacity, without qualifying its limits.

Practice question and response

Question: But I work to help people. Just because I cannot keep up with the quantity of information available, it surely would be unethical of me to refuse to answer questions when people are seeking help?

Response: It may be both unethical and a matter of negligent misstatement to give wrong, even though well-intentioned, information. The most effective help is likely to result from a delayed but accurate response. An instant, albeit wrong response, may make you feel helpful but it may damage rather than help the recipient.

Negligence and the human services

The mass of material available about professional negligence claims is dispropor-tionate to their occurrence in the human services. The probability of a suit and the possibility are quite different. The major legal requirements have already been summarised. In addition, a claim must be lodged within times specified under relevant statutes of limitations. By the time many people realise the extent of their injury they may be out of legal time. The practical obstacles for most claimants, many of them disadvantaged, who wish to sue are often also considerable (Mann 2003). Legal representation may be unaffordable, and eligibility for legal aid a problem. Unless claimants have financial capacity, or can enlist an advocacy or similar group with resources, a negligence claim will not really be feasible for them.

This reduces the practical legal risk for human service agencies and workers who cause damage. However, it does not absolve them from moral and professional responsibility and it does not diminish the other risks they face. Litigation is on the increase, and as Brammer argues (2003, p. 111), it is easier to establish liability at the operational rather than at the policy level, which increases the vulnerability of front-line work decisions. Cases that do eventually establish negligence precedents in the human services in Australia might catch deserving or even undeserving agencies and/or workers. The 'undeserving' point requires a little explanation. If a negligence suit does go ahead the court will focus only on the details of duty, breach, and damage on the occasion in question. It will not be attentive to the fact that the agency and/or worker respondents usually conduct themselves impeccably.

Practice question and response

Question: Are you really suggesting that I could make one mistake and be found at fault for it when I normally operate at above average levels?

Response: Yes, in a negligence case. The court will only hear evidence about that particular mistake or conduct, in relation to duty, breach, and damage. So if your mistake did not come within the parameters of reasonable care, although it was an aberration for you, you could be found liable. However note that courts demand reasonable care, not perfection, of professionals.

Breach of statutory duty under common law

There is a common law action akin to that of negligence where a plaintiff alleges damage as a result of a defendant's failure to perform a statutory duty. The plaintiff must show that the defendant did have a statutory duty, that the plaintiff was in a class that the duty was meant to benefit, that the defendant did not carry out the duty, and that damage resulted. Reynolds (1995) argues that these sorts of actions may have broader scope than those in negligence. If he is right, cases of this type may attract the interest of advocacy groups in the future. But again, all the obstacles that attend negligence actions apply here, and there may be legislative limitations too on these claims. For example, private claims of this kind are not permitted when there has been a breach under the *Social Security Act 1991* (Cth) (Sutherland and Anforth 2001).

Defamation and breach of confidence

These topics will be covered in the following chapter. They are two more examples of private legal actions against agencies and/or workers who are careless with information and opinions.

Breach of professional association codes

What happens if a professional association code of ethics is breached? The codes technically only pertain to members, and members who breach may have disciplinary action taken against them or have their membership terminated, under the constitutional rules. These associations, such as AASW and AIWCW, have no jurisdiction over the majority of Australian human service workers who are not members. Even for members, the risks of sanction are not great. Many associations do not have complaint procedures in place, and lack the resources to investigate and process allegations. Given the broad statements in the codes, it is very difficult to prove a breach (Coady 2002; Stone 2002). In addition, potential complainants often do not know of the existence of relevant associations and reporting processes, let alone the membership status of workers. If a worker's behaviour is bad enough for an association breach case to succeed, chances are it has already attracted employer and possibly other legal sanctions.

Complaints and investigatory bodies

If there has been a breach of statute the state may lay charges and agencies and/or workers become defendants. If private law action is taken the agency and/or worker become respondents in a civil case. These are examples of direct legal action. But there are other legal mechanisms that might be activated when parties have concerns and/or complaints about agencies and/or workers. For example, there are many formal complaints and investigation bodies, created and empowered by legislation.

Complaints bodies are an increasingly common phenomena in the health (Devereux 2002) and human services. There are also an increasing number of general investigation and audit bodies, such as Ombudsmen and the Independent

Commission Against Corruption (ICAC) in New South Wales and the Crime and Misconduct Commission in Queensland, especially applicable to public officials. These bodies have diverse powers, some statutory, of investigation and reporting rather than sanctioning. Their activities may be paralleled or followed by more direct legal action. For example, a worker's treatment of clients could be investigated by one of these bodies and a recommendation made for criminal charges. These charges could be laid by the state, while a negligence claim is simultaneously mounted by the clients against the worker and employer.

There are many critiques of the fairness and effectiveness of these bodies, particularly complaints ones (e.g. McMahon 1997; McCullough 2002; Wilson 2002), but even if agencies and workers who come under their scrutiny are not seriously penalised, the attention can absorb resources, expose poor practice, and cause embarrassment.

A mosaic of expectations, risks, and possible outcomes

A quantity of material has been canvassed thus far about rules that might be broken, and standards and sanctions that might apply when they are. But how can agencies and workers struggling to assess legal and other risks on a daily basis organise and contextualise this material? As figure 3.1 shows, law is only one component of the complex contextual mosaic of interlocking expectations, risks, and sanctions in which human service practice takes place. Legal explorations of questionable human services practice outside of this wider context are incomplete and potentially misleading for the practitioner.

For most situations in which an agency and/or worker have underperformed, the outcomes, if any, are not easily predicted. Much hangs on the seriousness of the wrongdoing, the political sensitivity around that conduct at the time, who detects it, the powers of the sanctioning bodies, and even more on the resources and tenacity of the complainants. There is generally not a simple linear relationship between action and sanction. The rare transgressor may be sanctioned while the persistent one is untouched. In addition, many aggrieved people seek other than legal means of redress. They may for example go to the press or complain to a member of parliament. It is hard to predict what sorts of consequences, if any, will apply in these cases. However, the processes can take up considerable agency and worker time and energy and may cause considerable embarrassment. Yet other people may threaten physical retribution. This is not unknown in the human services and it must be factored into thinking about work and personal safety.

In respect of inadequate performance in the human services, the law is akin to a sleeping giant. It has a greater potential for action than is realised. When it is awakened, agencies and workers can expect to be significantly challenged. The notion of a legal duty of care is a useful reminder to human service agencies and workers about their responsibilities but it does not define the full scope of their obligations and on occasions it will not even exist when other obligations do.

Key points for practice

- Errors and mistakes are an accepted and expected part of human service and any other practice. They cannot be eliminated but agencies and workers can and should make efforts to minimise their frequency and impact.
- Very few incidents of 'getting it wrong' in human services work are ever addressed directly by the law. The majority go unnoticed and unsanctioned by the law. This may leave workers less constrained legally, but perhaps more exercised in terms of ethics and personal values.
- Agencies and workers who do come to the attention of the law will not usually be able to rely on their usual or general competence as a defence. The circumstances of that specific incident and conduct will be the sole interest of the law.
- Workers who 'get it wrong' are more at risk of action by their employer than they are of independent legal action.
- Because of the many different ways in which the law can be activated, generally competent workers might be sanctioned, while persistently poor performers may not experience any scrutiny by the law.
- Good intentions are a poor defence if the law is involved when things have gone wrong. Well- and ill-intentioned behaviour can equally result in damage or potential damage to others.
- Agencies and workers do need to be familiar with contemporary knowledge and widely accepted ideas about sound practice in their fields. Parochial assessments of standards of performance do not encourage good practice, and are not acceptable to courts.
- Aggrieved people will often pursue other than legal actions. These may not result in any legal scrutiny or sanctions but they too can be very painful for the agencies and workers involved.
- Wise agencies and workers always act as if they may come under direct legal scrutiny. This attitude is likely to engender better practice, and it certainly prepares for rational justification of actions if the law is ever applied.
- A legal duty of care should prompt more careful practice but it does not define the full range of human service obligations.

Some useful web sites

Negligence

http://revofneg.treasury.gov.au/content/home.asp
www.lawcouncil.asn.au/journal/LCA/LCA+Brief

Investigation commissions

www.icac.nsw.gov.au/
www.cmc.qld.gov.au/

Ombudsman

www.ombudsman.gov.au/
www.ombudsman.wa.gov.au/
http://act.ombudsman.gov.au/
www.ombudsman.vic.gov.au/
www.nswombudsman.nsw.gov.au/csc/index-csc.html

Health complaints

www.justice.tas.gov.au/health_complaints/home.html
www.hccc.nsw.gov.au/health-public-affairs/you/02.htm

6

Managing Information

What does managing information mean?

It includes confidentiality and more

Consider these human service situations:

- A worker at a party is asked about a client in their agency.
- Client files are left on the photocopier.

These are relatively obvious situations of client related confidentiality. But confidentiality is a taken-for-granted concept that is used too loosely in the health and human services and is subject to myth-making.

Exploding the myths about confidentiality

- There is an enduring myth in the human services that confidentiality is absolute. Charlesworth (1993, p. 6-2291) says social workers withhold information necessary for effective client management in professional teams because of a mistaken understanding of confidentiality.
- Human service workers maintain a myth that they are especially vigilant about confidentiality. Again Charlesworth (1993, p. 6-2291) claims that social workers have a reputation for being righteous about confidentiality while not being careful about it themselves. Other human service workers should be included in this critique.
- There is yet another myth that client information is most in need of protection from 'outsiders'. However 'insiders' in health and human service systems are a big threat to client confidentiality. For example, they browse electronic client data bases (Kelly 1998) and are careless about talking together in public places like lifts (Vigod, Bell et al. 2003).

Beyond confidentiality

Not only is confidentiality a misunderstood concept, it is only one of many aspects of information management in the human services. In the following situations, some but not all involving clients, workers also face difficult questions about how to handle information:

- Nepotism in agency tender and contract processes is rife.
- Emails about a senior job appointment are mistakenly sent to a worker.
- A worker suspects that one of their clients may be a threat to another person.
- A worker comes across a colleague's pornographic web site.
- A colleague acts frequently as if mildly drug affected.
- An agency to which a worker refers clients constantly mishandles those clients.
- Sensitive work files are commonly carried in the worker's private car.
- Fascinating details of a high profile sportsperson are accessible to workers on an agency electronic data base.

Here there are questions about reporting information or not, putting information at risk, accessing information or not, acquiring information advertently or otherwise, and so on. Thus this chapter addresses the various obligations, legal ones in particular, that are relevant to human service agencies and workers managing all sorts of information in diverse circumstances. The familiar concept of confidentiality is explored and the myths about it challenged. However, it is deliberately contextualised in a wider treatment of information management. Like all other information matters, confidentiality is subject to a complex pattern of social, legal, employer, and personal imperatives that have been emphasised earlier in this book.

The chapter is structured around an information management cyclic schema and covers issues of data collection, recording, storage, and access. As always, the law and the human services are seen as interactive and potentially mutually reinforcing.

Interaction of human service practice and law

Traditionally, information issues have been left largely to organisations and practitioners, although there has been legislation in each jurisdiction about the management of government records, instanced by the *Archives Act 1983* (Cth). The situation has changed with comprehensive privacy legislation enacted by the Federal Government and by many states more recently. The *Privacy Act 1988* (Cth) originally applied to the operations of Federal Government departments and contained eleven Information Privacy Principles (IPPs) concerning the collection, use, security, and disclosure of personal information. The *Privacy Amendment (Private Sector Act) Act 2000* amended the original Act so that it now applies also to private organisations including not-for-profit ones with an annual turnover of more than $3 million, and any practitioner or private organisation offering health services, or collecting personal information. Through it, ten National Privacy Principles (NPPs), expanding on the original IPPs, have been enshrined in Schedule Three of the *Privacy Act 1988*. Most human service agencies are thus now covered by very wide-ranging provisions about how information should be handled and this is likely to be an area of increasing significance. But as always, the legislation is applied through human service procedures and practices.

The cyclic schema in figure 6.1 includes a number of information management topics or phases, consistent with the Federal Privacy Principles. It also depicts a symbiotic relationship between legal and human service practice factors in good information management. It is argued that:

- quality professional information management practices will generally satisfy legal requirements
- legal requirements will be generally consistent with quality professional information management practices.

Because of this fusion there is some artificiality in trying to segregate and focus on legal aspects, even though that is what this chapter will attempt. The cycle is followed by discussion of legal points relevant for each of the phases. A considerable amount of attention is devoted to access and the two persistent relevant legal questions—what are the imperatives to refuse access or not disclose, and what are the imperatives to disclose?

The agency and worker and their purposes are positioned at the centre of this cycle. The mandate and aims of the agency are critical in determining the *purpose* of each information processing activity no matter how big or small. This is a very important point as the outcome of any legal challenge is likely to depend as much on the defensible professional arguments put by the agency and worker as it is on a question of law. The agency has responsibility for ensuring that acceptable

Figure 6.1 Cycle of information management in the human services

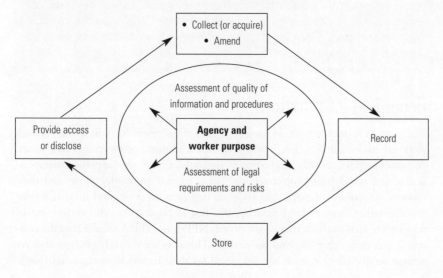

information policies, procedures, and practices are established and managed. The worker accommodates ethical, agency, and personal demands in their own practice. Both have responsibility for monitoring legal obligations and risks in their mutual and individual work activities. These points can now be illustrated by attention to the major legal issues at each position on the cycle.

Collecting (or acquiring) and amending information

What information is collected deliberately will depend on agency and worker purposes. How it is collected and by whom, and how it is amended will invoke in particular IPPs 1 and 7 and NPPs 1, 6, and 10. In summary the information collection must be consented to, necessary, lawful, not unreasonably intrusive, and the person about whom it is collected must be fully informed about what is being done and why. These collection principles may not apply to information acquired incidentally until it is recorded formally in some way and then principles about records and storage will apply. The collection principles are consistent with human service ones, but how they are operationalised in practice hangs on the word 'purpose', which is why it is positioned so centrally in the cycle.

Practice question and response

Question: Our case managers have responsibility for assisting young people to establish themselves in independent living and in work. Should they collect information, say, about clients' early biological family experiences?

Response: This is more a question of human service practice than law. The main thing is that the agency can justify its answer in terms of its mission, policies, program, intervention, and assessment models, and in terms of what would be seen more widely as acceptable human service practice in this area. So in brief, what is the intervention approach, is it reputable, and what sort of information is essential for it to be implemented? If these questions cannot be answered precisely it is likely that the parameters of information collection in the agency are similarly ill defined and indefensible.

Recording information

The types of formal records, in hard copy and/or electronic form in human service work are multitudinous. For instance there are minutes of meetings, case notes, assessment reports, emails, court reports, logbooks, case or service plans, correspondence, and research or project reports. What records are made, when, and their content, structure, language, and style are largely matters of good human service practice rather than of legal prescription. But as far as personal information in documents such as client files is concerned, NPP 3 and IPP 3 require that the content is accurate, complete, and up-to-date. This may seem overly obvious and yet human service client records are renowned for their technical inaccuracies (Kagle

1991) and their incompleteness, particularly about reasons for and details about intervention activities (Swain 2002b).

If the law becomes involved in a question about records, it will be interested in credibility of sources, comprehensiveness, logic, rationale, balance, relevancy, and concurrency of records and events. In determining appropriate standards for record keeping, courts might consult academics with knowledge of record keeping and professional education (e.g. Kagle 1991; Ames 1999; Kane, Houston-Vega et al. 2002), agency policies and codes, and/or professional associations and registration boards (e.g. American Psychological Association 1993; Australian Association of Social Workers 1999; Symons 2002).

Practice question and response

Question: What should be recorded and how much written?

Response: There is any number of answers that could be acceptable both in practice and in law. The critical thing is that the agency and worker answers are justifiable in terms of policies and procedures consistent with privacy law, and in terms of what would be seen more widely as acceptable human service practice.

Storing information

Much could be said about practical questions of space and organisation, not least about the particular challenges posed by electronic records systems (e.g. Jackson 2001). But here three legal questions are concentrated on.

How should the records be stored?

The answer here, from a position of both law and human service ethics, is 'safely'.

NPP 4.1 (*Privacy Act 1988* (Cth) Schedule 3) says 'An organisation must take reasonable steps to protect personal information it holds from misuse and loss and from unauthorised access, modification or disclosure'.

But what are reasonable steps? Guidelines promulgated by the Office of the Federal Privacy Commissioner help determine them (Office of the Privacy Commissioner 2001). Many organisations have developed their own policies and procedures about how and where data will be stored and accessed. This latter issue is relevant to many workers now who are carrying information with them from place to place, including office to home. The agency policy on this will be important to their defence if anything goes amiss, and the agency policy in turn will need to be consistent with privacy guidelines and general human service standards.

How long should they be stored?

Governments increasingly prescribe, through legislation, regulations, policies, and state records schemes, the length of time that it is necessary for some organisations and practitioners to keep client records and about destruction of information (see

NPP 4). Much of this activity at state and territory level has been prompted by the federal privacy legislation. For example, the Victorian *Health Records Act 2001* and the New South Wales *Health Records and Information Privacy Act 2002* require that health practitioners keep adult client records for seven years after last attendance and child records until that person turns 25. In addition, the *National Enquiry into the Separation of Aboriginal and Torres Strait Islander Children from their Families* (Wilson 1997) recommended that records of those children removed from their families never be destroyed and state records schemes are incorporating this requirement.

Agencies and private practitioners need to know whether or not they are covered by an Act, regulations, or scheme, either directly or under the terms of a contract with government for outsourced work. If they are not, they will still be judged by general standards of acceptable practice if they face legal challenge. Thus it is important that they have retention policies consistent with recent legislation and government policies. The implication for all workers is that their day-to-day work records have a legal life that may be even longer than their own. This is surely a stimulus for workers to think carefully whenever recording something, as being called to account for records many years after they were made is a disconcerting prospect.

Permitting or denying access to information

All human services agencies should have in place policies and procedures for determining who can access agency and client information and under what circumstances. There are legal reasons for this but again, human service practice considerations are also vital.

Practice question and response

Question: Should clients be allowed to read their own files?
Response: This is as much a question of professional ethics and agency policy and practice as it is one of law, although freedom of information and privacy law are premised on rights of access. Both NPP 6 and IPP 6 entitle the individual to have access unless exceptions apply, for example it will pose a threat to the life of someone or to the privacy of a third party. In good human service practice, the articulated service ideology and intervention approaches being used by an agency will indicate the appropriate procedures and practices for sharing or not sharing information with clients. It is argued here, based on both legal and human services principles, that clients have a right to know what is documented about them unless there are compelling reasons otherwise. Adequate practical safeguards must be in place to help clients understand and cope with this information, and to protect the confidentiality of others referred to in their records.

There are two overriding sets of legal imperatives that bear on questions about access to or release of information. These may at times seem contradictory and as always, competing demands need to be balanced and prioritised. One set of imperatives protects information, and the other compels disclosure.

Legal imperatives to protect information

Common law duty of confidentiality

Confidentiality is accorded value for similar reasons in both the law and professional ethics. The AASW Code of Ethics calls attention to the 'responsible use of information obtained in the course of professional service', which implies care with information beyond that related to clients (Australian Association of Social Workers 1999, p. 14). It addresses information privacy/confidentiality in respect of clients quite comprehensively in clause 4.2.5. The AIWCW Code of Ethics is much less detailed, but values confidentiality of client information in clause 3.1 and respect for employer policies and practices in Part 5 (Australian Institute of Welfare and Community Workers Undated). Other human service professional codes, like those of the Australian Association of Rehabilitation Counsellors (Australian Society of Rehabilitation Counsellors Undated) and the Australian Psychological Society (Australian Psychological Society Ltd 2002), contain similar provisions.

As to the law, there is a common law general duty of confidentiality, albeit a technically confused one (Tucker 1992; Jackson 2001). If an agency or worker breaches the duty of confidentiality, one or both of them could be sued, by the damaged party, in a private or civil suit for breach of contract, negligence, or perhaps breach of confidence. The plaintiff in a civil suit will have to prove three things (Pearson 1997, pp. 187–8):

- that the information was not already widely known
- that the information was gained in circumstances that implied an obligation of confidentiality
- that the disclosure of the information injured the person who was entitled to want it kept secret.

The remedies may be an award of damages or perhaps an injunction to prevent continued or further disclosure. The defences to a breach of confidence action involve public interest and legal compulsion arguments and these will be returned to soon. For all the reasons discussed in the previous chapter, private legal actions of this sort against human services agencies and workers are hitherto uncommon in Australia. But that is no reason for complacency. It is only a question of time before actions are taken and it will be a hapless human service agency or worker who sets the precedent for breach of confidentiality.

Exceptions to confidentiality

Despite the general duty, confidentiality is not absolute in the human services and there are many exceptions to it. They are outlined here and some will reappear later under compulsion to disclose.

Where consent is given for disclosure

Informed consent in contemporary human services seems to cause confusion. Consent to disclosure is enshrined in privacy principles and it is consistent with ethical professional practice. In consenting, the client, or relevant person, must understand the specific reasons for and details about collection, intervention, and/ or disclosure. But putting flesh on the legal and ethical principles is again a matter of often quite complex process, procedure, and practice issues. For example, professional judgments are exercised in deciding how much information is given to clients to help them understand what they are consenting to and in what form it is given. To give one example, if work involves potentially dangerous clients, the agency might use a protocol that includes client consent to release of information about their risk to others (McBride and Tunnecliffe 2001). These protocols will have implications for the development of positive worker–client relationships but they are not insurmountable.

Ironically, given the anxiety about client consent issues in the human services, consent for research purposes is often forgotten. Projects and evaluations involving perusal of client records, for instance, often go ahead without client consent and this is contrary to both law and ethics. There is evidence that most people are willing to have their records used in research as long as they are asked for consent (Willison, Keshavjee et al. 2003).

Practice question and response

Question: It isn't legal now under privacy law for an agency to disclose client information to other agencies is it?

Response: This misconstrues the spirit and letter of the law. Information can be released as long as the client knows exactly what is to be released and why, and specifically consents to it. The question suggests that the agency does not have comprehensive release protocols in place and it would be wise for it to consult its legal officer. Refusal to release essential information is likely to impede effective intra-agency and interagency intervention. It could even constitute negligence at law if the failure to pass on information puts the client or other people at foreseeable risk in some way.

Where there may be a duty to warn because of a threat to life, or a public interest
These exceptions are relevant where the public interest in confidentiality is balanced by a public interest in unauthorised disclosure for a very important reason. The US case of *Tarasoff v Regents of the University of California* (1976) 551 P2d 334 is a much cited example of the duty to warn exception. The exception, if it applies, may then become a defence to a breach of confidence suit. But does it apply in Australia? McMahon (1992) and McSherry (2001) conclude that it is unclear without Australian precedents. Certainly NPP 2.1 allows for unauthorised disclosure on threat or public safety grounds, and there is a Ministerial Determination covering public interest and law enforcement purposes under the *Social Security (Administration) Act 1999* (Cth) (Sutherland and Anforth 2001). McMahon (1992, p. 16) provides four useful criteria for deciding to warn without consent, and as possible defences in a *Tarasoff* type suit. These are:

-    the victim is clearly identified
-    the plan to kill is specific

- the client has the means to act out the threat
- steps to protect the victim are practicable.

There are a number of other overseas cases indicating how courts may attempt to balance the public interest and confidentiality. The British case of *W v Egdell and Others* [1990] 1 All ER 83, and the more recent Canadian case of *Smith v Jones* [1999] 1 SCR 455, involved psychiatrists passing on their reports about prisoners, and potentially breaching confidentiality, when they were concerned about significant dangers posed by these prisoners. The House of Lords confirmed the primacy of the public interest over professional confidentiality. The Canadian Supreme Court also found for the public interest. The majority ruling in the *Smith* case can be used to extend McMahon's four criteria above to include:

- the victim can be an identifiable group (e.g. prostitutes in the *Smith* case)
- the danger is imminent.

Where disclosure is reasonably necessary for the enforcement of law
This may be the same as the public interest exception above and similarly has not really been tested in Australian courts. In the case of *R v Lowe* (1997) 2 VR 465 the Court of Appeal of the Supreme Court of Victoria confirmed the subordination of private confidence to the broader public interest, by ruling evidence from psychotherapy sessions as admissible, in a murder trial (McMahon 1998).

Where disclosure is authorised or required by law
Examples were given in the previous chapter. Other instances include:

- *Children and Young Persons (Care and Protection) Act 1998* (NSW) s 27 requires the reporting of child abuse and neglect by certain groups of people which includes many human service workers.
- *Corrections Act 1986* (Vic) s 90 places reporting duties about offender behaviour on community corrections officers.
- *Nurses Act 1999* (SA) s 43 requires health professionals to report to the Nurses Board if the physical and mental capacity of their nurse clients is impaired.

In some cases legislation of this sort will contain indemnity clauses, such as s 29 of the *Children and Young Persons (Care and Protection) Act 1998* (NSW), which protects the notifier from a number of possible legal suits such as defamation, or breach of a code of ethics.

Legislated protection of information

As explained in the previous chapter, many workers and ex-workers are covered by statutory provisions which prevent them from disclosing information, or protect them from being compelled to do so. For example, some protections are as follows:

- Under the *Family Law Act 1975* (Cth) s 19 and s 19n, Family Court counsellors in accredited agencies and some mediators are bound by an oath of secrecy about client recounts and these are not admissible in evidence.
- The *Evidence (Confidential Communications) Act 1998* (Vic) exempts some evidence of medical practitioners and counsellors about victims of sexual offences. The *Evidence Act*

1929 (SA), for the same offences similarly exempts the evidence of counsellors and therapists on the grounds of public interest. In this case the public interest is in maintaining confidentiality and not in breaching it.

Non-disclosure requirements more commonly derive from the employer organisation's general legislative mandate. All public servants are covered by secrecy provisions under relevant state or Commonwealth acts and regulations. More specifically, for example:

- *Health Services 1991* (Qld) s 51 prohibits disclosure of information gained through work.
- *Mental Health Act 1990* (NSW) s 289 is a similar provision to that above.
- *State Service Act 2000* (Tas) s 9 is a general confidentiality provision for public servants.
- Under s 28 of the *Disability Services Act 1986* (Cth) workers are bound by secrecy provisions. However here is an interesting example of multiple legal requirements as these provisions expressly exclude disclosures relevant to the purposes of the *Social Security Act 1991* (Cth).
- *Northern Territory Criminal Code* s 222 is interesting in that it makes the unlawful acquisition of confidential material and use for personal advantage, a crime, for which the penalty is imprisonment for three years.

So a worker who breaches these statutory provisions may well have much more to fear than in a private suit by an injured party. The full force of the state will be brought to bear on them if their breach is detected and pursued and the penalties involve fines and even imprisonment. For instance, unlawful disclosure about client information under the *Social Security (Administration) Act 1999* (Cth) s 204 can result in imprisonment for up to two years or an equivalent fine (Sutherland and Anforth 2001). This section also covers former employees and subcontractors.

Contract law and non-disclosure

Confidentiality may well be an implied term in any contract between human service provider and client (Devereux 2002). Thus a breach of confidence by an agency or worker could result in a civil suit for breach of contract.

Express or implied terms prohibiting disclosure of information are also common in employment contracts. All employees are bound by the implied or explicit terms of their employment contracts. For workers in non-government agencies that are not covered by the types of legislation just outlined, the employment contracts will be particularly relevant to matters of information management. For instance, if there are agency procedures for consent to release of information and/or access to client information systems, and workers fail to comply with them, they may face disciplinary action if not dismissal under industrial law.

Privacy legislation and non-disclosure

It will be evident from this chapter so far that governments are actively legislating about information privacy. Disclosure and access are only two, but fundamental, elements of privacy law. There are several IPPs that address the need to guard personal information very carefully. For example IPP 4 covers secure storage, 9 its use for relevant purposes only, 10 the limit on use without consent, and 11 restrictions on disclosure. Likewise NPPs 2 and 4 cover use and disclosure and security. The Privacy Commissioner can investigate alleged breaches of the *Privacy Act 1988* (Cth) and if they are substantiated, redress including compensation may be ordered, although only the Federal Court or Federal Magistrates Court can enforce a determination (Office of the Federal Privacy Commissioner 2003).

There is a diverse pattern of government activity within states and territories around privacy and some of them are still in the process of enacting sets of legislation or developing schemes consistent with, or complementary to, that of the Commonwealth. Through these, state government operations will be subject to similar information handling requirements that cover federal departments and private organisations. There are variations in things like scope of regulation, power, exemptions, and penalties. The Commonwealth legislation applies in the Australian Capital Territory. New South Wales has had a specific *Privacy and Personal Information Protection Act (1998)* for some years and the *Health Records and Information Privacy Act (2002)* is expected to come into operation in 2004. In Victoria there is a new comprehensive scheme underpinned by the *Information Privacy Act (2000)* and the *Health Records Act (2001)*. In Western Australia, South Australia, and Tasmania, administrative instructions currently apply to government agencies (Waters 2001), although Western Australia is in the process of enacting privacy laws.

Most human service agencies and workers now are likely to be caught at some point within the scope of National Privacy Principles and/or state or territory equivalents. As with storage, agencies and workers need to be informed about the Acts or schemes and organisation codes that are relevant to their practice. Proven breaches under privacy Acts or schemes can result in agencies having to take various forms of corrective action. Breaches caused by a worker, particularly if the worker in turn infringed agency codes, can lead to disciplinary action or dismissal.

Defamation and disclosure

This may seem a curious topic to include here. However it relates to the communication of sensitive information or opinion, and the risks that attend this behaviour. It is most likely to come into play when workers are discussing and writing about each other and it is speculated that it may become more prominent in future. It may be particularly relevant in relation to email and Internet use (Jebb 2003). Defamation law attempts to balance the public right of free speech with the private right to protect one's reputation. Anything that damages a person's reputation, even ridicule, may be defamatory. If spoken it is slander and if written it is libel. For example, the following actions could perhaps raise the question of defamation:

- Emailing others that the boss, Ms X, is incompetent.
- Writing to others that a client, Mr Y, is crazy.
- Saying to others that referral agency Z failed in its duty to a client.

This is a complex area of law as there are currently eight sets of common law and/or legislative schemes with a mix of civil and criminal provisions, across the Australian states and territories (Pearson 1997). However, the Commonwealth

Government is proposing a uniform code to replace these schemes. Currently, there may be defences to a defamation action of truth, fair report and opinion, or public interest and duty, or qualified privilege. For the purposes here it is enough to note that all workers make defamatory assertions frequently as they go about their work. Some of these are gratuitous and some are intrinsic to the work itself. As to the former ones, all workers need to be mindful that they are taking a legal risk. As to the ones intrinsic to work, they will and should continue, but it is more likely that a defence will succeed if the information is true, accurate, balanced, necessary to the purpose of the work, and divulged only to those who need it. In other words, good human service practices can again interact with the law to the benefit of the practitioner and service.

Legal imperatives to release/disclose information

The legal imperatives to protect information are offset by a range of other compulsions to inform, disclose, or provide access. Some of these have been covered in the section on exceptions to confidentiality and they will only be mentioned briefly here.

Right of access to information

Freedom of information (FOI) legislation

There is Commonwealth legislation, and legislation in all other jurisdictions but the Northern Territory (Paterson 1998), that allows citizens to have access to information about government activities, for a fee and within specified limits. This sort of legislation, unlike the privacy legislation, covers more than personal information; so under it, citizens can seek access to departmental records. There is provision for indemnity for disclosure under these types of Acts. It is worth noting here that as with the more recent and comprehensive privacy legislation, information is being seen by the law as accessible to those with rights. Thus workers have to be ever mindful of the range of potential readers of their records, both client and agency ones. In addition, they will be increasingly involved in helping people access, correct, make sense of, and come to terms with information in their records.

Other access law

All Australian states and territories have legislation that gives rights of information access, and veto, to adoptees, birth parents, and adoptive parents (McDonald and Slaytor 2002). Similarly, states are in the process of deciding how to deal with access to sperm donor information. Again there is a prevailing general principle that people have a right to know about their personal information held by others. This rule may prevail even in situations where the informant and information collector did not consider or assume later disclosure. Again, the message to human service agencies and workers is that the law is increasingly sensitive to access rights and records have very long lives.

Privacy legislation

The access principles have been covered earlier in this chapter.

Practice question and response

Question: Some parents of 14- and 15-year-old clients say that they have a right to access records concerning their children. Is this correct?

Response: There is no simple answer to this question (see Milne 1995). It will depend on the maturity of the young person, their understanding, their capacity to make decisions, their independence, the sensitivity of the information involved and who, if anyone, is paying any fees. The Guidelines on the Health Sector under the NPPs (Office of the Privacy Commissioner 2001) advise that parents do not have automatic rights of access if the young person has decision-making capacity. It is essential that agencies dealing with young people have clear policies and procedures about others' access to their information and that clients are informed about these. These policies must show respect for the rights to privacy of the young people, even if they are legally minors.

Absence of legal professional privilege

Many human service workers are surprised that they, unlike lawyers, do not have a common law right of legal professional privilege. That is, they are not protected from court demands for information about their work. Because their codes of professional ethics value confidentiality so strongly, it is perhaps assumed that they are immune from court requests—but they are not, and they and their records can be subpoenaed by courts. This holds unless they are covered by a legislative protection such as s207 of the *Social Security Administration Act 1999* (Cth) that provides protection for Centrelink to resist court and tribunal demands for documents (Carson 2002). Without such a protection, workers must appear or tender the requested information to avoid being in contempt of court. The question of how to approach a subpoena will be canvassed in the next chapter. Again it is underscored that a worker's records always have a range of potential future and perhaps unexpected readers.

Duty to report or warn

This has been canvassed in the previous section on exceptions to confidentiality.

Practice question and response

Question: Given all these problems about access to records and limits on confidentiality isn't it better to record nothing or very little?

Response: No it is not. As Swain (2002b) and Ames (1999) argue on professional practice and accountability grounds, it is unethical to deliberately not record. For similar reasons Symons (2002) says that independent standards consultants would disapprove of lack of records. Thus the law will look unkindly on the absence of records and any worker who has avoided making them could be subpoenaed to give oral evidence anyhow. It is better and wiser practice to communicate the limits of confidentiality and to concentrate on relevance and rationale in documenting in sensitive situations.

Statutory obligations to report

It has already been explained in this and the previous chapter that there are many legislative requirements for particular groups of people to disclose or report things concerning, for example, certain infectious diseases, road traffic, social security and workers compensation matters, and misconduct of colleagues. One of the most important of these for most human service workers is child abuse and neglect under the legislation of each state and territory.

A legal duty to report crimes?

There is no automatic legal duty requiring human service workers to report intended or past crimes that they receive information about. As just mentioned there are some specific legislative reporting requirements about some criminal activities, for example child abuse. As to serious crimes such as rape and murder, the picture is more one of moral, ethical, and public interest considerations. The criminal offence of misprision of a felony which once required anyone to report serious crimes that they found out about, seldom now exists. In some states, for example under s 316 of the *Crimes Act 1900* (NSW), it is an offence to conceal information about a serious indictable offence unless that information is gained in the course of professional work as prescribed in the regulations. The regulations include social workers and counsellors. However while not reporting, and impeding police investigations are two different things, they can merge in practice. Workers who actively refuse to report what they know about serious crimes may find themselves charged under state and territory law provisions about obstructing police investigations. They could also, as previously discussed, face a negligence suit if their knowledge concerns an intended and identifiable crime and victim.

Practice question and response

Question: But in my work with young people at risk, I am legally obliged to report when they tell me about their car stealing, aren't I?

Response: You may not be obliged by legislation in your jurisdiction to voluntarily report this kind of offence. However, your agency may have crime reporting procedures that are intrinsic to its philosophy and its intervention approaches. If this is the case and you do not report, your job may be in jeopardy because you have not complied with your contract of employment. You may also be required to divulge this information if you are subpoenaed to appear in court. Clients should be fully informed about all reporting requirements and possibilities.

Whistleblowing

This topic warrants special attention beyond the figure 6.1 cycle because it concerns extraordinary dilemmas of information management.

Whistleblowing entails exposing organisational corruption, misconduct, fraud, and/or poor administration in the public interest. It is relevant where there is endemic or systemic wrongdoing in an agency, where there does not appear to be any internal management will to act, and where the problems are of public concern. Whistleblowing is becoming an increasingly important and troubling issue in all work arenas. In fact De Maria (1996, p.17) describes whistleblowing as an important form of dissent for social workers and refers to it as the 'ultimate public service'. In the following examples workers are faced with very difficult choices about information that comes to their attention:

- Many staff are systematically stealing and selling agency drugs.
- Staff workloads are so high that serious errors of judgment are recurring.
- Agency funds are used consistently to purchase nonessential expensive IT equipment.
- Board of management members consistently appoint friends to new positions in the agency.
- A particular client group is routinely and actively underserviced or refused service.
- Staff are regularly bullied, threatened and intimidated by a group of managers.

Whistleblowing situations raise moral, ethical, legal, and practical quandaries for workers in large and often conflicting measure. Given the very nature of organisational corruption it is often difficult or impossible to report problems within the organisation itself. Decision-making in these circumstances is a notoriously difficult balancing and weighing exercise (Blonder 1996; Martin 2000) and whistleblowing is only one of many possible responses. Ultimately, faced with the sorts of scenarios above, workers must make hard personal decisions.

These things said, what are the legal considerations? There are basically three of them:

- First, 'there is no general right or legal duty to disclose wrongdoing' (Vernon 1998, p. 232), which affirms the necessity for personal decision-making.
- Second, there are legal obstacles to whistleblowing in the imperatives for secrecy covered earlier in this chapter. That is, there may be statutory and/or other legal barriers to an individual passing on information about the workplace to outsiders.
- Third, there are limited protections and indemnities from reprisals for whistleblowing under whistleblowing legislation if it is done appropriately. Additionally, some protection against retaliation after whistleblowing may be provided by the *Public Service Act 1999* (Cth) s 16 for Commonwealth employees, under changes to the *Corporations Act 2001* (Cth), and by state or territory legislation if it exists. To be protected, the informing behaviour has to be caught within the scope of the relevant legislation. Protective schemas generally require that the reporting be made in the public interest, to appropriate internal or statutory investigative bodies, which do not include the media.

The Queensland *Whistleblowers Protection Act 1994* (Qld) only covers disclosure by public officers of misconduct, maladministration, improper management, and dangers posed in the public sector (Criminal Justice Commission 1995). The Victorian *Whistleblowers Protection Act 2001* also only covers exposure of public bodies. The South Australian *Whistleblowers Protection Act (1993)* applies in addition to illegality or corruption in the private sector. The *Protected Disclosures*

Act 1994 (NSW) provides some defence if the internal disclosure is frustrated and the official then goes to a Member of Parliament or a journalist (Pearson 1997). The protections under these statutes may not seem very comforting to the would-be whistleblower facing trauma and retribution. Under the South Australian Act for instance, a whistleblower who suffers retaliation may make a civil claim in tort, or take action under the *Equal Opportunity Act 1984* (SA) but a civil action may be costly and proving retaliation may be difficult. These Acts may also indemnify whistleblowers against civil and criminal actions, which provides some additional consolation.

In the absence of whistleblowing legislation, or even where it exists, how reporting of wrong practice is responded to and investigated will be largely a matter of agency policy and procedures. If the agency is already compromised at high levels there are inherent difficulties with internal processes. In any action the whistleblower may be a lone individual lined up against the might of very large and powerful opponents. The position of the whistleblower is never an easy one and it is likely to be their own values (see figure 3.1) that determine their actions, rather than external imperatives from, say, law or the agency.

Key points for practice

- All information obtained and handled through human service work has legal risk potential.
- Beware categorical responses to questions about information management. For most situations, including those involving confidentiality, there are qualifications and these must be made very clear to clients in particular.
- It is essential that agencies have policies and procedures promulgated to staff and clients for collecting, recording, storing, accessing, and amending information and that these policies are consistent with both federal and relevant state and territory privacy law and associated schemes.
- The extent to which these policies have substance and offer specific guidance to workers will depend largely on how clear the agency is about its mandate, purpose, and approach to service delivery.
- It is essential that workers are familiar with agency policies and procedures concerning information management and comply with them. If agency policies do not exist or are deficient then workers should ask that they be developed.
- Records should always be kept with the possibility of later legal scrutiny in mind.
- Always question the source and authority of unfamiliar claims made about information handling. Both worker and client interests may be served by knowing what imperatives really exist, how they can be utilised, and/or what risks are associated with non-compliance.
- Workers will be required to exercise discretionary professional judgment in many information handling situations. In circumstances involving questions of access/disclosure it may be useful to go through a checklist of the legal pressures for and against release before deciding on a response.

Some useful web sites

Privacy

www.privacy.gov.au
www.privacy.gov.au/act/casenotes/

Whistleblowing

www.whistleblowers.org.au/

7

Workers, Courts, and Tribunals

Images and anxieties

The quotes that follow concern particular professional groups and areas of work but their point can be generalised; giving evidence in court is a major cause of professional anxiety. 'When tested by lawyers in an adversary proceeding, the reaction is one of affront and personal injury and they [case workers] tend to become polarised, in the belief that they are protectors of the child against legal charlatanism' (Bates, Blackwood et al. 1996, p. 40 quoting Tamilia 1971). 'Difficult and distressing for all participants' is another description of the adjudication of child protection matters (Sheehan 2003, p. 38). Court phobia and humiliation often characterise the perceptions of psychologists about giving evidence (Stevens 2003). Clinical social workers are claimed to 'march bravely to the stand like martyrs' (Vogelsang 2001, p. 1). Social workers feel that their practice and evidence is held in low regard by courts compared with the respect paid to medical and psychological expertise (Braye and Preston-Shoot 1997). There is in fact evidence that courts rely on legal knowledge and discretion more than they do on the information from child protection services (Sheehan 2003). The law and human service cultural differences discussed in Part I are particularly conspicuous in court work.

The litany of woes about human services work in courts could continue, compounded no doubt by popular images of witnesses being savaged by smart barristers. But not all of these often US-based images are accurate reflections of general human service worker experience in Australia. Civil litigation has been less common in this country, and human service workers appear here less commonly as expert witnesses. Nonetheless, these workers are generally apprehensive about courts, lack confidence in their performance skills and knowledge, feel undervalued, believe that their causes or values are disregarded in courts, and are distrustful of the legal system and lawyers. This is not a formula for success, and moreover some of their fears are justified.

For many human service workers, court appearances are irregular or infrequent and/or yet to happen. It is hard to see what might be done in advance to prepare for these often unexpected and commonly feared events. But writing about psychologists in courts, Wardlaw (1984) makes a useful distinction between evidence and courtroom performance. He argues that skills in building up sound evidence through good practice can be rehearsed daily by beginners and experienced workers alike, regardless of courtroom experience. This point allows the theme from the previous chapter to be extended here. That is, although the experience of giving evidence in court is generally testing and sometimes traumatic, human service workers can minimise damage to their self-esteem and increase their effectiveness by having confidence in the quality of their own work practices and their evidence. If they report simply, carefully, and honestly about their professional actions, which they have ensured are appropriate and well documented, they are less likely to be destabilised by what confronts them in court.

As previously indicated, the symbiosis between sound human service practice and satisfaction of legal requirements is a constant refrain in this book. This chapter moves next to an overview of the range of human service activity in various courts and tribunals, and then to how the law works with witnesses and information or evidence in court. From there it shifts to preparation for, and actually appearing as a witness, or as a supporter of others who are in courts or tribunals.

Courts, similar bodies, and dispute resolution

Courts are the traditional, recognisable forums in which litigation is adjudicated. But there are now many other bodies in which disputes are resolved, and methods other than litigation for disposing of them. The 'informal justice' movement in Australia and elsewhere is reflected in the burgeoning number of quasi-legal bodies for determining disputes and reviewing decisions; for instance there are tribunals, boards, authorities, and commissions. It is also characterised by the proliferation of alternative dispute resolution approaches (introduced in Part I); that is, negotiation, mediation, conciliation, facilitation, independent expert appraisal, and arbitration (Astor and Chinkin 1992; Mendelsohn and Maher 1994). Some of these approaches are now used in court systems. For example, mediation has been incorporated into Family and Federal Court processes, and many state courts can direct on to mediation. Conciliation and arbitration are entrenched in industrial courts. Court annexed arbitration also increasingly applies to state courts (Astor and Chinkin 1992). ADR approaches are common in quasi-judicial bodies. They are even more prevalent in agencies that offer dispute resolution services, for example community legal or justice centres, and neighbour, family, and commercial conflict resolution services, auspiced by any number of organisations.

However, in this chapter courts and quasi-judicial bodies are the focus because the process of testifying in them particularly challenges human service workers.

There are enduring debates about definitions of and differentiation between courts, tribunals, and other quasi-legal bodies (e.g. Allars 1990). For present purposes, these are sidestepped, and the term tribunal is used loosely to cover a range of quasi-judicial bodies that have relevance to human service work. Also in the interests of simplicity, the term 'court' may be used to include both courts and tribunals unless a differentiation is otherwise indicated.

Scope of human service activity in courts and tribunals

Human service workers have a number of main roles across a range of courts and tribunals.

Main roles

- *Witness of fact, character, or as an expert*: these roles will be elaborated later. Briefly, workers may give factual evidence about events that they have witnessed; they may give evidence about the good character of someone who is a respondent or defendant in a case; and they can testify as to opinions based on their specific expertise.
- *Report writer*: sometimes human service workers prepare reports, for example a pre-sentence report in corrections, and/or documents to inform courts. They may or may not actually give oral evidence in court about these documents.
- *Petitioner, applicant, or plaintiff*: human service workers may initiate actions, commonly under a statutory power, for example a child protection application, even though a lawyer or barrister is likely to conduct the case. The applicant will often also be a key witness of fact about for instance, parental behaviour. Human service workers may also be applicants in their own cases, for example in employment or injury actions.
- *Respondent or defendant*: human service workers who are the subjects of action, become respondents or defendants. For example, if sued for negligence, or charged under criminal matter law, or cited as the offending decision-maker under a number of appeals processes, these roles apply to them.
- *Lay advocate*: human service workers assist others to make applications, prepare submissions, and appear on their behalf, in particular before tribunals.
- *Supporter*: human service workers often support others who are involved in legal proceedings.
- *Arbitrator, negotiator, mediator, conciliator, and facilitator*: these roles in court-related processes are assumed by human service workers and, as explained in Part I, by others including lawyers.
- *Member/adjudicator*: some tribunals require one or more members to have backgrounds in social welfare, for example the Administrative Appeals Tribunal (AAT), the Social Security Appeals Tribunal (SSAT), and state guardianship bodies.

Advocates of a kind

Two points about roles are highlighted. One is that human service workers often imagine themselves, rather superficially, as perennial advocates for the oppressed. However in a significant amount of tribunal activity in particular, they work for the organisations whose decision-making is in question; or they are the applicant for an order which may deprive an individual of, say, liberty or housing; or they may actually alone or with others sit as tribunal members. In terms of simple if not entirely accurate stereotypes they represent 'might' as much as 'right'. Yet again the importance of the principles of administrative law outlined in Part I are underscored; both in relation to the worker as original decision-maker and in their tribunal work.

The second point concerns the term advocacy itself. Human service advocacy roles are to be differentiated from the conduct of specific cases in courts and tribunals. The latter is legal advocacy and not the province of human service workers, other than in the limited role of lay advocate. Human service workers do work in partnership with lawyers to achieve desired outcomes, and a desire to protect and/or advocate is often activated in them by the court process. But in the giving of fact or opinion evidence, they are not advocates; they are witnesses responsible for giving the best evidence so that the adjudicating body can make the best decision. Human service workers who are provoked into assuming a legal advocacy role when giving evidence are easily brought unstuck in the witness box. Those who demonstrate disciplined, thorough, and objective preparation for and performance in court, may help produce a desired result. Thus they may still be striving for an advocated outcome, but not by advocating as a witness.

Practice question and response

Question: But surely human service workers are advocates?
Response: Yes, advocacy is one of their important functions. They advocate for individuals in many arenas, for systematic change, and for many causes in between. But the carriage and conduct of court cases is legal advocacy and the province of lawyers.

Range of courts

The main types of courts relevant to human service work are as follows:

- *Criminal*: workers may be witnesses of fact, for example they may have seen an assault; they may be report writers and/or provide oral evidence pertinent to sentencing; they may give character evidence; on occasions they may be the defendant. A few are called as expert witnesses. Charlesworth (1993) argues that they could be useful advisers to lawyers in the preparation and conduct of criminal cases, for example through social assessments of the role of the defendant in the family and community.

- *Civil*: workers may be applicants and respondents, witnesses of fact and character, and possibly even expert witnesses.

- *Children's and Youth Courts*: in these courts, where questions of adoption, juvenile offending, need for care, neglect, and abuse are decided, human service workers are commonly key witnesses of fact, report writers, and sometimes applicants.

- *Family court*: Counsellors and Welfare Officers for this court established under the *Family Law Act 1975* (Cth) are usually social workers and psychologists. They may conduct case conferences to resolve disputes about children, prepare reports about the welfare of children in divorce proceedings, or report on any matter determined by the Court, relating to the proceedings. They are witnesses of fact, and experts, as they give professional opinions.

- *Special courts*: for example domestic violence courts, drug courts (Freiberg 2002; Makkai and Veraar 2003; McGlone 2003), mental health courts, and Koori (Hulls 2002) or other Indigenous courts. Human service workers may act as witnesses and service the courts as liaison, assessment, intervention, and support workers.
- *Coronial inquests*: human service workers may be witnesses of fact if and when deaths related to their work are investigated.

Range of tribunals

Tribunals commonly deal with the outcomes of administrative decision-making. Thus many exist in areas relevant to the human services, and workers commonly engage with them. Tribunals, operating under state or federal legislation, vary in terms of their composition, decision-making powers, and procedures. In some the adversarial system applies, while in others a more inquisitorial approach is taken, along with ADR modalities. Some permit legal representation and some do not, in some the rules of evidence apply and in some they do not, in some oral evidence is taken and in others only written submissions are accepted. Human service workers are often applicants, respondents, witnesses, lay advocates, and/or preparers of documents. Major areas of experience, some to be returned to in later chapters, are as follows:

- *Immigration*: the Migration Review and Refugee Review Tribunals cover the ground here, both established under the *Migration Act 1958* (Cth). Workers may be Department of Immigration and Multicultural and Indigenous Affairs employees who investigate and document, or associates of the groups who support applicants in preparing submissions about visa applications, refusals, and refugee status.
- *Administrative review*: the AAT, a federal review body established under the *Administrative Appeals Tribunal Act 1975* (Cth), can review decisions across the whole area of Commonwealth administration, some other tribunals, and non-government bodies. Workers may prepare documents though their employment in government departments, or assist applicants to prepare and give evidence.
- *Mental health*: Matters of involuntary detention and treatment are dealt with by state boards for example the Mental Health Review and Patient Review Tribunals in New South Wales. Workers may make applications, assist those who are the subject of applications, or work with those for whom orders exist.
- *Health*: a number of bodies, generally established under state or territory legislation, review health decisions and complaints. For example the Northern Territory Health and Community Services Complaints Commission investigates and conciliates complaints from service users. Human service workers may be employed by the commission, may assist complainants, or be the subject of complaint.
- *Workers compensation*: at state and territory level there are bodies, for example the South Australia Workers Compensation Tribunal, which adjudicate compensation disputes.

Human service employees of return-to-work case management agencies commonly have involvement with them. Injured human service workers may themselves be applicants.

- *Victims of crime*: some statutory bodies at state level, for example the Victorian Victims of Crime Assistance Tribunal, determine compensation matters for victims, and human service workers may assist the board and/or the applicants.

- *Substitute decision-making for adults*: bodies established under state statutes make and monitor guardianship and administration decisions, for example the Guardianship and Administration Board in Western Australia, and the Guardianship Tribunal in New South Wales. Human service workers may make applications to these Boards for orders for individuals whose capacity to function independently is questioned, or work with those for whom orders already apply.

- *Discrimination*: the Federal Human Rights and Equal Opportunity Commission (HREOC), and many state bodies, for example, the Tasmanian Anti-Discrimination Tribunal, hear complaints about discrimination within their jurisdictions. Workers may support clients through these processes, or find themselves and/or their agencies, the subject of complaint.

- *Social Security*: the Social Security Appeals Tribunal (SSAT) reviews benefits decisions. Human service workers may assist and lodge appeals for individuals, or respond to appeals in their capacity as employees of Centrelink.

- *Residential tenancies*: bodies established under state and territory legislation deal with disputes between landlords and tenants, for example the New South Wales Residential Tribunal, and the Residential Tenancies Tribunal in South Australia. Human service workers may assist tenants through these tribunal processes. But increasingly, human service agencies are themselves landlords and their staff make applications, for example, to terminate leases of clients/tenants who have not complied with tenancy agreements.

- *Corruption*: there are a number of generally state-established bodies with power to investigate corruption. For example, ICAC in New South Wales investigates complaints about the corrupt conduct of public officers. Human service workers may be applicants, respondents, or lay advocates in relation to these bodies and their proceedings.

Court processes, evidence, and witnesses

Human service workers can do several things in preparation for work in courts and tribunals. By familiarising themselves with courts, the law of evidence, and the functions of particular types of witnesses, they can begin to desensitise themselves to an alien system.

Court arrangements and processes

Familiarisation with the physical characteristics of courts, the personnel, and the rhythm of activity in them, is an invaluable preparatory activity. There are many courts and some tribunals in most jurisdictions, for example the AAT, which are open to the public. By watching proceedings, asking questions of court staff, and by reflecting on their own emotional responses, human service workers can test and extend both their confidence and their composure in court settings.

Evidence

Yet another form of preparation is to learn something about what evidence means in law. The law of evidence deals with information differently from the human services where sequential, common-sense narratives based on deductive social science modes of enquiry normally apply. Evidential rules are strictly applied in criminal proceedings, but are not mandatory in many tribunals (O'Neill 1996). However it is sensible to heed them as they are intrinsic to legal thinking and may be used to assess weight of evidence (Forbes 2002). Evidence collected and presented by human services workers in accordance with rules of evidence is also likely to have greater credibility in courts (Bates, Blackwood et al. 1996). It is added that sensitivity to the rules makes for better human service information data collection and interpretation practices. Some general points about evidence follow:

- Evidence is information elicited in courts, generally through examination of witnesses, according to complex, technical, historical, common law rules now overlaid by legislation. All jurisdictions have evidence legislation, for example the *Evidence Act 1995* in New South Wales. The *Evidence Act 1995* (Cth) applies to Commonwealth jurisdictions and the Australian Capital Territory and some of its provisions apply to all Australian courts.
- In the adversarial system, evidence about the particular situation is elicited and contained by both sides, each attempting to satisfy the burden and standard of proof which applies. In the inquisitorial system the court itself may elicit evidence.
- The party making the claim generally has responsibility for putting forward the evidence to prove their claim.
- Witnesses are generally only allowed to give evidence of facts; that is, what they have experienced directly through sight, sound, touch, smell, and taste. Opinion evidence, where interpretation of or inference from facts is involved, is the province of expert witnesses. This will soon be elaborated.
- Evidence may be oral, documentary, or real. Real evidence can be experienced directly by the court. For example it may be shown a knife or picture, or listen to a song or visit a location.
- Although the rules of evidence permeate legal thinking, they may be relaxed or abolished in some jurisdictions by legislation. For example under the *Workers' Compensation and Rehabilitation Act 1981* (WA) s 84ZD and the *Administrative Appeals Tribunal Act 1975* (Cth) s 33(1)(c)(c), they have been abrogated. Conversely the *Evidence Act 1995* (Cth) does apply to proceedings before the Family Court and the rules do apply to proceedings under the *Community Protection Act 1994* (NSW) s 14.
- Evidence varies as to admissibility and weight. The law of evidence is largely concerned with allowing into court information that is material and relevant, while excluding that which is unnecessarily prejudicial. Relevance is a matter for the court to determine and it hangs on whether evidence, either direct or circumstantial, helps to prove or disprove a fact in issue. If evidence is ruled admissible, it may be accorded greater or lesser weight depending in some part on the credibility of the witness who provides it. Many human service workers who testify are frustrated when their narrative explanations of events are interrupted and segmented by lawyers. They are also prone to take offence when their evidence is not given the weight they think it warrants.

- There are certain classes of witnesses about which the law has traditionally been cautious, unless their evidence is corroborated or verified by others. The testimony of complainants in sexual assault cases and of children generally, are two such examples. Legislation has now generally abolished the old common law requirements about corroboration warnings to the jury in such cases, for example the New South Wales *Evidence Act 1995* s 164 does this, but the distrust may still be evident in legal attitudes.
- There is a general rule precluding the admissibility of hearsay evidence in courts, especially in criminal cases. That is, second-hand versions of events in question are excluded, and evidence from witnesses who have direct knowledge and can be cross-examined in court is favoured. For practical reasons there are now many technical amendments to this general rule and some hearsay evidence is allowable. However, there may be legal argument about the admissibility of specific evidence in particular cases. Much of the evidence that human service workers can offer is hearsay: for example a client has told them about a rape or they heard about an assault on a child. Their evidence may fall within exceptions to the hearsay rule. For example, they may hear confessions from alleged offenders, or have 'recent complaint' evidence (Cossins 2002) through contact with victims of sexual assault. There are two implications of this. First, notes should be taken carefully and immediately as soon as this sort of evidence is obtained. Second, this human service worker evidence may necessarily be the subject of legal argument. If it is, taking the argument personally is a waste of precious emotional energy.
- The law also has a long tradition of rejecting character or propensity evidence, especially in criminal cases. That is, evidence that goes beyond the specific facts of the immediate proceedings and shows the accused to be generally a person of bad character is likely to be inadmissible.

Practice question and response

Question: These ideas about corroboration, hearsay, and character reflect objectionable institutional responses to the clients in my service. How can they be justified and maintained?
Response: These rules have developed over time out of valid concerns to safeguard the rights of defendants to fair trials. However you are not alone in your concerns, changes are occurring and there are calls, many of them from lawyers, for continuing change (e.g. Australian Law Reform Commission 1997; Cossins 2002; Eastwood 2003). These are the sorts of matters about which human service workers too can validly take on advocacy roles in the interests of systemic change.

The rules of evidence are a mystery and source of frustration to many people outside of the law. However human service workers have a particular duty to reach a resolution in their thinking about the rules because their own well-being and sometimes that of their causes may be at stake. Remember to distinguish between an objective critique of the rules and an emotional, subjective rejection of them. When human service workers take the latter position a vicious cycle results. Their effectiveness and credibility in the court system are reduced and they in turn feel increasingly victimised and estranged. It is possible and empowering to take a critical objective position on the rules, while learning to manage their practical requirements more adeptly.

Witnesses

Witness roles and their relevance to the human services are explored a little more fully here.

Witness of fact

These witnesses testify to what they have direct evidence of; what they saw or heard or otherwise acquired through their senses. They cannot give opinion evidence other than on matters of everyday experience. Anyone can be a witness of fact if they have relevant evidence to give. An example of fact testimony relevant to the human services would be where a worker in a residential establishment witnesses a fight. If charges are laid and a trial results, the worker can be called as a witness by the prosecution or the defence and cross-examined about the event. They will be allowed to answer about what they saw and heard and any opinions, professional or personal, that they may hold about the situation will not be permissible, no matter how relevant they might believe them to be.

Practice question and response

Question: But I am a professional. Why would my interpretations be unwelcome?
Response: It is not a question of unwelcome or 'second-class status' (Albert 2000, p. 261), but rather about how witness roles are categorised in law. Your fact evidence alone might well be crucial, and certainly welcome.

Expert witness

These witnesses give opinion evidence. Under common law and legislation, they can assist the court by drawing inferences from evidence, explaining technical subjects, giving expert factual testimony, and/or giving specialist hearsay evidence (Hodgkinson and Scarman 1990). Traditionally they have been called by one or other side in a case, although there is a move in some arenas to court appointed experts (e.g. in negligence, Commonwealth Treasury (Ipp Report) 2002). The fact that these witnesses are called expert does not mean that fact witnesses are not experts in their work. The term 'expert' here is a legal one denoting a particular function of the witness.

Courts have been long troubled by experts for many reasons. To start, there are problems of assessment. How is expertise in an area to be determined; does a field of expertise really exist or is it 'junk science' (Loevinger 1992), and how can an expert be recognised? Then experts may engage in battles that confound rather than assist courts. Experts are expensive and may command big fees. Their evidence and their conflicts may consume enormous amounts of court time. Historically experts have not been permitted to comment on the 'ultimate issue' in any case (e.g.

defendant motivation or state of mind at the time of the alleged offence), as this is the question for the court to determine. Although legislation such as the Commonwealth *Evidence Act 1995* s 80 has abolished this rule, legal sensitivities about expert evidence that addresses the central legal question, may still exist. Likewise courts are touchy about witnesses being called to give expert evidence about what they consider to be common knowledge and thus within the purview of the court. The concepts and language of much human service activity do not seem technical or unfamiliar to others, and can appear to be within the ordinary knowledge of laypeople. Thus courts may be inclined to reject the need for human service expert evidence. Again, this common law rule has been abolished by some legislation such as the *Evidence Act 1995* (Cth) s 80, but vestiges of it may remain in legal attitudes.

Ultimately, questions about whether a field of expertise exists, whether it will help in a particular case and whether or not a particular witness qualifies as an expert in a case will be determined by the court. A worker may qualify as an expert in one case and not in another. This is a surprise to many professionals who are accustomed to their expertise being determined by their formal qualifications. Expert witnesses generally are very experienced and may or may not hold formal qualifications. Also it is the court, not the experts, which ultimately decides which facts and which inferences or opinions are the most convincing.

Practice question and response

Question: Surely all human service workers have expertise?
Response: Yes, they probably do. But that is different from saying that they would all satisfy technical legal tests, in a particular case, involving a particular set of facts in a specific area, which the court needs assistance in interpreting.

Many workers actually find themselves in hybrid witness positions, more common in tribunals than in courts, which result directly from their professional responsibilities. As outlined before, many human service workers operate in jurisdictions where the rules of evidence have been abolished and they testify to both facts and opinions. So for example, a worker covered by the *Children's Protection Act 1993* (SA) s 45 (1), which abrogates the rules of evidence, may be called to testify about a child's situation. They may be questioned about what they saw and heard during interviews and in the family house; that is, they will give fact evidence. They may also be asked to draw a conclusion about the state of the house and the children in it. However despite the invitation to opinion, they still will not have expert witness status in the strict legal sense, and need to be mindful of overstepping that invitation. The fact witness giving opinions is in an ambiguous position legally, and one which tends to exercise both courts and workers (Bates, Blackwood et al. 1996; Barker and Branson 2000).

Human service workers, psychologists apart, have seldom been used as expert witnesses in Australia in contrast to the USA where forensic social work is an active industry. Charlesworth (1993, p. 6-2231) puts this down to lack of social work interest in the task, lack of demand by lawyers for their services, limited time and encouragement for state or non-government organisation (NGO) employees to take on the task, and a small human service private practice sector. In addition she notes the inclusive character of social work knowledge, and this is even more a problem for the wider spectrum of human service workers. This makes it difficult for lawyers and courts to know what unique and specific expertise these workers have, and in the past they were likely to fall foul of the common knowledge rule. But to give an example of how they may be used, a social worker was qualified to give expert evidence on the extent of social work practice recognition of child sexual abuse in the 1960s, in *Radnedge v State of South Australia* (1997) 192 LSJS 131.

Being called to appear

Human service workers may be asked to appear and do so voluntarily, or be given notice, or be subpoenaed. As explained in the previous chapter they must appear if subpoenaed. Some workers prefer to be subpoenaed rather than appear voluntarily because that process may mitigate any breaches of confidentiality. It is often forgotten by human service workers that they will be called by one side in the dispute in adversarial proceedings and have its legal assistance. Thus there is one legal team that has a vested interest in them performing well. In tribunal proceedings where there are no lawyers or only some parties have them, human service workers who are appearing will need to be more self-reliant.

Preparing court and tribunal reports

What follows is a list of general principles about reports, many of them client related, which are given orally or in writing to courts. The principles will be fleshed out by the practices and protocols of the courts and organisations involved, and by human service practice knowledge and experience.

- Summary information about the report, for example date, client name, agency, and so on is clearly listed on the front or at the top.
- The purposes of the report are clearly explained.
- The client's social and service context is acknowledged.
- Information sources and their limitations are acknowledged.
- Content is accurate and precise.
- Content is neither duplicated nor assumed.
- Content is balanced and comprehensive.
- There is a logical sequence of headings.
- Fact and opinion are distinctly separated.
- Opinions are supported with and justified by evidence.
- Technical terms and/or jargon are avoided and if they must be included they are explained.
- Gratuitous, biased, or discriminatory language is avoided.
- Complex situations, events, or relationships are outlined as plainly as possible, perhaps in dot point form, or with the assistance of visual aids such as genograms (Brammer 2003), tables, or maps.

- The style, language, and content are chosen with the readers' rather than the writer's needs in mind.
- The style is clear, concise, and unambiguous.
- The style and tone appear objective.
- Proofreading and editing have been carefully attended to.
- Conclusions are based on the data and flow logically from it. Writers need to give attention to matters of degree (Carson 1990, p. 49) or in other words 'strength of opinion... [expressed through] graduated scales of concern[s]' (Stevens 2003, p. 24).
- Authorship and title/position are evident.

Are recommendations to be included in court reports? This will depend very much on the legislation, if any, under which the report is prepared and the preferences of the court. However a few suggestions are offered. It may be possible and desirable in some jurisdictions to outline a range of possible options to the court and the advantages and disadvantages of each (Brammer 2003) rather than making a single recommendation. However, Chisholm (1997, p. 10) from his perspective as a Family Court judge, argues in general that the writer should 'put their cards on the table' rather than leave the court guessing at what they actually do conclude. Bates et al. (1996) advise writers to inoculate themselves against distress when their recommendations are not followed. Courts weigh all considerations in decision-making, and there may be contrary evidence about which individual witnesses have no knowledge.

Practice question and response

Question: But aren't these principles just the same as for any human service report?
Response: Yes, while specific courts may have particular preferences and formats, the general human service principles of solid data collection and report writing apply here too.

Preparing to appear

Attitude and presentation of self

Given the prevalence of human service worker concerns about testifying in courts, it is sensible for those who are called to prepare themselves mentally. Part of this process involves accepting that courts are 'theatres' and that they along with other witnesses will have to 'perform' (Brammer 2003, p. 97). Belief in the integrity of one's position is not enough to carry the witness role. It is equally necessary to think about presentation, projection of confidence, and perception by others. Carson (1990) emphasises the significance of stance, appearance, speech patterns, use of eyes, and prefatory phrases to sustain others' interest and manage interruptions.

Appearance is a vexed matter. Carson (1990, p. 10) proposes 'sober clothes'. Vogelsang (2001) advises, among other things, that men avoid pony tails and women dangly earrings when giving evidence. These sorts of suggestions can cause indignation among human service workers as edicts to 'sell out' or to present falsely. The obvious rejoinder is that adaptability and integrity are not mutually exclusive. Workers must decide if personal affront is to be given priority over the matter that brings them into court. Adaptability may produce the result that the worker desires, on behalf of the client or the cause, while stubborn adherence to 'normal' presentation style may help defeat it. After all, appearing in court is not a usual experience for most workers and it does call on unusual responses. Again it is worth recalling the difference between an objective critique of systems and a subjective rejection of them. A worker can go into court with a critical mental set and perform well because they are intellectually open and alert. Workers who emotionally reject the process are more likely to be confused and defeated by it.

Managing concerns about confidentiality

As explained in the previous chapter, human service witnesses can be compelled by subpoena to appear and give evidence unless they have legislative protection. But courts will weigh up public interest concerns against those of confidentiality before compelling witnesses. Davidson's (2002) advice for private psychologists about responding to subpoenas has useful general applicability:

- check the validity of the summons and if it is flawed challenge it
- write to the court about confidentiality, especially third party concerns
- help the court to limit and specify the information that is really relevant
- seek release from the confidentiality agreement that underpins the information sought
- write to the party issuing the subpoena explaining the desired limits on information sought
- seek legal advice [employees should receive this through their employer organisations]
- comply with the final decisions of the court.

Getting organised

Perhaps the most important preparatory activity for witnesses is to revise their own work relevant to the case and clarify their justifications for intervention and/or action. It is important to be clear about what happened, why, in what sequence, and where. Challenges and questions can be anticipated. For example, the witness's qualifications may be a point of vulnerability, or there may be professional disagreements about how a client has been handled, or there may be weaknesses in the way an issue has been managed. All these things are facts of life, not to be denied and hidden, but confronted so that the most sensible answers can be offered if they are pursued in court. If a report has been written, the witness must be familiar with it. Files and notes should be put in order, but not amended, for taking into court, even though they may not be used during testimony. A full and accurate witness curriculum vitae (CV) should be available. This may be required in court, particularly if the witness is being called as an expert. Even if a CV is not requested, the process of compiling it helps witnesses to review their own qualifications and scope of expertise, which is in itself useful psychological preparation.

It is crucial that witnesses are briefed by the lawyers who have called them, and that the hearing process is fully explained; in a court this will mean an overview of examination-in-chief, cross-examination, and re-examination. Possible areas of concern to both the human service witness and lawyers can at this stage be aired and worked on. It is in the interests of the human service worker to initiate this contact if the lawyer does not.

For human service workers going into court as part of their statutory work Braye and Preston-Shoot (1997, p. 291) outline a number of helpful actions:

- be clear about agency mandate and procedures and about own role in court
- request clear directions from the court
- get advice from within the agency about unanticipated issues, and questions of resourcing
- have a manager in court to assist in complex cases
- ensure involvement of the agency lawyer
- understand possible involvement and role of other experts and own agency position on these.

Actually giving evidence

Skill in testifying requires experience. The skills are covered more fully is specialist literature (e.g. Carson 1990; Charlesworth 1993; Barrett 1999; Vogelsang 2001; Stevens 2003). They are also likely to be the subject of specialist inservice training and/or later professional development. However the following list of general guidelines may encourage thinking about the task and can be used to reflect on others observed giving evidence:

- project voice and present as confidently as possible
- take time to think and answer
- remain calm and polite and avoid becoming defensive
- try and rely on memory but ask to refer to notes if necessary
- adopt an attitude and demeanour of trying to help the court. The adjudicator in turn is more likely to assist the witness in coping with the examining lawyers
- maintain an open, nonpartisan manner without conceding on own conclusions
- do not guess at answers
- say 'I do not know' when this is so
- listen fully to questions in all their complexity and answer each part carefully
- think very carefully before answering leading questions that promote a particular response
- answer only the questions put unless the question forces an inappropriate 'yes' or 'no' response. If this happens explain that a yes or no is not possible and then answer
- do not anticipate future questions by adding extra information in early answers
- if previous testimony is misinterpreted in a new question, correct it before answering
- avoid 'sugar coating' testimony, perhaps because it concerns a client or someone who is in court (Barker and Branson 2000, p. 46)
- limit responses to own area of expertise and resist answering questions beyond it.

Stevens (2003) also advises witnesses to behave and speak discreetly in court waiting areas where they may be observed; to accept that their own early performances may disappoint them; and to resist taking the process too personally.

Accompanying others attending court

Human service workers frequently assist others who are attending court. For example, a case worker may accompany a victim of domestic violence giving evidence about assaults. A case manager may accompany a young person charged with an offence. A worker may support a victim of a crime in developing a victim impact statement; or another person making a discrimination complaint before a tribunal. Another worker may be assisting a colleague distressed about the outcome of a court case and the list could go on. In these cases the worker will be reassuring, explaining, interpreting, liaising, and counselling, but of course never giving legal advice. Thus it is important that workers can navigate their way competently around court buildings, personnel, and processes. All that troubles human service workers about court processes may be similarly preoccupying those they are assisting. Having a reasonable knowledge about courts and their workings is not only critical for workers' well-being but also for that of their clients. The trick for workers is to harness their own anxiety in the interests of empathy, while not infecting other people with a negative or hostile mental attitude.

This chapter started with tales of woe about the human services and court work. It ends with notes of optimism about how the process can be made less intimidating, and even exciting, if workers understand it, their roles in it, and the challenge of 'performing'.

Key points for practice

- Court work requires mental priming and acceptance of different professional approaches:
    - the different cultures of law and human services work will be exhibited and perhaps exacerbated in courts
    - courts are the home ground of another professional group and it is normal for human service workers to be unnerved by them
    - courts are the public arena for a joust between adversaries and in them confrontation, difference, and challenge are the norm
    - the law of evidence is technical and complex.
- Recognise these professional differences but resist stereotypical perspectives on foe, friend, wrong, and right. Lawyers and human service workers are often on the same side and share the same views about outcomes. Human service workers are frequently on the side of the 'authorities', facing lawyers who are advocating for the 'victim'.
- Human service workers are not in courts as lawyers and should not judge themselves or be judged against lawyers' standards. They assist the court on matters within their human

service experience and expertise. It is against good human service practice standards that they should prepare, give evidence, and be evaluated.

- Having good-quality human service evidence is half the battle of work in courts and tribunals.
- Reports and other documentation prepared for courts should comply with all the usual principles of good human services information management.
- Witnesses must perform. This requires preparation, practice, attitudinal flexibility, and resilience.

Some useful web sites

Courts and tribunals

www.hreoc.gov.au
www.aat.gov.au/
www.federalcourt.gov.au/
www.familycourt.gov.au/
www.supremecourt.wa.gov.au/
www.courts.act.gov.au/
www.lawlink.nsw.gov.au/lawlink.nsf/pages/courts
www.courts.qld.gov.au/
www.courts.sa.gov.au/
www.courts.tas.gov.au/
www.vcat.vic.gov.au/
www.justice.vic.gov.au/

Part III

SERVICE DELIVERY— DIVERSE POPULATIONS AND JURISDICTIONS

8

Crimes and **Victims**

Features of the criminal justice system

For many people, criminal law is what they first think of when they hear the phrase 'the law'. It is certainly true that the criminal law forms a fundamental part of our society. As Carvan (2002) explains, the criminal law is part of the public law. All of society is subject to it, and ideally protected by it. On a very basic level, every society needs a criminal justice system to avoid anarchy. Crime affects everyone in society, and promises to 'get tough' on crime are perpetual vote winners for any political party (e.g. Hogg and Brown 1998). However, the development of a criminal law system that fulfils the role society has cast for it has never been simple, and every jurisdiction wrestles with issues such as punishment, and the role of retribution and rehabilitation. This is due to the complex and multifaceted nature of the criminal law and its task. Law is, in part, a reference point, ideally establishing standards and parameters that will enable society to function at its best. This is seen in few places as clearly as in the criminal law, yet criminal law is about more than simply defining a code of prohibited behaviour and prescribing punishment. It operates on both an individual and a generic level, and is concerned not only with crimes, but also with victims.

Workers may encounter the criminal justice system directly. Some workers may potentially face criminal sanctions for misconduct, as outlined in Part II. Other workers may themselves have been victims of crime, but these issues are not the focus of this chapter. Instead, this chapter will address the basic features of the criminal justice systems in Australia for adults and juveniles, as well as family violence. Pertinent practical issues facing both human service workers dealing with clients who are encountering the criminal justice system, and those in non-direct service areas such as policy development with new diversionary courts, report writing, and court liaison will be canvassed. Some of the related thematic issues currently facing criminal law and efforts in reform will also be explored.

What is crime?

Most people if asked would be able to provide a definition of crime. Usually it would incorporate such notions as 'doing something wrong' or 'breaking the rules'. Yet all such actions could be punished as civil wrongs. The person responsible could be sued and made to compensate injured parties, as explained in an earlier chapter. The consequences of committing a criminal offence stand in marked contrast to those of civil litigation. Thus for a person's action to merit criminal punishment, it must be of such a nature as to offend against society's standards to a significant degree. Changing social circumstances therefore impact the criminal law in the changing dynamics and community attitudes regarding which conduct does or does not constitute an offence. The law is necessarily reflective of societal standards at any given time.

The criminal law is different to some areas of law in that it prescribes standards of conduct according to the wishes of society, expressed through their elected representatives. Thus the law treats criminal offences as acts against society as a whole, and not primarily against the victim of the specific crime. This perspective has two main effects. First, it means it is possible to commit a crime that does not involve a readily identifiable victim, or easily identifiable damage that has occurred. This can be contrasted with tort law in which there must be a plaintiff and a defendant; one person suing another for a specific reason due to particular damage. Second, it means that when a person is charged with a criminal offence, it is not the victim who prosecutes, as the victim may be the community as a whole. The state prosecutes, termed 'R' or 'The Queen' in case titles. The victim of the crime may be the main prosecution witness, but the case is not their responsibility to prosecute or to pay for.

Another distinguishing characteristic of criminal offences compared to other breaches of law lies in the penalties imposed. Again in civil law, punitive measures taken tend to be financial in nature. However, imprisonment (what people usually think of as the punishment for criminal behaviour) is a very severe consequence for an action, no matter how long or short the sentence imposed. Even the existence of a criminal record with its attendant stigma can have wider ramifications for individuals than a history of civil litigation, depending on the circumstances.

All jurisdictions have legislation governing sentencing principles. In each case, the future consequences of a criminal record are one factor that courts must consider when determining the appropriate sentence for the offence, especially for younger adults. Imprisonment is only one possible sentence and is less commonly imposed than the other options, which include fines, community service orders, good behaviour bonds, suspended sentences of imprisonment, or even recording the conviction against the offender.

Sentencing

Deterrence and punishment are the two main factors that are traditionally given as justifying the sentences imposed for criminal offences. There are other factors such as rehabilitation and the protection of society. One clear approach taken to sentencing is the old adage 'prevention is better than cure'. Deterrence has traditionally been seen as the main way to accomplish this. For this reason deterrence is a heavily weighted factor in sentencing: to discourage the individual from reoffending (specific deterrence) and also to discourage other people from committing the same crime (general deterrence). However a related question is that of whether there are alternative methods of achieving deterrence rather than simply imposing severe penalties, and how much practical deterrence is achieved by such sentences. Research suggests that alternative forms of punishment more directed at rehabilitation may more effectively reduce recidivism (e.g. Howells and Day 1999). For this and other reasons, the sentencing options available for criminal offences are diverse. There is extensive ongoing debate over the extent to which the differing sentencing principles should influence sentencing, and which should be given the most weight in individual crimes.

The Australian legal system does not approach sentencing as being primarily about retribution for its own sake. The main concern is what is best for society as a whole. For example, the purposes of the *Sentencing Act 1997* (Tas) as outlined in s 3, focus on the protection of the community but include establishing fair sentences for individual offenders and preventing crime by using both sentences of deterrence *and* of rehabilitation, and 'recognising the needs of victims' also. Alternative methods of sentencing and resolution of some criminal offences are being explored in different jurisdictions, particularly for juveniles (e.g. Strang and Braithwaite 2002), some of which were canvassed in chapter 7. Initiatives in this area are reflective of the nexus between human services and law, explained in Part I. More recent alternatives have also been introduced and/or trialled for particular offences, for example people charged with certain drug offences, or for particular groups, such as Indigenous defendants. One standard requirement to have a case heard through such diversionary methods, especially those not involving a court hearing, is that the defendant admits their guilt. Cases in which the defendant has chosen to plead not guilty must still be processed through the mainstream system.

Preventative (or indefinite) detention of offenders deemed a danger to the public is a controversial issue in sentencing. So too is mandatory sentencing, in which a minimum sentence is imposed for all offenders regardless of their individual circumstances with no discretion given to the court to impose a lesser sentence. In recent years Western Australia and the Northern Territory have introduced controversial mandatory sentences for property offences, which received a great deal of publicity across Australia. However all states and territories have mandatory sentences for certain offences. Many regulatory offences have mandatory minimum sentences, such as minimum terms for loss of licence or fines for some driving offences. Additionally, murder carries a mandatory sentence of life imprisonment in South Australia, the Northern Territory, Queensland, and Western Australia. In the other jurisdictions, the maximum term is life imprisonment, but the exact sentence imposed is discretionary.

Criminal law in Australia

Jurisdictions

Australia's criminal law follows two main jurisdictions; that of each state or territory, and that of the Commonwealth. Criminal conduct of any given offender may be either a state/territory offence or a Commonwealth one. Commonwealth criminal offences are typically either offences committed on exclusively federal property (such as in airports), or against federal officials.

In Australia the criminal law derived originally from the English common law. A measure of consistency and predictability in these decisions was provided by the doctrine of precedent, by which the common law obtains its authority. Courts make decisions on a case-by-case basis, but if each could be decided according to different rules it would be chaotic. Therefore cases are decided using precedent. This means that cases on the same subjects must be decided in line with previous decisions. The point of law decided in an individual case becomes a rule that must be applied to cases involving the same point of law in the future (see generally Staller and Kirk 1998).

Codifying the criminal law

The criminal law in South Australia, Victoria, New South Wales, and the Australian Capital Territory is still based on the common law. Even though those states and territory have enacted their own legislation that forms part of the criminal law, their legislation supplements but does not entirely supersede the common law. However, several jurisdictions have replaced the common law by enacting Criminal Codes, which *are* intentionally substituted for common law. Code states still have the doctrine of precedent, but instead of interpreting the common law, the courts now interpret the Criminal Code. Queensland, Tasmania, the Northern Territory, and Western Australia are code states. In addition to state jurisdictions, there is also a federal jurisdiction of criminal law operating in Australia. For a number of years there has been a move towards developing one single criminal code, which would apply across all jurisdictions. This has not yet occurred. There is of course a federal criminal jurisdiction, which is primarily governed by the Commonwealth Criminal Code, introduced comparatively recently in 1995. This Code covers different offences to those covered under each state's jurisdiction. Additionally the High Court, as the ultimate appellate court, hears criminal cases also. It applies the criminal law from the individual jurisdiction in each particular case. The High Court has made it clear however, that Australia has one uniform system of common law, and not a different system for each individual state (see generally Bronitt and McSherry 2001).

Elements of criminal offences

It is important to have an awareness of the nature of criminal responsibility as understood by the legal system. The reason for this is deceptively simple; some human service workers may have clients who have been charged with offences, do not have a lawyer, and who are mistaken about whether they are guilty or not. This is absolutely not to suggest that human service workers should act as 'stand in' lawyers in this situation. Human service workers must be vigilant in not giving legal advice to their clients. However, workers who understand that there may be more to a client's guilt than meets the eye are in a better position to encourage their clients to seek legal advice. For this reason, a brief rudimentary account of basic criminal responsibility and how it is assessed by the criminal law is included.

Criminal offences are categorised differently according to their severity and their nature. Additionally, many are classified according to certain elements; physical elements and mental elements.

Physical elements

All offences, regardless of their nature, involve physical elements. These are commonly thought to be the action that constitutes the offence, but the concept is broader than that. The physical elements of a specific offence include all circumstances that need to be established in order for the offence to be made out and the accused to be found guilty. This will include physical actions of the offender, but can also include, for example, specific circumstances of the victim or the time at which the offence occurred, if these particular factors are part of what makes the conduct an offence.

Mental elements

Not all offences have a mental element, but many of the most serious offences do. The mental element is basically the state of mind that an offender must have possessed in order to be guilty. The mental element might be intention, knowledge, recklessness, or negligence, or sometimes two or more of those as alternatives.

These elements are best illustrated in their application. Consider the following example of a fictitious offence. A city council has responded to concerns over attacks on children after dark in its locality by persuading the state parliament to enact the following new offence: 'No person shall intentionally assault a minor in the city at night'.

Clearly in this example 'intentionally' is the mental element. If a person does not commit the crime intentionally, they are not guilty. 'Assault' is quite clearly a physical element. It is the action that is considered criminal. However, the offence is not to 'intentionally assault' just anyone. This offence is to intentionally assault a *'minor* in the *city* at *night'*. Thus the status of the victim (a minor), the location of the crime (the city), and the time it occurs (at night) are also physical elements that the prosecution must prove. If the mental element, and any of those additional physical elements are not present (and proved beyond reasonable doubt) then the accused will not be guilty of this particular offence, although they may well be guilty of some other offence.

Practice questions and responses

Question: If someone hits another person deliberately, how could they not be guilty of assault?
Response: This demonstrates the differences between lay and legal understandings of terms, as well as the more complex dynamics involved in issues of criminal liability. It is a highly legal and highly technical area. Self-defence, intoxication, and mental health may all affect liability in individual cases. It is important to be aware of such factors, even though as a human service worker you may not be conversant with their details.

Question: What happens if they didn't know the person was a minor, or that they were within the Central Business District or something?
Response: Good question. The discussion above focuses on the physical elements for the offence, and your question concerns the mental element. Defence counsel may well want to argue that the offence was not made out for those sorts of reasons, and it would be up to the court to decide, unless the legislation itself specifically addressed those issues.

Categories of offences

As mentioned above, not all offences have a mental element. Some offences (known as 'absolute liability offences') require proof of the physical elements only. Many driving offences are an example of this. If someone were speeding, it is no defence to argue that they didn't know they were going too fast or didn't intend to—the prosecution only has to prove the physical elements; that they were driving and the car was exceeding the speed limit. Other offences (known as 'strict liability offences') may contain no mental element, but instead have built-in defences available to exclude people who made honest mistakes about the facts. These offences tend to be more regulatory in nature. The majority of minor offences are either strict or absolute liability offences. In the final analysis, while it is important to be aware of the general scope of offences and issues surrounding their categorisation, decisions regarding appropriate charges are initially a matter for police, and ultimately, for the courts.

Clients charged with offences

Most people who are charged with criminal offences plead guilty (Mack and Anleu 1998). This has many ramifications for workers, especially those with adult clients who do not have access to the range of diversionary options available to young offenders. Many clients do not have a lawyer and may not know how to best represent themselves, what information to give the court, or the issues surrounding the charges against them. They may also be unaware of their rights and options (such as seeking an adjournment to give them more time to prepare their case) and the assistance that is available to them even if they are unrepresented in court.

Some clients may plead guilty and not be aware that they have a valid defence to a charge, or that one of the physical or mental elements of the offence is arguably not present and they may well *not* be legally guilty even if they *were* involved in the situation. Others may prefer to plead guilty and 'get it over with', not realising how damaging this can be to future employment and other opportunities. Obviously providing any level of specific advice on these types of issues is not possible (and is professionally unwise) for human service workers, but it is certainly possible for workers to highlight complexities involved in the process that the client is not aware of. This leaves clients better able to seek appropriate legal advice, and/or argue their own case.

There is also fundamental information that the court will need in order to determine an appropriate sentence, such as employment history, character references, community activities, and the defendant's dependants. If their client has a lawyer, workers may have a role in liaising with them and providing this type of relevant information about their client to assist in the lawyer's own preparations prior to sentencing. It is even more critical for unrepresented defendants to know the types of issues that can be raised when making sentencing submissions to the court, since they will do so themselves without a lawyer. Unrepresented clients may not know this information is needed, and the court may or may not ask specific questions about such matters.

Other practical information is also helpful. Each Magistrate's Court has a duty solicitor available to provide some basic assistance to unrepresented defendants; this is certainly crucial for an unrepresented client to know. Workers may find themselves discussing a bail application with a client, or perhaps providing information directly to the court as to their client's suitability for bail, and will need to be familiar with the main issues involved in that area also.

Indigenous Australians and the criminal law

Overrepresentation of Indigenous people in custody is an issue that is common to both the adult and juvenile justice systems. Indigenous Australians make up a vastly disproportionate number of individuals currently incarcerated across Australia (McRae, Nettheim et al. 2003). Recent statistics show that Indigenous Australians form 20 per cent of the prison population and are incarcerated at a rate 13 times greater than that of non-Indigenous offenders (Australian Institute of Criminology 2002). One method often floated to address these issues in part is the use of traditional tribal punishments as alternatives to custodial sentences in some cases. The place of Indigenous customary laws within the Australian legal system has been debated judicially since the early 1970s, and this debate increased after the landmark native title case of *Mabo v Queensland (No 2)* (1992) 175 CLR 1, since that case recognised, among other things, the existence of Indigenous customary law (McRae, Nettheim et al. 2003). Recognition of Indigenous customary laws is fraught with both practical and ideological difficulties, since the nature and role of such laws defy easy comparison with non-Indigenous law. Customary laws certainly involve more than traditional forms of punishment, but are rather 'the application of cultural values and principles to indigenous community life' and for this reason they do not need to be restricted in their application to people living in traditional communities (Clark 2002, p. 7). Despite this, it is the traditional punishment component of customary law that is most often considered within general criminal law.

In 1986 the Australian Law Reform Commission recommended the recognition of customary law where it does not conflict with general law and where it is in the interests of justice (Australian Law Reform Commission 1986). A proper consideration of the issues raised in this debate is outside the scope of this book, however two points need to be emphasised. First, while Australia does not recognise customary law as a parallel alternative system, facets of such law are incorporated within the framework of the general law in specific situations, especially regarding initiatives such as Indigenous Courts for adults, community justice programs, and restorative justice (McRae, Nettheim et al. 2003), some of which were discussed in chapter 7. The assistance of the Aboriginal Legal Rights Movement is also available. Indigenous juveniles may be involved in family conferencing (discussed later in this chapter), although its cultural appropriateness has prompted arguments both for and against (e.g. Blagg 1997; Braithwaite 1997). However it has been advocated that general restorative justice principles be applied more broadly to communities living according to customary law as it may well lead to a reduction in levels of violence. Traditional punishments are used as part of restorative justice in some of those communities, and those communities tend to experience low levels of violence (Sarre and Wilson 1998, p. 12). Customary laws arguably provide scope for such initiatives, as they are 'more a process of governing social relations' than a set of rules, thus inherently providing a greater role to be played by Indigenous community justice groups in addressing breaches of law (Limerick 2002, p. 15).

Second, despite this approach to several aspects of customary law, there is widespread reluctance to formally recognise and allow a place for traditional punishments in the general criminal law. Instead, recognition of these punishments tends to occur rarely, only for accused people living in a tribal community, and on a case-by-case basis (Sarre and Wilson 1998). Thus the fact that an Indigenous offender living in a community that observes customary laws will be subjected to a traditional form of punishment for their offence could be a mitigating factor in their sentencing before the court, but will rarely be considered as an alternative sentence in its own right.

Juvenile justice

The most fundamental point to bear in mind regarding juvenile justice is also the source of much of the controversy surrounding this area: although charged with the same offences, children are sentenced and processed differently from adults under the criminal law in each state or territory. The exception is that children can be dealt with as adults for very serious offences such as murder. Each jurisdiction has wrestled with determining how their juvenile justice system should be structured, due in no small measure to the difficulties society has faced in answering questions of the status of children, their rights, responsibilities, and capabilities. Juvenile justice historically has been approached from either a welfare model or a justice model (Braithwaite 1996). The welfare model involves more paternalistic active intervention by the state in the lives of individual young people accused of offences, with rehabilitation of the offender as its primary sentencing goal. Partly due to this model, at one time young offenders and children in need of care were all dealt with as one group in many jurisdictions. Some jurisdictions that have a strong emphasis on the welfare model continue to do this, commonly incorporating child protection and young offender provisions into the same legislation. In contrast, the justice model approaches children as much more akin to adults, requiring them to take responsibility for their actions. It does also highlight their legal rights as individuals, however there is significant debate over whether children are able to utilise the rights given to them under the law (Gale, Naffine et al. 1993).

South Australia is a good example of the differing approaches. Its juvenile justice system was once based primarily on the welfare model. The *Children and Young Offenders Act 1979* (SA) dealt with child protection and juvenile justice in differing sections. It was replaced in 1993 by the *Children's Protection Act* and the *Young Offenders Act*. The long title of the *Young Offenders Act*, states its purpose is to 'reconstitute the juvenile justice system' of that state, which operates fundamentally out of the justice model. Each state or territory varies in the chosen legislative balance between these competing notions and the extent to which children should be treated the same as adults under the law, but all have drawn from both models. From these differences it is possible to draw points of commonality, and these will be the focus here.

Features of juvenile justice systems

Purpose and structure

Generally, the juvenile justice system of a given Australian jurisdiction has a more rehabilitative focus than its adult system equivalent; however under a justice model, a substantial reason for that focus is community protection. Police often have wider discretionary powers regarding the progress of a young person through the system than they have regarding adult offenders. Typically, police have discretion regarding adults at the very beginning of the process; that is, whether or not to arrest or charge a particular individual and with which specific offence. In contrast, much of the discretion given to the police is ordinarily focused at keeping young people out of the court system, whereas in the absence of a diversionary system, the majority of adults charged with criminal offences have no other option but to have that charge dealt with through the courts.

Despite being designed with a greater rehabilitative and diversionary potential than their corresponding adult systems, the juvenile justice systems in most jurisdictions are still based on the adult systems. Although historically there has been recognition of the need to formulate a model of criminal justice better suited to young people and one which solves the problems encountered in previous models, many of the flaws inherent in the adult systems are transferred across and at times exacerbated when applied in a juvenile system. There is thus a corresponding need to achieve a juvenile justice system that can balance the needs of all stakeholders without having to put up with such inherent flaws to do it. 'Mimicking adult justice ... seems an odd solution to the perceived deficiencies of children's justice' (Gale, Naffine et al. 1993, p. 16).

All states and territories have a legal presumption that a child under the age of 10 years is not able to commit a criminal offence. They are presumed not to understand the consequences of their actions, nor to understand right from wrong to a sufficient level to justify imposing criminal liability on them for their actions. Due to this, children under this age are not charged with criminal offences. State intervention may occur regarding very young children who behave antisocially; however this would be through welfare and alternative care systems or perhaps by placing them under state guardianship.

Limitations exist in all states and territories also on the extent to which details of a young person charged with an offence can be reported in the media. A common example is that their name or details that would tend to identify them are not reported. This aims at safeguarding their reputation and at preventing stigma from attaching to convicted offenders in order to facilitate rehabilitation. This is in marked contrast to the position of an adult defendant who is usually identified by name in any media reports on alleged offending, which may have a lasting effect on their reputation notwithstanding that they may in fact later be acquitted, often unbeknownst to the public.

Juvenile courts

Young people charged with criminal offences do not appear in the same courts as adults. Each jurisdiction has a separate court to hear charges against young offenders. These courts are variously named but have the powers of Magistrate's Courts. They also have different rules governing their daily activities, for example limitations on who is admitted to the courtrooms and who can watch proceedings. This safeguards the privacy of the defendants. Their procedures are also designed to reduce the factors inherent in usual court proceedings that may contribute to young people becoming repeat offenders. For example in Victoria, the Criminal Division of the Children's Court is required to conduct its proceedings in a manner that minimises any stigma to the young person or their family.

Diversion and community protection

In each state or territory, young people accused of offending are diverted around the formal court system if at all possible, due to the greater emphasis of juvenile justice systems than adult systems on rehabilitation to prevent future offending. This link between rehabilitation and the wider community protection interest in reducing future offending is consistent with the justice models that again predominate in Australian juvenile justice systems. Family conferences are now a commonly used alternative method of resolution in some jurisdictions to court appearances. Although not suitable in all cases, they are available for minor offences and a prerequisite is that the young person acknowledges their guilt (Daly and Hayes 2001). If they maintain their innocence they will necessarily have to go to court. A family conference typically involves the young person and the victim(s) of the offence meeting and engaging in a mediated discussion of the offending and its consequences accompanied by supportive adults such as relatives, a teacher, or human service workers. Conferencing gives the victim in particular much more input than they have in the adult court system (Alder and Wundersitz 1994; Daly and Hayes 2001). An agreement is drawn up which sets out the decided penalties. It typically includes compensation to the victim and community service among other options. If the young person does not comply with all requirements the matter is referred to the court.

Penalties

Unless a young person is charged as an adult and tried in the adult criminal courts, the penalty regime for young people convicted of criminal offences differs from that of adults. Under the *Children and Young Persons Act 1989* (Vic) the Children's Court may require, among other things, that a young person who is convicted of an offence enter into undertakings governing their behaviour, pay compensation to victims, enter into good behaviour bonds, or pay fines. Additionally young people 15 years or over may be ordered to perform community service hours (called a youth attendance order) as an alternative to a sentence of detention, or serve weekend detention. If sentenced to detention, children between 10 and 15 are placed in youth residential centres, whereas young people between 15 and 18 years are placed in youth training centres.

Restorative justice

'What does justice involve?' This question is much debated and one answer is that it should involve 'restoration'. Restorative justice involves a sentencing process focused on the restoration of victims, offenders, and the community (Braithwaite 1996; Daly and Hayes 2001), which maximises the involvement of each of these groups in the process. It not only makes offenders directly accountable for their actions but also ideally provides them with an opportunity to take responsibility and thus have the impetus for change. Restorative justice occurs in more than juvenile justice alone, but features predominantly in that sphere. The precise mechanisms used in restorative justice can vary, but family conferencing is one common example (Alder and Wundersitz 1994), and Indigenous community justice groups that advise magistrates are another. The goal is to address competing sentencing aims, which have not been successfully achieved by either the welfare or the justice models standing alone (Braithwaite 2002).

Focus on responsibility, consequences, and victims

The movement away from the welfare models of juvenile justice has seen a greater emphasis on young people taking responsibility for their actions and facing the consequences directly. Where family conferences occur, they arguably face those consequences far more directly than many adult offenders, and all levels of those juvenile systems that are diversionary require an acknowledgment of responsibility by the young person. Victims of offences have a very direct role in some levels of the system—in particular family conferences. Victims have the opportunity to express clearly what they consider is required to provide restitution and the system has been structured with that emphasis.

Practice question and response

Question: This is all very well, but what about young people of Indigenous or culturally diverse backgrounds? Family conferencing is hardly suited to them, surely?

Response: It is important not to generalise or categorise groups too broadly or quickly. However, the cultural appropriateness of conferencing for many such young people and the suitability of close police involvement and potential power imbalances have all been hotly debated in different forums (e.g. Blagg 1997; Braithwaite 1997; Daly and Hayes 2001). It is also arguable that family conferencing is no less alienating for culturally diverse and Indigenous young people than many court processes already are, and family conferencing is at least more adaptable to cultural needs than a court hearing.

Police interviewing

Another facet of the criminal justice system in which human service workers often become directly involved is that of police interviews. Young people are not meant to be interviewed by police in relation to an offence without an adult present, and that adult may be a human service worker if there is no other adult (typically a family member) who is able to attend. When involved in these interviews the worker must be very clear on their role, and ask questions to clarify this if necessary. It is essential that a client who is interviewed answer the questions asked of them personally, rather than having that information provided by the worker.

An informed worker has the opportunity to ensure that clients are aware of their rights and police responsibilities. For example, police in each jurisdiction operate under guidelines for interviewing persons charged with offences, including fundamental issues such as maximum lengths of interviews. Workers in the area should become familiar with these in order that appropriate information can be passed on to clients where necessary.

Practice question and response

Question: Surely it is my responsibility to advocate for my client in the face of police questioning?

Response: No. In this situation, that form of 'advocacy' is understood as the role of the lawyer, which you are not. In the wider sense of advocacy, you will best serve your client by supporting, observing, taking notes, interpreting your client's needs and physical and emotional state to police, and by later following up any concerns you may have about the conduct of the interview.

Victims of crime

Many victims of crime do not go to the police and thus have no contact with the criminal justice system. Support of such victims, particularly of sexual abuse or assault, or domestic violence is certainly undertaken by various human service workers and agencies, however the focus here is on support offered to victims who are involved with the processes of the criminal justice system.

Victim support services and agencies operate in all Australian jurisdictions. In the early 1980s the focus of the victims' movement was on victim's rights, leading to a raft of legislation aimed at protecting victims giving evidence in court and providing for the use of victim impact statements, with most jurisdictions adopting a Charter of Victim's Rights (Cook, David et al. 1999). Additionally, recent amendments to some jurisdictions' criminal injuries compensation legislation has provided for the inclusion of victims in the criminal justice process, for example in the South Australian *Victims of Crime Act 2001* and the Queensland *Criminal Offence Victims Act 1995*. In the 1990s this focus began shifting to the support of victims, and 'only secondarily [to] lobby[ing] for structural and systematic change to the criminal justice system' (Cook, David et al. 1999, p. 86). Human service workers play a key role in the ongoing fulfilment of various agency mandates in victim support.

Compensation for victims

In all jurisdictions it is possible for a victim of crime to obtain a compensation payment from the state or territory government. These payments are funded by levies paid by all people found convicted of any criminal offence. This provides an alternative to civil action, which is generally not a viable option for victims of crime to take, either due to their own or the offender's financial position, or because the identity of the offender(s) is unknown. The amount payable is assessed on a sliding scale according to the level of injury sustained by the victim, with maximums differing in every jurisdiction, from $10,000 under Tasmania's *Criminal Injuries Compensation Act 1976*, to $75,000 under Queensland's *Criminal Offence Victims Act 1995*. Compensation payments are thus far less than amounts available as common law damages. Another problematic issue regarding these schemes is the difficulty of defining compensable injuries, especially for sexual assaults and domestic violence, and for quantifying the appropriate compensation in those cases (see generally Forster 2002; Baron 2003; Johns 2003).

Family violence

Legal response to domestic violence in Australia

The law has been slow to develop an approach for dealing with issues of domestic violence, now increasingly subsumed in the wider term 'family violence'. Family violence includes spousal abuse but also violence against other family members such as siblings, parents, and extended family members. Traditionally, domestic violence was not perceived by the criminal law as a distinct area of offending. Any prosecution for violent conduct against spouses was under the general law of assault. A legion of difficulties impeded such prosecutions, ranging from reluctance of victims to make complaints, to police reluctance to arrest, coupled with a pervasive sense among the community that violence occurring in the family home was private and best resolved internally given the dynamics involved. In more recent years, domestic violence has come to be understood as a serious offence against the community, no different in that respect from other areas of the criminal law (Commonwealth Office of the Status of Women 1995). It is also an area of rapid development in law and human services and of interdisciplinary work between the two fields (for an overview see Urbis Keys Young 2002). An example of this is seen in the major national framework for addressing domestic violence, Partnerships Against Domestic Violence, which is a federally funded joint initiative of the Commonwealth and all state and territory governments. To date it includes nineteen Commonwealth and fifty-five state and territory projects.

The idea that violence in Australia occurs mostly out in the community, for example between strangers or in fights at the local pub, is a myth. In fact, 42 per cent of all assaults occurred in a residential location in 2001. This is greater than for any other single location, including those in the community. For the same year, 71 per cent of all assaults on women occurred in a residential location (Australian Institute of Criminology 2002). Statistics from the Commonwealth Office of the Status of Women for 2001 (2001) indicate that 50.1 per cent of women who had been assaulted in the previous twelve months were assaulted by their current or previous partner. Domestic violence is clearly prevalent in Australia, although like much intra-familial violence or abuse it is quite hidden.

It is trite to say that domestic violence involves more than legal issues. It involves emotional, social, behavioural, and psychological factors and dynamics, the treatment of which is beyond the scope of this book. Responding to situations of domestic violence likewise involves issues that are 'extremely complex in themselves, quite apart from any legal or policy considerations surrounding ... the process' (Law Reform Commission 2002, p. 3). It requires change on a societal and attitudinal level. For this reason the approach taken by human service workers seeking to assist clients who have experienced domestic violence requires 'a wider understanding than merely a knowledge of the legal remedies [but instead a] holistic approach' (Alexander 2002, p. 1). A worker who brings this approach to their interaction with clients is in a strong position to provide effective service and support. While acknowledging these dynamics and encouraging workers to develop their own understanding of them, the focus here remains on the legal issues and options in dealing with domestic violence.

State or territory legislation provides individuals who have been subjected to domestic violence with two main options. Criminal charges may be laid against a perpetrator if the conduct falls within assault provisions, or constitutes stalking (discussed below). Restraining orders may also be sought; these are often contained within legislation specific to domestic violence. These options are not alternatives

t from a state or territory court even if the parties are involved in Family
t proceedings.

Finally, a general restraining order may be obtained under state or territory
lation. These orders may be sought against any other person; they are not
ited to situations of domestic violence. For this reason they are the only option
most jurisdictions for a homosexual or lesbian person who experiences domestic
lence, as most state or territory domestic violence orders and the Family Court
junction are not available to same-sex partners. These restraining orders are also
e only option for other people experiencing intra-familial violence from an
ffender who is outside their jurisdiction's legislative definitions. Like domestic
iolence restraining orders, general restraining orders are available whether or not
assault charges are laid, but they still cover a narrower range of conduct than most
domestic violence legislation.

Key points for practice

- In all dealings with clients encountering the criminal justice system, workers must be
vigilant in ensuring they do not provide legal advice to clients, nor give clients the
impression that their assistance and advice is all that the client needs.
- A worker's focus, as always, should usually be on providing general information that
alerts clients to significant issues and options, exploring avenues for ensuring that they
receive legal advice where possible, and referral. When providing more specific
information care should be taken that it is still given in the context of general advice.
- As discussed in Part I it is necessary to develop a solid understanding of the criminal law
independent from any emotional response to deficiencies within it or within its implementation. The law does not fix complex social problems, but rather forms part of the
framework from which to address them, along with policy and effective service delivery.
- It is vital to approach domestic violence as a multilayered issue even where a worker's
mandate is specifically on the legal issues involved.
- The paramountcy of workers developing strong working relationships and knowing where
to refer clients for additional assistance and support cannot be overstated. Networks and
contacts among local police, lawyers, court staff, and other human service workers are
invaluable resources.

Some useful web sites

Criminology and criminal law

www.aic.gov.au
www.alrc.gov.au
www.ncp.gov.au/
www.police.tas.gov.au/police/police2001.nsf/W/Headings/CCAS-5GG864/?Open

---

to each other but it is not uncommon for a restraining order to be sought without
criminal charges being laid even where the conduct did involve assault. Many
factors influence a person's wish not to have criminal charges brought against their
partner, which will not be addressed here. Police may be empowered to lay charges
even where the victim of a crime does not want charges to be laid (Department of
Justice 2002; Law Reform Commission 2002). However, in practice this rarely
occurs since it is difficult to obtain a conviction without the evidence of the victim,
unless there is other evidence apart from their testimony.

Stalking

In all jurisdictions, stalking provides a relatively recent criminal charge as an
additional alternative for some situations of domestic violence. Stalking itself is not
limited to the domestic context, but much stalking occurs within this sphere
(Pearce and Easteal 1999; Ogilvie 2000). It is clear that classifying particular behaviour as stalking depends largely on its context and the intent of the accused, and
for this reason legislators have struggled to articulate definitions that are effective
yet do not risk criminalising innocuous behaviour. Stalking legislation tends to
focus on both the conduct of the accused and the reaction that conduct engendered
in the victim, either using broad or comprehensive definitions. It typically proscribes
conduct that constitutes stalking and the required mental element of the accused,
as well as including a requirement that the victim felt threatened by the conduct.

There is much debate about whether the legislation should have a subjective
focus on victims, which turns on the person's actual reaction, or an objective one,
hinging on the responses, actions, and expectations of a reasonable person faced
with that conduct. There is also debate about whether or not an accused must have
intended the victim to experience fear or intimidation, as this can be difficult to
prove beyond reasonable doubt, especially for conduct that may have an 'innocent
explanation' to many people, such as sending flowers (e.g. Blaauw, Sheridan et al.
2002). Most jurisdictions require the stalking behaviour to have occurred on more
than one occasion, although in Queensland, one instance will be enough if it is
protracted. International studies, however, consistently show that stalking rarely
occurs on only one occasion (Blaauw, Sheridan et al. 2002).

Restraining orders

The essential difference between a restraining order and bringing a criminal charge
is that a person against whom a restraining order is granted has not been convicted
of a criminal offence. A restraining order is a preventative measure designed to
guard against future violence rather than imposing a penalty for previous violence
(Alexander 2002). This is a fundamental reason for the structure and implementation
of restraining orders designed for domestic violence and the debate surrounding their
appropriateness and effectiveness (Law Reform Commission 2002). As a civil order,
they have a civil burden of proof, due to the fact that they are preventative in nature
and do not carry with them the stigma or consequences of a criminal conviction.
Additionally, although the issuing of an order is a civil matter, it is a criminal offence

to breach one. Other than these similarities it is clear that the domestic violence orders are broader and more suited specifically to domestic violence situations.

In addition to being seen as an easier alternative to criminal charges by some victims, restraining orders are easier to obtain than a criminal conviction. There has been some concern that police may be opting to use restraining orders rather than assault charges to respond to domestic violence for these and other reasons (Department of Justice 2002). Restraining orders for all offences, domestic or not, enjoy a mixed reputation. Problems surrounding their implementation and enforcement, as well as publicised breaches of orders are well known (e.g. Young, Byles et al. 2000). Some of these problems arise out of the hybrid nature of orders, which sit somewhat awkwardly in the system. They are not criminal in nature since they are preventative and thus they require a lower standard of proof; yet it is a criminal offence to breach one. The implementation of domestic violence restraining orders is also affected by the complex dynamics inherent in such incidents. Nonetheless, there has been an increased focus in recent years on reforming restraining order provisions to maximise their effectiveness in situations of domestic violence. 'Restraining orders do not work effectively without support and coordination. [They] work best where they are one element of a broader package involving government and community support' (Department of Justice 2002, p. 4). This is one area in which human service workers can play a vital role.

A combination of court and police intervention is also crucial to the effectiveness of any restraining order. Breaches need to be followed up on, and victims need to be able to have confidence that police will attend, listen to them, and take appropriate action. Much progress has been made in this area in recent years. Police regions increasingly now have a domestic violence unit (variously named), with officers who are specifically trained to handle call outs to domestic situations that may involve violence, and to assist in applications for domestic violence or general restraining orders (Young, Byles et al. 2000; Law Reform Commission 2002).

Practice question and response

Question: This all sounds rather idealised. Everyone knows that in reality, restraining orders are a waste of time. Women and children still get injured and killed with impunity.

Response: At times they do, and there are problems with restraining orders. These problems warrant a closer look, however. Are they due to the legal framework that is in place? The response of police and other agencies, and courts in imposing sentences for breaching orders has been improving but there is a long way to go. Nonetheless, it is clear that the effectiveness of restraining orders is largely about implementation, and therefore strong interagency work is needed. The problem is more than just a legal one.

Availability of restraining orders

Restraining orders specifically available for domestic violence are covered under legislation in each state and territory jurisdiction. In some states such as South

---

Australia and Queensland there is separate legislation t lence; other states such as New South Wales simply incor provisions into their existing criminal law statutes. The determining the availability of domestic violence restraining whether the person subjected to violence is within the clas the order is available, and whether the conduct concerned violence'.

Definitions of 'domestic violence' differ across the jurisdict ably broader than assault, allowing restraining orders to be obt such as threatening harm and damaging property. The New South provides a good example of this breadth: an apprehended domest may be obtained under the *Crimes Act 1900* (NSW) s 562AE to p committing any offence of personal violence under the Act, includ threatening with violence, as well as intimidation and harassment (have to involve threats of violence).

In New South Wales, the apprehended domestic violence order is protect a person who is in a 'domestic relationship' with the perpetrator. dictions define such a relationship as a spousal relationship (either in m as de facto heterosexual spouses). New South Wales and Queensland inclu sex relationships within the definition of a spousal relationship. New Sou also defines a 'domestic relationship' as including platonic personal relatic Therefore, in that state other relatives and members of a household would covered, extending the added protection of a domestic violence restraining or other forms of interfamilial violence. Queensland has also recently broadened application of the *Domestic and Family Violence Protection Act 1989* (Qld) similar vein, and additionally includes people who are in an 'informal care relatic ship'. These wider definitions allow for a greater range of interfamilial violence be addressed, either for those experiencing violence from immediate family mem bers other than a spouse, or for those people living in extended family households for cultural reasons. This is advantageous for Indigenous Australians in particular, who are at greatest risk of violence of any group in Australia (Carrington and Phillips 2003).

Other restraining orders

There are two other types of restraining orders applicable to situations of domestic violence. The first is an injunction under the *Family Law Act 1975* (Cth) s 114. This injunction is for the 'personal protection of a party to a marriage' or to protect the child of a de facto marriage. This injunction is thus only available to a married person and must be sought from the Family Court on the initiative of the person experiencing the violence. If the order is breached they must return to the Court to seek sanctions, and the process is generally far more costly and time-consuming. In contrast, state or territory orders can be obtained within a day in extreme situations, are easier to apply for personally, and police are available to apply and assist with the process. In fact, a domestic violence restraining order may usually be

Restorative justice
www.aic.gov.au/rjustice/
crj.anu.edu.au/
www.restorativejustice.com.au

Domestic violence
www.padv.dpmc.gov.au
www.lgcms.com.au/Kids&dv.htm
www.austdvclearinghouse.unsw.edu.au/

Victim support
www.lawlink.nsw.gov.au/vs/voclink.nsf/pages/victim_support
www.restorativejustice.com.au/victim_support_services.htm

9

Families and **Children**

The centrality of an interdisciplinary perspective

As mentioned elsewhere, a legal problem always has more than legal dimensions. It has both a human service context and consequence. The interrelationship of issues and disciplines so common in human service law is manifestly seen in family law. Increasingly, anecdotal and empirical evidence suggests that the effectiveness of the law in these areas is inextricably connected to its ability to integrate what have traditionally been viewed as 'human service' approaches into its processes, and to learn from the knowledge base of human service workers. Human services have endorsed inter-organisational collaborative approaches for many years, although in some areas the rhetoric has not been matched in practice. The collaborative inter-disciplinary approaches and integration discussed in Part I similarly have much to offer and are to be encouraged between the law and human service in the area of families and children. Many legal professionals and academics now advocate such reciprocity as a crucial element in the law's response to child sexual abuse in particu-lar (Brown, Sheehan et al. 2001; Eastwood 2003; Sheehan 2003). This approach starts with each individual lawyer and worker.

Crucial to any interdisciplinary approach is a clearly focused mandate for both law and the human services. Particularly in child protection work, human service workers have traditionally had one of two reputations in legal circles: either that of whingers who constantly point out the flaws in the system to little effect and who are influenced too much by their own emotions and attitudes in their decision-making, or that of highly effective agents for change who fulfil their roles and advocate with great impact. The area of families and children is one in which it is most difficult for workers in both the law and human services to remain objective and dispassionate. While it is true that a person's beliefs, values, and experiences will inevitably influence decision-making to some extent, it is crucial that this does not occur at the expense of the objectivity necessary to provide excellent and effective service and where appropriate, convincing advocacy.

Human service workers fulfil diverse roles in the area of families and children. Their child protection work may be the most publicly visible, but is only one facet of this complex area. They are involved in drafting legislation, advocacy, they run women's legal centres or shelters, are involved in family counselling and a great deal of front-line case management in the alternative care system. They are youth workers, run intervention programs, or work with drug and alcohol or gambling services, they work as Family Court counsellors, and the list goes on.

By its nature, virtually every area of human service work impacts families and children to some degree. However, this chapter concentrates on child protection and family law. Both are contentious areas and the subject of current reform. The chapter will consider two main areas of family law: marriage and divorce proceedings and arrangements for children, child protection at a state or territory and federal level, and issues for human service workers involved in all of these areas. Notable by their absence are child care regulation and education systems, as well as domestic violence. The latter is covered in chapter 8, on criminal law, for the simple reason that while it is perpetrated against family members, it is first and foremost a criminal offence. The same must be said of child abuse and neglect, however its unique position as a discrete area of human service work requires its separate treatment.

Marriage and divorce

Family law is in itself an incredibly complex area of federal law. The main piece of legislation covering this area, the *Family Law Act 1975* (Cth), is being amended and updated at time of writing, and indeed always has been, due to changing social conditions. As seen in other areas, the law mirrors, follows, and sometimes leads community attitudes as illustrated in figure 3.1.

Marriage and divorce are covered by the *Marriage Act 1961* (Cth) and the *Family Law Act 1975* (Cth). It is neither possible nor necessary to provide a great deal of detail regarding the law in these areas, however there are several key areas that impact upon human service workers generally, and their potential clients and interaction with those clients in particular.

Since 1975, with the introduction of the *Family Law Act*, Australia has operated under the 'no fault' principle regarding divorce. This principle simply means that the reasons for a marriage breakdown do not affect the rights of the parties to that marriage once it has broken down. Historically and in some other countries, the reasons for the divorce affected what each party could walk away with, and at times rights regarding their children. The *Family Law Act 1975* (Cth) however, introduced the concept of no fault divorce by providing for only one ground of divorce instead of several. In Australia, the only ground for divorce (termed 'dissolution of marriage' in the Act) is 'irretrievable breakdown' of the marriage. It is demonstrated by twelve months continual separation. The reasons for that breakdown do not affect the legitimacy of either party's claims under the Act. Applications for divorce can be made jointly or may be uncontested if the parties wish to simplify and speed up the processing of their documentation and hearing of their case. As of November 2003, all applications for dissolution of marriage must be filed in the Federal Magistrates Court.

'No fault' divorce means that it is also not possible to oppose a divorce just because one party does not agree to it. To oppose a divorce a party must argue that the breakdown has not occurred (i.e. the parties have not been separated for twelve months) or that the breakdown in marriage is not irretrievable. This last criteria is difficult to establish given that one person has applied for the dissolution of the marriage.

Property orders

Property division is an area of the Act currently being substantially reformed. The *Family Law Act 1975* (Cth) provides for orders to be made for division of property of the parties to a marriage. ('Property' here includes personal property, real estate, and financial assets, including business assets.) The Act does not cover de facto couples or the division of their property.

Important factors and misconceptions

Many people do not understand their rights to property under the law. In particular some people may think that they have less rights to property if they have not been contributing to the relationship financially in a direct way. However, the Court will consider both direct and indirect contributions to property, as well as property brought into the marriage. Thus a wife who stays at home to care for the couple's children while her husband works full time may well be found to have made an indirect contribution to their finances by freeing him up to work and saving money on child care arrangements. Direct and indirect contributions can be considered to be of equal value, depending on the individual circumstances, especially the length of the relationship.

Other factors such as future earning capacity, responsibility for the care of any children, and future superannuation payouts will also be considered. Superannuation entitlements can now be considered as 'property' capable of being subject to a property order in the Family Court under recent amendments.

Misconceptions can do a great deal of damage as many people (and thus many potential human service clients) may be labouring under them. Ideas such as jeopardising their rights by leaving the matrimonial home, or being able to retain property that was owned or purchased individually are simply not correct. The Court weighs many factors in deciding these issues. Workers' awareness of such misconceptions will aid in assisting their clients.

This highlights another important issue: where possible it is far preferable for the couple to negotiate their own arrangements regarding property division and provisions for any children in particular. One reason for this is largely financial. If the parties themselves cannot do it, then orders can be sought from the Court. However it is important to bear in mind that clients may not feel able to negotiate such arrangements confidently depending on their circumstances, perhaps because of intimidation, or else a lack of awareness as to what a 'fair' distribution would be. A worker should not hesitate to encourage a client who is in this position to seek legal advice.

Practice question and response

Question: This all sounds fine but as Alexander (1999) argues, in practice women are still disadvantaged under the current family law system, *especially* regarding property division!
Response: The law does not unilaterally solve social problems, and will always need to be amended and changed, as reflected by current developments (see also Braye and Preston-Shoot 1997). Perhaps it is not changing quickly enough. As always it is important to differentiate between an emotional response to and a critique of the law. Consider how you might direct and harness your energies congruent to your work, whether at a micro, mezzo, or macro level.

Property and de facto couples

Where jurisdictions have transferred aspects of their power to legislate regarding de facto property to the Commonwealth, the Family Court *can* deal with those matters. For example, Western Australia, Queensland, and New South Wales have recently introduced Bills referring their power to legislate for superannuation for separating de facto couples to the Commonwealth Government.

These exceptions aside, division of property for de facto couples is generally covered by relatively new state or territory legislation, under which state or territory courts follow a procedure broadly similar to that of the Family Court for parties to a marriage, making orders for property division. Some jurisdictions also provide for maintenance orders in some circumstances. Additionally, couples can lodge their own agreement making provision for such matters in the event of a breakdown of the relationship. In some jurisdictions de facto property matters are covered by separate legislation, such as the *De Facto Relationships Act 1999* (Tas) or incorporated within broader property law statutes, such as the *Property Law Act 1958* (Vic). Since 2002, the Western Australia Family Court, which is vested with both state and federal jurisdiction, determines property and maintenance issues for de facto couples under the *Family Court Act 1997* (WA).

It is important to recognise at the outset that the term 'de facto' is given various definitions in different pieces of legislation, and thus some states and territories define it differently for the purposes of property division than for other areas. In addition to this, eligibility under de facto property provisions varies between jurisdictions in one fundamental respect. Some jurisdictions do not include same-sex couples within the definition of de facto relationships. Queensland, the Australian Capital Territory, Western Australia, and New South Wales do. Queensland makes provision for property orders for same-sex couples, but not maintenance. Additionally, the various de facto property Acts do not apply to all relationships. The Court will look at many factors to determine whether or not the parties can be classed as 'de facto partners', including their commitment to a shared life, the existence of a sexual relationship, the length of the relationship, and whether they relate and identify as a couple.

People in relationships falling outside the jurisdiction of applicable de facto relationships legislation for any reason will instead have any property issues determined by common law, either contract law and/or general property law.

Family law and children

Although family law does differentiate between people who are married at law and people who are living in de facto relationships, it does *not* differentiate between children on that basis. Under the *Family Law Act 1975* (Cth) each parent is responsible for their child jointly until the age of 18 unless a Court orders otherwise, under sections 61B and 61C of the Act. This responsibility continues regardless of the parent's marital status. The term 'parental responsibility' is used instead of guardianship. The terms 'custody' and 'access' are no longer used under the *Family Law Act 1975* (Cth). Instead, 'residence' and 'contact' have replaced them. 'Guardianship' has also been superseded at least in this part of the Act by 'Specific Issues'. This is partly due to a subtle yet important shift in the law's understanding of the rights of children. It was considered that custody and access perhaps erroneously implied that parents have a right to see and live with their children that is more important than the corresponding rights of the child. 'Residence' and 'contact' instead imply that such parental contact is actually important first and foremost for the well-being of the child and thus it is the *child's* right. The Court will consider the right of children of divorced parents to maintain their relationship with both parents to be incredibly important. Any disputes regarding arrangements for children are decided by reference to the child's welfare as the paramount concern. The Act encourages parents to make informal arrangements themselves if possible for the ongoing care of their children as variations to court orders must be made by the Court which can be problematic if plans change suddenly and the parents wish to alter arrangements quickly. Residence, contact, and specific issues are provided for in Parenting Orders, in Division 5 of the Act. Section 64B(2) provides:

> A parenting order may deal with one or more of the following:
>   (a)   the person or persons with whom a child is to live;
>   (b)   contact between a child and another person or other persons;
>   (c)   maintenance of a child;
>   (d)   any other aspect of parental responsibility for a child.

The wishes of children are taken into account as much as possible depending on their age. Their own lawyer, called the Separate Representative, may represent them in the Family Court. The role of the Separate Representative will of course vary from case to case depending on the individual child and their ability to convey their wishes.

Family law and child abuse allegations

In Australian civil law there are two jurisdictions operating with respect to child abuse: the child protection system of each respective state or territory and the federal family law system, comprising the Family Court and Federal Magistrate's Service. Child abuse is often revealed or raised in the course of divorce proceedings. The Family Court takes allegations of child abuse seriously, and their impact is seen primarily in disputes over residence and contact orders (Turner 1997). The Court will not make a residence or contact order in favour of a parent accused of abusing the child if there is an 'unacceptable risk' of abuse occurring as a result. This was decided in the seminal case of *M v M* (1988) 166 CLR 69. However, the overlap between the child protection system and family law system is in itself both problematic and contentious. It is recognised that a more collaborative approach to child protection is needed between the state and federal levels in order to ensure that children are not lost between the two jurisdictions (Family Law Council 2002). This is especially so given the respective functions and powers of the jurisdictions. In particular, the states and territories fulfil an investigative function whereas the Family Court and Federal Magistrates Service do not, and as private individuals instigate family law matters, state or territory child protection services are seldom a party to those actions (Parkinson 2003, p. 4). Further, the mandates fulfilled by the respective bodies are different both in purpose and in jurisdiction: '[State child protection services] do not have a general investigatory role in child protection. Their mission is tied to their statutory responsibilities' (Parkinson 2003, p. 4). This means that child protection services will not necessarily be able to provide the Family Court or Federal Magistrate's Court with the particular information needed to answer the specific questions it faces, as the two jurisdictions have different foci. Recommendation 1 of the Family Law Council's report, *Family Law and Child Protection*, is the establishment of a federal child protection service, to investigate allegations of child abuse in proceedings before the Family Court or Federal Magistrate's Court that are not subject to state investigation (Parkinson 2003, p. 5).

The Standing Committee of Attorneys-General is establishing a working group to discuss these issues. It will particularly focus on the 'one court' principle recommended in *Family Law and Child Protection* (Recommendation 13). This would allow all issues regarding family law and child protection to be heard in the same court rather than have one family involved concurrently in two court processes in separate jurisdictions (Family Law Council 2002). Further developments in this area are likely. Significant research shows that the kind of interagency collaboration advocated between the law and human service work is also critical in ensuring a family law system that provides a strong protective element for the children it encounters, especially regarding allegations of sexual abuse. Recommendation 4 itself incorporates such a multidisciplinary approach in the proposed federal child protection service.

Programs are also being developed to minimise the trauma experienced by children whose parents were involved in Family Court proceedings where abuse or neglect is raised as an issue. Project Magellan was one such pilot program, the success of which at the Melbourne and Dandenong Registries of the Family Court has prompted its consideration elsewhere (Brown, Sheehan et al. 2001).

Practice question and response

Question: But aren't most allegations of child abuse raised in the Family Court just a false smokescreen allowing the accuser, usually the mother, to get favourable residence and contact orders?

Response: It is important to be wary of stereotypical assertions; statistics regarding allegations of abuse raised in the Family Court do not support this contention (Turner 1997).

Child support

Child support is somewhat unique in that it does not only arise on the breakdown of a marriage. Child support payments affect many families in Australia, and while calculated according to a prescribed formula, are a complicated and subjective issue. A discussion of precise payment determinations will thus not be attempted, but only a broad coverage of the scheme's framework and resulting issues for human service workers. Child support payments are regulated by Commonwealth legislation; namely the *Child Support (Registration and Collection) Act 1988* (Cth) and the *Child Support (Assessment) Act 1989* (Cth). The current scheme was introduced by those Acts, and thus does not apply to all children and parents. The previous scheme applies if the parents separated before 1 October 1989, or if all the children of the relationship were born prior to that date. Thus the majority of child support payments are made under the current scheme, and it is this scheme that is discussed below. The required payments are both assessed and collected by the Child Support Agency, which manages the scheme.

It is important to note that an assessment is only made by the Child Support Agency if a child's parents are unable to reach an agreement between them as to the amount of child support that is to be paid. These agreements can then be registered with the Child Support Agency as a child support agreement. The Child Support Agency can assist parents who wish to attempt to reach such an agreement with mediation. Alternatively, parents may choose to keep their agreement private and not register it with the Child Support Agency.

Parents who wish to have the amount payable under a child support assessment altered may apply to do so if their circumstances have altered in certain respects, including changes in parental income, legal obligations to care for other dependants, or living circumstances. It is also possible to seek to have most decisions made by the Child Support Agency reviewed, and this process, at least at its initial level, is very informal, needing only to be done in writing within twenty-eight days. If the issue is not resolved at that point, the parent may appeal to the Family Court or Federal Magistrates Court. Child support assessments and disagreement with them may evoke strong emotions and frustration from clients. It is critical that they be aware of the options available to challenge decisions and of the normalcy of the appeal process generally in legal culture.

The Family Court fulfils several roles in this area. It still determines child support payments for children who are under the old scheme. Additionally, it hears appeals from decisions made by the Child Support Agency, and can also order continued payments for children under the new scheme who are over 18 but in tertiary education, or who are in special circumstances, as these decisions are beyond the power of the Child Support Agency.

Child protection legislation

Australia has two jurisdictions dealing with child protection. An outline of federal involvement has already been provided, however responding to child abuse and neglect is predominantly the legal purview of states and territories, and it is this law that is discussed here.

The administration of child protection legislation is founded generally across all states and territories on the principle that the primary responsibility for a child's care and protection lies with the child's family and that a high priority should therefore be accorded to supporting and assisting the family to carry out that responsibility. Most Acts accordingly contain broad and varied powers in order to respond to the myriad of issues involved in family structures and parenting. A typical example of the breadth of most legislation in this regard is Victoria. Under the *Children and Young Person's Act 1989* (Vic) the Family Division of the Children's Court is empowered to:

- Order that written undertakings be entered into for up to twelve months by the parent, child, or person with whom the child resides, if the person consents to making that undertaking. Undertakings contain any conditions considered by the Court to be in the best interests or welfare of the child.
- Make a supervision order, which leaves existing custody and guardianship of the child unaffected but gives the Secretary the responsibility of supervising the child.
- Make an interim protection order while the case is being investigated.
- Grant custody of the child to a person other than the Secretary, either with or without an accompanying supervision order.
- Make consequential orders to protect the child.
- Remove a child from the guardianship or custody of their parent/guardian if the child is at risk from a person other than their parent/guardian but their parent/guardian is not willing or able to protect the child from that risk.

These powers are in addition to making either short- or long-term custody and guardianship orders, which are less utilised than may be thought. The relevant court is meant to have the necessary flexibility to make orders providing for the best outcome possible in the circumstances, and to allow the family to stay together or be reunited at some point, as long as it would not endanger the child.

Table 9.1 sets out some aspects of child protection legislation in each state and territory. Commentary regarding common themes and features is included below. The table provides an abbreviated summary, which is intended to be read in conjunction with the legislation in each jurisdiction, rather than as a substitute. It compares and contrasts such areas as definitions of abuse, the scope of the child protection legislation, and duties of workers in each jurisdiction. While points of commonality are clearly evident, there are notable differences between jurisdictions also.

Table 9.1 State and territory child protection legislation

ITEM	South Australia	New South Wales	Victoria	Northern Territory
Legislation	Children's Protection Act 1993.	Children and Young Persons (Care and Protection) Act 1998.	Children and Young Persons Act 1989.	Community Welfare Act 1983.
Application of Act; where child is...	At risk.	In need of care and protection OR at risk of harm.	In need of protection.	In need of care.
Level of risk required for intervention	If child has been, is being, or is likely to be abused or neglected.	If current concerns exist for the safety, welfare, or well-being of the child due to prescribed circumstances.	Suffer or be likely to suffer significant harm.	Substantial risk of maltreatment.
Mandatory notification threshold	Suspicion on reasonable grounds formed in course of official duties.	Suspicion on reasonable grounds formed in course of the person's work.	Belief on reasonable grounds formed in course of official duties— only physical injury or sexual abuse.	Belief on reasonable grounds.
Mandated notifiers under legislation	Medical practitioner, pharmacist, nurse, teacher, day care worker, police officer, dentist, psychologist, social worker, community corrections officer, volunteers, or employees in public or private organisations working with children.	A person who delivers services as part of employment or paid work in: health care, welfare, education, children's services, residential services, or law enforcement wholly or partly to children.	Medical practitioner, psychologist, nurse, teacher, school principal, day care worker, youth, health or welfare worker, publicly employed youth and child worker, probation officer, police officer, youth parole officer, or prescribed class of persons.	Police officers are mandated to notify and carry out investigations. 'Any person' is mandated as a notifier, without restriction.
Uses abuse or neglect as grounds for intervention	Occurrence or risk of physical or sexual abuse, emotional abuse, or neglect.	Not specifically.	Yes, covers harm resulting from all forms of abuse and neglect.	Not specifically.
Uses harm or other grounds for intervention	No.	Yes, if current concerns exist for safety, welfare, or well-being.	Yes, but not as a replacement for 'abuse and neglect'.	Substantial risk or occurrence of 'maltreatment', including physical or sexual abuse or exploitation; and neglect.
Includes 'emotional abuse'	Yes, and includes serious psychological injury and detriment to well-being.	Not specifically.	Yes. Includes emotional and psychological harm.	Yes, includes serious emotional or intellectual impairment caused by child's home environment.
Includes exposure to domestic violence	No.	Yes, if therefore at risk of serious physical or psychological harm.	Not specifically.	Yes, as above.
Includes risk of female genital mutilation	Yes, specifically included; FGM also defined.	Not specifically.	Not specifically.	Yes, specifically included as a type of maltreatment.

Table 9.1 State and territory child protection legislation (cont.)

ITEM	Queensland	Western Australia	Tasmania	ACT
Legislation	Child Protection Act 1999	Child Welfare Act 1947	Children, Young Persons and Their Families Act 1997	Children and Young People Act 1999
Application of Act; where child is...	In need of protection.	In need of care and protection.	At risk.	In need of care and protection.
Level of risk required for intervention	Suffer or be at unacceptable risk of suffering harm.	11 grounds for being declared in need of care and protection, including ill treatment.	Occurrence or likelihood of abuse or neglect.	Child has been, is being, or is likely to be abused or neglected.
Mandatory notification threshold	Belief on reasonable grounds.	No current mandatory notification provisions at time of writing.	Belief or suspicion on reasonable grounds, formed in the course of official duties.	Reasonable suspicion formed from or in the course of the persons work—sexual or physical abuse only.
Mandated notifiers under legislation	Medical Practitioners under the Health Act 1937. Authorised officers under the Child Protection Act or an officer or employee of the Department or an employee of a licensed care service must notify regarding children in residential care.	Not applicable. WA research has indicated mandatory reporting does not increase the protection of children in that state and focus instead on preventative intervention programs with families.	Medical practitioner, dentist, dental hygienist, nurse dental therapist, police officer, police department employee, probation officer, any teacher or principal, child care workers, Government agency employees/volunteers or Government-funded organisations in health welfare, education or residential services to children; prescribed persons.	Medical practitioner, dentist, teacher, police officer, school counsellor, nurse, child care worker, family day care worker, public servant providing services relating to the health or well-being of children, young people or families, the community advocate, the official visitor, a prescribed person.
Uses abuse or neglect as grounds for intervention	No, but types of abuse and sexual exploitation are given as specific examples of 'harm'.	No.	Sexual abuse, physical or emotional injury.	Physical or sexual abuse, emotional abuse or neglect, exposure to domestic violence.
Uses harm or other grounds for intervention	'Harm' is any detrimental effect of a significant nature on the child's physical, psychological or emotional well-being.	Uses 'ill-treatment'.	No.	No.
Includes 'emotional abuse'	Yes, as well as psychological abuse.	Not specifically. Some provision for living conditions that jeopardise mental physical or moral welfare.	Yes and includes serious psychological harm and detriment to well-being.	Yes, defines it as causing significant detriment to wellbeing.
Includes exposure to domestic violence	Not specifically, but broad definition of harm allows for it.	As above.	No.	Yes.
Includes risk of female genital mutilation	As above.	No.	Not specifically.	Not specifically.

It can be seen from table 9.1 that although there is great similarity between the jurisdictions, there are also significant differences. Some require only that the child is either being or is at risk of being abused or neglected. Others require a greater risk or likelihood of abuse or similar conduct, such as Tasmania. Note that Victorian legislation focuses on *significant* harm or risk or damage caused by the various types of conduct or circumstances in order to determine the appropriateness of state intervention. Still other jurisdictions do not use notions of risk. The broadest range of criteria for intervention is seen in Queensland and New South Wales. As discussed above, instead of categorising risk according to abuse or neglect, these Acts utilise the concept of 'harm'. Harm is defined as including abuse or neglect, but also ensures that the legislation can be invoked in situations where there may be dispute about whether particular conduct is classed as abuse or not, yet the child is still at risk of harm. In South Australia's recent review of child protection it was recommended that the concept of 'significant harm' be adopted as the benchmark for intervention of the state instead of the current use of 'abused or neglected' (Layton 2003).

Common to all states and territories but not included within table 9.1 are the additional alternative circumstances for children to be considered in need of care and/or protection. For example, for a child to be declared to be in need of care due to abuse or neglect a standard requirement in most jurisdictions is that the child's parents be unwilling or unable to protect the child. In New South Wales the *Children and Young Persons (Care and Protection) Act 1998* stipulates a range of circumstances in which current concerns may exist for the safety, welfare, or well-being of the child or young person. If at least one of those circumstances is present they will be considered at risk of harm. These factors are:

(a) the child's or young person's basic physical or psychological needs are not being met or are at risk of not being met,

(b) the parents or other caregivers have not arranged and are unable or unwilling to arrange for the child or young person to receive necessary medical care,

(c) the child or young person has been, or is at risk of being, physically or sexually abused or ill-treated,

(d) the child or young person is living in a household where there have been incidents of domestic violence and, as a consequence, the child or young person is at risk of serious physical or psychological harm,

(e) a parent or other caregiver has behaved in such a way towards the child or young person that the child or young person has suffered or is at risk of suffering serious psychological harm.

Note that there is no specific additional requirement included in (c) that the child's parents or caregivers be unwilling or unable to protect the child. This means that although a failure to protect may well have occurred, in New South Wales it is not a prerequisite to having a child removed from the household because of the sexual or physical abuse. A failure to protect the child could fall within (e), as could emotional abuse. The broader definitions used in this Act focus on the end results of conduct and the effect it has on the child or young person, rather than trying to anticipate and include every precise way that the risk of harm may arise. Many jurisdictions have also adopted the use of broader definitions for these reasons.

Other differences occur between jurisdictions due to the varied nature of child protection investigations and the way notifications are received and processed within the departments and agencies. For a detailed treatment and comparison of these, see Australian Institute of Health and Welfare (2002).

Practice question and response

Question: So much for all these legislative provisions to detect and stamp out child abuse! We all know that it is one of the most hidden crimes in the community. I can't count the number of friends I know who were abused as kids and never had any intervention by a child protection agency! The law needs to change, and our work just won't get any easier until it does.

Response: While your criticisms are well justified and problems with child protection are widely acknowledged by legal and human service professionals in the system, it is important to disentangle the legal, resource allocation, and service delivery issues and reach a point in your own approach that allows you to respond as effectively as possible to them.

Child protection definitions, proceedings, and advocacy

Although the terminology may vary, child protection legislation allows for proceedings to be commenced where a child is in need of protection. This need is commonly established when the child is suspected to have been abused, and there are reasonable grounds for this suspicion.

As seen above, abuse is usually broadly defined. It covers emotional, physical, and sexual abuse, as well as neglect. For comparison with the table, the *Family Law Act 1975* (Cth) s 60D (1) defines abuse as:

(a) an assault, including a sexual assault, of the child which is an offence under a law, written or unwritten, in force in the State or Territory in which the act constituting the assault occurs; or

(b) a person involving the child in a sexual activity with that person or another person, in which the child is used, directly or indirectly, as a sexual object by the first-mentioned person or the other person, and where there is unequal power in the relationship between the child and the first-mentioned person.

State and territory jurisdictions tend to either provide broad inclusive definitions of abuse or neglect, or to use alternative terminology altogether. As mentioned above, the *Child Protection Act 1999* (Qld) does not use the term 'abuse' as a requirement for instituting child protection proceedings. Under s 10 of that Act, a child is considered to be in need of protection if they have suffered harm, are suffering harm, or are at unacceptable risk of suffering harm, and do not have a parent who is willing and able to protect the child from that harm. 'Harm' is defined even more broadly than abuse. It specifically includes physical, psychological or emotional abuse, neglect, and sexual abuse or exploitation as examples of harm. However, s 9 specifically provides that it does not matter how the harm was caused, and 'harm' itself is defined simply as 'any detrimental effect of a significant nature on the child's physical, psychological or emotional wellbeing'. This indicates the desired focus in child protection decision-making is the effect of conduct on the child. Despite differences in terminology, abuse or neglect is still the benchmark in most cases leading to the child protection system becoming involved. For this reason a closer look at these terms is warranted.

Emotional abuse

Any form of abuse does emotional damage. 'Emotional abuse' however does not refer to this damage, but to a separate form of abusive conduct. Emotional abuse is a pattern of behaviour. For example, the term does not refer to a caregiver losing their temper and calling a child an idiot on an isolated occasion, although that behaviour is self-evidently wrong. Emotional abuse occurs over time. It is also defined by reference to its consequences, involving the damaging of a child's self-esteem and/or emotional development. Emotional abuse is also considered to occur through being exposed to domestic violence, and this is reflected in the child protection legislation of most jurisdictions in some way. The *Children and Young Persons (Care and Protection) Act 1998* (NSW) does not use the phrase 'emotional abuse'. In that Act, s 3 defines abuse to include 'exposing or subjecting a child to behaviour which psychologically harms the child' instead.

Physical abuse

Physical abuse involves physical injury deliberately inflicted on the child. It is also partly defined by its consequences; reference is made to the child's physical or psychological development being jeopardised by the abuse, and also to detriment of the child's well-being.

Sexual abuse

Sexual abuse is a term of broad application. Many jurisdictions have a similar approach to that of South Australia. The *Children's Protection Act 1993* (SA) includes the term within the definition of abuse, however like most child protection legislation, the Act does not separately define it. The South Australian Mandatory Notification Guidelines instead describe it as occurring: 'when someone in a position of power to the child or young person uses his or her power to involve the child/young person in sexual activity' (Family and Community Services Undated, p. 5). 'Sexual activity' is itself a broad term. It is not limited to oral, anal and vaginal sexual intercourse. It includes any activity of a sexual nature either on or involving the child. Thus the term 'sexual abuse' used in legislation may potentially include such conduct as sexual suggestion, showing pornography to a child, and exhibitionism.

Another approach is taken by Queensland, which includes 'sexual exploitation' within its legislative definitions in addition to sexual abuse.

Neglect

Neglect involves failing to provide for the child's essential needs (e.g. food, shelter, clothing, health). For example, the *Children and Young People Act 1999* (ACT) s 151 defines neglect as constituting 'a failure to provide a child or young person with a necessity of life that has caused or is likely to cause significant harm to his or her wellbeing or development'. Such lack of provision does not have to be deliberate to constitute neglect.

Mandatory notification

Social workers and any human service workers providing service delivery to children are mandated notifiers of child abuse and neglect under the relevant child protection legislation in most states and territories, yet there is significant debate regarding the effectiveness of mandatory notification in reducing incidence of abuse and protecting children generally, in part because of the very real potential for alienation of clients and families. Omitted from that section of the table is Western Australia, which at time of writing does not have a mandatory notification requirement within the *Child Welfare Act 1947* (WA). This is partly due to the different nature of service provision in that state, which has protocols requiring maltreatment of children to be reported by certain government-employed workers or publicly funded agencies (Australian Institute of Health and Welfare 2002). In 2002, the Harries Report into child protection services in Western Australia found that mandatory notification was not likely to reduce the rate of child abuse and neglect (Harries and Clare 2002). Instead that jurisdiction focuses resources on family support services. Western Australia is in the process of introducing legislation to replace the *Child Welfare Act 1947* and reviewing its system generally.

In all jurisdictions, any person may voluntarily notify the relevant government department of suspected child abuse and neglect. Victoria and the Australian Capital Territory specify this option within their legislation at the commencement of the mandatory notification sections. Tasmania goes one step further. It provides that any adult who has reasonable grounds for suspicion has a *responsibility* to report, though it stops short of mandating that responsibility within the legislation and proscribing a penalty for non-compliance. In contrast, the Northern Territory has the broadest and the simplest mandatory notification provisions. All adults are mandated notifiers in that territory.

In addition to voluntary notifications by members of the general public, certain professional and volunteer workers are required by law to make such notifications. Precise mandatory notification requirements differ between jurisdictions, principally regarding the professionals required to report and the circumstances in which the duty arises. Individual workers must take care to be aware of their precise obligations regarding mandatory notification.

South Australia is typical. In that state, a duty to report (or notify) abuse arises under the *Children's Protection Act 1993* (SA) when the worker forms a suspicion on reasonable grounds that a child has been or is being abused or neglected. The Layton Report (2003) comments that South Australia has one of the broadest itemised group of mandated notifiers in Australia, and recommends extending the group further still. It is important to be aware, however, that the suspicion must arise in the course of an individual's work or official duties for notification to be mandated under the South Australian legislation.

Practice question and response

Question: Are you saying that despite being a worker, I do *not* always have to report suspicions of child abuse and neglect?

Response: In the eyes of the law in most jurisdictions that is correct. Generally, individuals who are mandated because of their professional position are only required by law to report instances that they become aware of in the course of their work. It is important to be aware of the precise requirements of your jurisdiction in this regard. Additionally, you may have moral and/or professional imperatives that affect your decision whether or not to make a notification.

'Reasonable suspicion'

'Reasonable suspicion' or a belief or suspicion on reasonable grounds must be formed in order for reporting to be mandated under most legislation. This phrase is and has always been notoriously hard to define (Swain 1998).

Despite these difficulties two points can offer guidance: suspicion is required, not certainty or proof; and there needs to be some evidence on which the suspicion is formed.

Additional examples are commonly given in Mandatory Notification Guidelines issued by child welfare departments. The Family and Youth Services Department Guidelines in South Australia (Family and Community Services Undated) contain the following examples of practical situations leading to a reasonable suspicion being formed: a child tells a worker they have been abused, not necessarily using that term; through the worker's own observation of the child and their behaviour or circumstances; someone else tells the worker that the child is being abused, and they are in a position to know this (a relative, neighbour, friend etc).

Child protection proceedings

All material covered in chapter 7, on courts and tribunals, is relevant here, as issues of child abuse and neglect may lead to criminal proceedings or, more commonly, child protection proceedings, and workers may conceivably encounter both. The Youth Court or Children's Court in each jurisdiction hears child protection proceedings. They do not determine criminal guilt for offences committed against children. For this reason they differ from criminal matters procedurally in two key ways, both regarding the hearing of evidence.

Standard of proof

Care and protection proceedings are decided based on a lower standard of proof than that required for criminal proceedings precisely because these proceedings are not criminal in nature. The standard of proof for child protection proceedings is the balance of probabilities. Thus it must be shown that it is more likely than not that the child is, for example, 'in need of care'. This is easier to prove than establishing the risk beyond a reasonable doubt. If criminal charges are also laid because of abuse, those are dealt with as a completely separate matter in the relevant adult court, and those proceedings must be proven beyond reasonable doubt.

Rules of evidence

An ongoing concern regarding child protection is the need to minimise the trauma caused to children by court proceedings. The traumatic effects of criminal proceedings against perpetrators on child witnesses have been well documented, and are seen as a key reason for the underreporting of child abuse by victims themselves, especially for child victims of sexual abuse (Eastwood 2003).

Procedures for giving evidence in court are more flexible than in criminal proceedings. Children in child protection proceedings do not usually give evidence personally, and they are sometimes protected from doing so. For example, s 112 of the *Child Protection Act 1999* (Qld) specifically provides that a child cannot be compelled to give evidence in the proceedings. In all jurisdictions, the usual process is that the child's case worker and other professionals provide reports by affidavit detailing interviews with the child, findings, conclusions, and recommendations. Thus information is provided to the court to substantiate the allegation that the child is 'in need of protection', but this is often not given directly by the child.

This position can be contrasted to criminal proceedings for offences against children in all states and territories where children are required to give evidence directly to the court and be cross-examined, unless the accused has entered a guilty plea. Understandably this is a distressing experience for the child. In Western Australia, a different criminal jurisdiction is used to hear cases involving sexual offences against children. A central feature is that children give evidence to the court through closed circuit television from a remote location, and thus do not have to be present in court. Although they are still cross-examined on this evidence, most children report that it significantly eases the distress involved in giving evidence. A trial of a similar system has just begun in New South Wales, and has been recommended for South Australia also (Layton 2003).

Another difference seen in child protection proceedings relates to the nature of evidence admissible in court. As the traditional focus in evidence is on first-hand evidence given in person, problems are caused by the limited ability of younger children to give evidence in an adversarial system. They may not have the language skills to accurately explain events that occurred, for example. These problems are avoided in child protection proceedings by instead allowing second-hand or hearsay evidence to be given as described above. Child protection legislation in all jurisdictions specifically provides that the traditional rules of evidence do not apply to such proceedings, and the court can obtain the information it needs to make decisions in any way it considers necessary.

Separate representative must be provided for the child

The provision of a separate representative (the child's own lawyer) is another feature of child protection proceedings. The child is able to express their own views and wishes through the separate representative. The state or territory pays for this representation and the separate representative is independent not only from the parent's lawyers but also from counsel representing the minister who is seeking the orders from the Court.

In practice there is often a great deal of agreement between counsel for the minister and the separate representative, but either way, the child is able to contribute to the proceedings.

Children's rights

It is common knowledge among professionals in the area that child protection cannot be achieved by legal solutions standing alone. All jurisdictions use preventative and interventional programs in working with children and with parents. Some additionally feature other legislative frameworks for child support and advocacy, and for improving child protection services. In particular Queensland and New South Wales have both a Children and Young Person's Guardian and an Office of Commissioner for Children and Young Persons. Although the precise powers and functions vary between the jurisdictions, these statutory bodies have been introduced in recent years into those states, providing among other things another avenue for advocacy, review, and safeguarding of children. New South Wales additionally has a Joint Parliamentary Committee on Children and Young People. Its functions include monitoring and reviewing the Commission for Children and Young People, reporting to Parliament, and monitoring issues and developments affecting children and services provided to children and recommending reform. In Western Australia the Select Committee on Advocacy for Children (Appointment of a Commissioner for Children) is due to report in 2004 on the best method of establishing an advocate for children, whether that be through a Commissioner or an independent office for children. The establishment of both an Office of Commissioner for Children and Young Persons and a Children and Young Person's Guardian have been recommended for South Australia also (Layton 2003).

Key points for practice

- Workers will fulfil their mandate best in these emotive areas of law by being aware of the complex dynamics involved in family law and child protection matters and focusing on their specific role.
- It is important to be conscious of personal experiences and ideological positioning and their effects; as well as how to restrain or perhaps use these to best fulfil worker

mandates. Be aware of how to conserve and focus personal energies on superior service delivery and/or advocacy, rather than dissipate them in outrage and distress.

- Workers need to be very clear about legal responsibilities in these areas including precise mandatory reporting obligations and up-to-date knowledge of the law in their own jurisdictions. Child protection in particular is an area of continual reform and change.
- When dealing with clients involved in the family law system workers should be alert for misconceptions clients may have regarding their rights, options, and avenues for assistance, but as always take care not to provide legal advice, or to give the impression of doing so.
- Families and children are two of the more taxing and difficult areas of human service work but excellent, informed, and focused human service practice within them avails much, especially in achieving an effective legal response to these fundamental issues.

Some useful web sites

Families

www.familycourt.gov.au
http://law.gov.au/flc
www.familylaw.gov.au
www.aifs.org.au

Children

www.csa.gov.au
www.napcan.org.au/
www.aifs.org.au/nch/nch_menu.html
www.kidshelp.com.au/

10

Difference and **Vulnerability**

Big questions of rights, needs, and welfare

This chapter addresses some of the major ways in which the law attempts to restrain, enable, or protect those perceived to be different in some way and/or at significant risk to themselves or others. Life is generally attended by risk and all members of society may be the cause or victim of, for instance, a traffic collision, a theft, an unfair consumer transaction, a financial loss, or prejudice. Moreover some members of society, for example children, are seen as being more at risk than others. In all of these areas there is law designed to inhibit, protect, or punish, or in some other way constrain the behaviour of citizens. However in this chapter the more narrow focus is on matters that are particularly relevant to the human services, and adults. Vulnerable adults and their rights have not figured largely in this book hitherto, while some attention has already been paid to children. Discrimination and disability law will be outlined along with guardianship and mental health law. And last, refugee law and asylum seekers will be briefly considered. How does this seemingly strange collection of topics fit together? The unifying theme is difference, disadvantage, or vulnerability and the law's approach to these issues. It will be seen that the substantive law has many roles in this area, for instance it may endorse, and/or enable, and/or protect, and/or decide; it may legalise behaviour or proscribe it. The following scenarios set the scene for the chapter:

- What is the legal position when a person in a psychotic state refuses medication, has profound communication difficulties and does not eat, sleep, or attend to personal hygiene?
- Does the law have any way of responding to a confused and frightened older man who seems to be financing an adult son's gambling habit, and whose house is being sold by that son? Perhaps the other children of this man are concerned about his well-being. Is this purely a matter between siblings?

- If an adult refuses essential medical treatment on religious grounds can the law be invoked to authorise intervention?
- Are the resource problems faced by some people with disabilities attempting to live independently in the community anything to do with the state and the law or simply questions of individual choice?
- If an adult with brain damage and serious health problems is drinking excessively, requiring regular hospitalisation and facing death, is there any role for the law? And does anything change if, when drunk, that person threatens to harm others?
- What about the person who loses a job or is refused a service because they are pregnant, Indigenous, old, not Australian, female, or intellectually disabled? Does the law get involved in any way?
- When a family flees persecution in another country and comes to Australia in search of safety, how does the law respond? What if the family pays people smugglers to get it here? What if it comes on a tourist trip and stays on?

Readers may perhaps begin to feel uneasy about these questions. Words like self-determination, free choice, and paternalism may be occurring to them, along with others such as need for protection and human rights. If so that is a very healthy sign, because the questions mask profound philosophical and jurisprudential debates that are played out around the intent, shape, and amendment of the law at any point in time.

How are notions of universal human rights to be weighed against concepts like incapacity, welfare, and need (Jones and Basser Marks 2000)? To what extent is law part of the problem or part of the solution in questions of capacity? What is 'this thing called disability' (Davis 1998, p. 15)? What values and models do and should underpin legal responses to disability (Blencowe, Sampford et al. 1998)? How are autonomy and paternalism to be balanced? How can impairment and citizenship be integrated (Carney 2000)? What is competence, and legal competence in particular (Cooper 1991)? How is individual freedom to be weighed against community protection? How are rights to treatment and to refuse treatment to be reconciled? These are the sorts of contests that lie behind the relatively normative overview of law attempted in this chapter. Not all of the questions posed above will be canvassed in the following material, but the relevant legal terrain will be generally outlined.

In the context of vulnerability two collateral points are dispensed with before the chapter proceeds. The idea of informed consent is ever-present in contemporary health and human services but what does it mean? And similarly, the various meanings of the term guardianship often cause confusion.

Informed consent

This principle was mentioned in chapter 6 in the context of privacy principles. In the more general legal sense, consent validates treatment, intervention, or professional action, and it is a defence to a legal action in personal trespass or negligence that an individual consented to that action. This is also consistent with those professional ethical guidelines and standards of practice that underscore dignity, autonomy, and self-determination. The principle is raised again here because individuals who are subject to professional action or treatment are putting their trust and well-being in the hands of their workers. This exposes them, even if they are very competent people. If they lack competency or capacity they are even more vulnerable. The word treatment appears here because most of the relevant cases about informed consent in Australia have originated in the medical arena and must be extrapolated to the human services.

The seminal case is that of *Rogers v Whitaker* (1992) 175 CLR 479 in which Mrs Whitaker lost her sight after eye surgery. The High Court found that the doctor had breached his duty of care by not disclosing to her sufficient relevant information before the operation, that is, information about risks which would have been significant to her. This and subsequent cases have prompted most organisations to implement procedures for ensuring that clients have consented to intervention. Compliance with these procedures is essential in medical treatment where bodily integrity is at stake. But it is also applicable to human service intervention. So there are both legal and moral imperatives to ensure that clients know exactly what they are agreeing to. Comprehensive informed consent procedures should ensure that:

- the client has full information about the intervention procedure and its risks generally, and to them specifically
- consent is both intervention or activity specific and time limited
- information is presented in a form that can be comprehended by the client and that they have opportunities to clarify it
- the client has comprehended the information
- the client has genuinely consented to the intervention, preferably in writing
- the worker records their actions in giving information, eliciting and answering questions, and in obtaining consent.

The mechanistic form-signing processes seen in some human service organisations may not actually satisfy these consent procedures at law, nor in ethics. Similarly, forms that require clients to consent to a general range of activities may provide little legal protection for the agency.

Practice question and response

Question: My agency has consent forms for psychotherapy and for release of information. I always make sure that they are signed. You seem to be questioning this practice. What is wrong with it?

Response: There may be nothing wrong with it, if your clients really understand exactly what they are consenting to and its risks, and if they have genuinely consented.

Most human service agencies and workers probably accept the need for them to seek permission for their own clinical work with clients and for release of personal information but they may be less attuned to the consent aspects of advocacy work. However, workers engaged in advocacy work on behalf of others have a particular responsibility to ensure that those others know what the positive and negative outcomes of that advocacy might be. Advocacy intervention might, for example, delay a decision, or result in a financial cost or in closer scrutiny of the other's situation, and it is essential that these possibilities are declared and explored before the advocacy action happens so that the risks are fully understood.

The question of consent is obviously much more complicated when an individual's competence to consent is in doubt, or they are particularly vulnerable in some other way. However it is very important to appreciate that disability and mental incapacity are not synonymous. Many people with disabilities are perfectly competent to give informed consent and they are treated in law like anyone else. Even if someone's consent capacity is in doubt, the law will emphasise respect for their human dignity, and require the presumption of their legal competence to be rebutted before any decisions are made on their behalf (Jones and Basser Marks 2000). The case of *Re Marion (No 2)* (1993) 17 Fam LR 336 involved a question of consent to sterilisation for a person with intellectual disability. It determined that 'people with disabilities are entitled to individual inviolability' (Jones and Basser Marks 2000, p. 152) like anyone else, and that decisions about their treatment should be made on the basis of their individual needs and characteristics rather than their disability *per se*.

If the person is deemed to be incompetent, the law will investigate agents such as parents and legal guardians who might consent for them. If there is no agent, court- or state-appointed advocates will be invoked. This is a topic to be addressed below.

Several types of guardianship?

The word guardian has several past or present legal meanings which can confuse human service workers:

- The term may arise when parental rights and responsibilities concerning children are being referred to. This is generally quite correct as parents are generally the legal guardians of their children. But it is not appropriate terminology under the current *Family Law Act 1975* (Cth). It was seen in chapter 9 that the language of guardianship and custody has been replaced in that Act by the terms residence, contact, and shared parenting.
- The term may arise when minors are for some reason placed by law under the control of the state or individuals other than their parents. For example under the *Children, Young Persons and their Families Act 1997* (Tas) s 42, a care and protection order can result in a child being placed under the guardianship of the Secretary.
- The term may arise correctly when the legal competence of an adult is being addressed. This topic is covered later in this chapter.

Discrimination and harassment

Discrimination, in the sense of treating people differently on the grounds of their attributes, is a familiar phenomenon to human service workers. Many people are discriminated against, harassed, or vilified for the very things that may bring them into the human service sphere; for example physical disability, mental illness, sexual preference, or a prison record. Others experience similar responses for these and other characteristics that may be incidental to their human service client status. While most agencies and workers will at some time have to respond to discrimination or harassment against their clients or even themselves, others have a specific mandate to campaign against or work with discrimination issues. Yet others will work in agencies that consciously positively discriminate, for example in their staff selection processes or in who is serviced. These agencies may have exemptions under relevant Acts that allow them, for instance, to appoint people with particular religious affiliations or to only deliver services to women.

All agencies and workers need to know the general architecture of discrimination law. It permits some discriminatory actions. For example, it allows some affirmative action in some areas such as employment (Ronalds 1998), and it may in future permit some discrimination against drug addicts if mooted amendments to the *Disability Discrimination Act 1992* (Cth) are enacted. However, discrimination law is largely concerned with illegal discrimination and essentially provides remedies or rights of redress, in civil law, against behaviours that are specified as unlawful (Ronalds 1998). Discrimination law does not so much 'address underlying structural problems' as focus on the 'aggrieved individual complainant' (Bailey and Devereux 1998, p. 292).

The law in this area is largely statutory as parliaments have in relatively recent times responded to United Nations (UN) declarations that recognise social justice principles and the detrimental effects of discrimination. Two examples of these declarations are the Convention on the Elimination of all Forms of Racial Discrimination (CERD) and the Convention on the Elimination of all Forms of Discrimination Against Women (CEDAW) (Bailey and Devereux 1998). There are federal discrimination laws and also laws in each state and territory. At the federal level there is a set of relevant Acts. In chronological order the main ones are:

- *Racial Discrimination Act 1975* (Cth)
- *Sex Discrimination Act 1984* (Cth)
- *Human Rights and Equal Opportunity Act 1986* (Cth)
- *Disability Discrimination Act 1992* (Cth).

Some examples of major relevant state and territory legislation are:

- *Equal Opportunity Act 1984* (WA)
- *Discrimination Act 1991* (ACT)
- *Anti-Discrimination Act 1991* (Qld)
- *Anti-Discrimination Act 1992* (NT)
- *Equal Opportunity Act 1995* (Vic).

This arena of law is also dynamic as parliaments vary and extend the range of grounds, areas of activity, and remedies covered in accordance with changes in society and in community attitudes. For example an Age Discrimination Bill 2003 (Cth) has been introduced into Federal Parliament. If passed it will outlaw age discrimination in work, accommodation, education, and access to goods and services among other areas. It also provides for positive discrimination where bona fide benefits for a particular age group are involved, or measures to service age-related needs or reduce disadvantage. Breastfeeding has just been included as a ground covered by the *Sex Discrimination Act 1984* (Cth), as have carer responsibilities in the Equal Opportunity (Carer's Responsibilities) Amendment Bill 2003 (SA). It is proposed by the Federal Government that the *Disability Discrimination Act 1992* (Cth) be extended to cover state and territory education systems and the training sector.

There is another example of change in the contentious Australian Human Rights Commission Legislation Bill 2003 before Federal Parliament at the time of writing. Among other things this Bill aims to limit the power of the Human Rights and Equal Opportunity Commission (HREOC) to intervene in cases that raise human rights issues, abolish specialist commissioners, and limit the Commission's inquiry powers.

As Thornton (1990, p. 1) writes, not all different treatment is necessarily discriminatory. Some grounds and areas are covered in both state/territory and federal legislation and some are not. Some grounds may not be covered at all. Different grounds may be covered under different Acts as with the Commonwealth, or under one compendium Act as with the states and territories. Definitions may differ in different jurisdictions (Bailey and Devereux 1998). For example, the *Disability Discrimination Act 1992* (Cth) applies an inclusive definition of disability. But regardless of jurisdiction, the general nature and intent of the laws are similar although the details do vary.

Discrimination law specifies grounds on which discrimination is unlawful, and in which areas of activity or which 'ambit[s] of operation' (Thornton 1990, p. 102). Those who believe that they and perhaps their associates have experienced discrimination, may lodge a complaint. So, for example, it may be unlawful to discriminate on the grounds of race in housing, on age in education, or on marital status in employment. Ronalds (1998, pp. 5–6) provides a checklist for thinking through the legal dimensions of a discrimination issue, for which the burden of proof falls on the complainant. His main points are elaborated here:

- *Is the ground of discrimination identified as unlawful?* For example, mental illness as a ground is not covered by the South Australian legislation, and transsexuality is not covered by the Western Australian and Victorian legislation.
- *Has there been an act of direct or indirect discrimination or harassment?* Direct discrimination is determined by comparing the treatment of the person who alleges unfavourable treatment on the grounds of an attribute and treatment of other people who do not have that attribute. For instance, if a person of colour receives different treatment from that received by white people, then direct discrimination may be operating. When requirements that appear to provide equal treatment in fact have a disproportionately unfair impact on some people, indirect discrimination may be present. This is more complex than direct discrimination and it exercises the courts. In bare outline it disadvantages a

particular group whose members cannot, or cannot easily, comply, while those outside that group can more easily comply. For example while a requirement that a job be filled by a full-time person only may appear to have neutral impact, it is likely to affect women and men differently.

- *Did the discrimination occur in a specified area?* For example discrimination laws in all jurisdictions relate in some way to employment and all but the *Racial Discrimination Act 1975* (Cth) relate in some way to education (Ronalds 1998). Across jurisdiction there is a range of other areas that are commonly covered, for example access to premises, trade union and clubs, goods and services, and advertisements.
- *Does the action fall within one of the specified exceptions?* For example under the Age Discrimination Bill 2003 (Cth) inherent job requirements may permit positive discrimination on the grounds of older age.

An aggrieved person may lodge a written complaint with the relevant body if they believe that they have been discriminated against directly or indirectly or harassed, on the basis of a ground, and in an area covered by relevant legislation. In the case of Commonwealth legislation the body is likely to be HREOC. Under state and territory legislation there are different bodies. For example, there is a New South Wales Anti-Discrimination Board, in South Australia an Equal Opportunity Commission, and in Tasmania an Anti-Discrimination Commission. These bodies generally take a conciliatory approach to disputes rather than a formal legal one, but cases do go before the relevant tribunals if they cannot be resolved earlier. Employers may be found vicariously liable for the discriminatory, harassing, or vilifying actions of their employees or agents unless they have taken all reasonable steps to ensure that this behaviour does not occur. For example, they need to have appropriate policies, procedures, and training in place.

For many complaints there may be a choice of state or Commonwealth juris-diction. If there is choice, questions of access, cost, range of eligible complainants, and remedy are worth consideration. For some situations complainants may also seek redress through tort or employment law (Bailey and Devereux 1998).

Practice question and response

Question: You seem to be suggesting that only some discrimination can be dealt with. All discrimination is wrong and surely we as human service workers have a responsibility to take action whenever it happens?

Response: Remember that there may be good grounds for positive discrimination. Other discrimination may well be wrong and you might wish to take action. The main point is to act strategically within authority, and for maximum effect. In relation to legal grounds for action and areas, they are prescribed by the legislation and not all situations you encounter will be covered. If a situation is not covered you will need to seek other than legal recourses. Even if it is covered by the legislation you may decide that no response or a non-legal response is likely to be more productive.

Disability and the law

There are two main ways in which the law specifically addresses disability. One is through rights of redress and remedy under discrimination law as just outlined. The other is through legislation aimed to enhance the social inclusion of people with disabilities, reduce their disadvantage, and provide them with specific services. The Commonwealth *Disability Services Act 1986* (Cth) is the major piece of enabling or funding legislation in Australia. Through this Act Australia recognises its international human rights obligations. The principles and objectives of the Act stress quality of life, choice, actualisation and participation for disabled people, and concomitant requirements on disability services. For example services should provide advocacy support, respect rights of privacy and confidentiality, involve consumers in service planning, and so on. However there are criticisms that the Act is more service than consumer focused and that its definition of disability is too limited (Australian Law Reform Commission 1996; Rose 1998). From these criticisms flow recommendations that it should be more rights based.

There are also criticisms about the absence of a coordinated national approach to disability services (Rose 1998). While the Commonwealth provides considerable funding for disability services much of the administration and most of the service delivery is managed at state and territory level. Thus there is also a *Disability Services Act*, enacted in the early 1990s, in each state and territory, which is largely directed at funding, service contracts, and such like. In Victoria there is also a specific *Intellectually Disabled Persons' Services Act 1986* (Vic), which aims to promote human rights principles and to coordinate government polices and programs. However some of these state and territory Acts too are being amended progressively so as to give greater practical application to human rights objectives through, for instance, minimum service standards, complaints mechanisms, and service coordination. The *Disability Services Act 1992* (Qld) was undergoing a review of this type at the time of writing.

Most of the legislation outlined here becomes familiar to people working in disability advocacy services, disability policy areas, and disability service management. Direct service workers may be less aware of its existence but would do well to acquaint themselves with the objects and principles of the Commonwealth and relevant state or territory Acts. These can serve as lodestars for good practice, and help arm workers who are entering the fray as advocates for clients and others.

Guardianship and administration

It was recognised earlier in this chapter that the capacity of some adults to make important personal decisions is impaired. They may not be able to consent to medical treatment, manage their finances, or continue to live safely alone. Or they may be subject to abuse and exploitation. Any number of long- or short-term conditions may contribute to these difficulties, for example acquired or birth brain damage, dementia, unconsciousness, mental illness, and so on. To illustrate this issue of capacity:

- A person with dementia may refuse to eat, wash, or use a toilet. They have no family connections. Who could intervene here?
- A person with brain damage may refuse an essential medical procedure. Can anyone consent for them?
- A person with an intellectual disability may be subject to sexual advances. Can or should they be protected in any way?
- A person with a mental illness may be sleeping rough and subject to assault. Can anyone intervene here against that person's will?

These individuals may or may not need assistance in dealing with these situations. Everything will depend on their decision-making capacity, not the mere existence of their conditions or circumstances. However in all states and territories in Australia there is a legal regime for protecting the interests of people whose *decision-making capacity* is impaired, through the regulation of substitute decision-making. In general these regimes involve a suite of legislation that aims to protect people's finances and chosen lifestyles, educate the community, and appoint and monitor adult guardians.

The regimes vary a little between jurisdictions, for example their coverage may start at 16 years (e.g. New South Wales) or 18 years in the Northern Territory and Tasmania, and their terminology differs, but they have similar objectives and structures. In general they provide for:

- Enduring guardians to be selected by a person before they lose capacity.
- Financial/legal affairs (frequently called administration) and lifestyle (guardianship) and consent to medical treatment decisions to be considered separately, because people often have variable decision-making capacities.
- A state body/tribunal to hear guardianship and administration applications and appoint or vary guardians and/or administrators (e.g. the Guardianship and Administration Board in Tasmania, and the VCAT Administration List in Victoria).
- A state body to advocate for those with decision-making impairment, investigate orders and applications, and educate the community (e.g. the Public Advocate in Western Australia and Queensland and the Community Advocate in the Australian Capital Territory).
- A state body to manage peoples' financial and legal affairs (i.e. administrate) if there are no appropriate private alternatives (e.g. the Protective Commissioner in New South Wales and the Public Trustee in South Australia).
- Private guardians (e.g. family members) to be appointed by the guardianship body if appropriate.
- A guardian of last resort, that is a state officer or body, to be appointed by the guardianship body, if there are no private alternatives (e.g. the Public Guardian in the Northern Territory and New South Wales, Adult Guardian in Queensland, and Public Advocate in Western Australia).

In terms of declared principles, these legal regimes also generally attempt to ensure that:

- impaired decision-making capacity rather than impairment *per se* is the only justification for substitute decision-making
- the rights and integrity of the individual are paramount
- the least restrictive and intrusive arrangements are to prevail
- decisions made should be consistent with the person's own wishes if they were not incapacitated
- the wishes of the person are to be sought if possible
- informal arrangements are to prevail if at all possible.

Examples of relevant legislation in different jurisdictions are as follows:

Guardianship Act 1987 (NSW)
Adult Guardianship Act 1988 (NT)
Guardianship and Administration Act 1990 (WA)
Community Advocate Act 1991 (ACT)
Guardianship and Administration Act 2000 (Qld).

Practice question and response

Question: How on earth can I be expected to remember all these Acts and details, and where would I start if I had to deal with an adult competence issue?

Response: If you work with groups in which reduced decision-making capacity is a common problem, you will be surprised how familiar you soon become with the relevant state/territory legislation. If you only infrequently come across capacity difficulties you should be aware at least of your main state/territory Acts, and the relevant public education and guardianship bodies. Both are invaluable resources and the latter will assist you. Whether you work in these areas or not, you should read the objects or principles of the relevant guardianship Act because they will refresh your memory about individual autonomy. Good human service practice can always do with an occasional ideological boost or confirmation.

Human service workers enter the adult guardianship arena in different ways. Some of them sit on the bodies or tribunals that make the orders, or work in the related public advocacy offices. In the latter capacity they might be engaged in public education, investigating applications, orders, and complaints, and/or actually carrying out some of the functions of a guardian of last resort.

More commonly they work with individuals and families where guardianship and/or administration orders exist or are sought and in these capacities they are precluded from filling the role of legal guardian. These workers may support family members seeking orders from the relevant tribunals, or themselves make applications for orders for individual clients. This latter job can be particularly taxing for them. It is usually prompted by a complex set of circumstances in which ethical issues around self-determination are finely balanced against urgent practical/risk considerations. In addition it puts the worker and/or their report before a quasi-legal body with all the attendant tensions mentioned in chapter 7. The task will require the worker to present and argue an evidence-based case, consistent with the principles/objects of the relevant Act. Many of these activities have been the subject of other chapters in this book.

Human service workers also have a role in helping justice administration personnel such as police, and legal practitioners, recognise vulnerability and exploitation in situations where all these workers may be involved. Few lawyers specialise in the rights of older people (Setterlund, Tilse et al. 1999) or have extensive knowledge of intellectual (McGillivray and Waterman 2003) and other disabilities, which are relevant to mental capacity. They like many justice personnel often need to be educated and advised about the physical, mental, and life problems experienced by people with impaired decision-making capacity. With this sort of support from human service workers, their own work with such people is likely to be more informed and more effective.

Mental health

This area overlaps with guardianship in that individuals whose decision-making capacity is impaired by mental illness may be subject to guardianship applications or orders. Like substitute decision-making, mental health law is largely a matter of state or territory legislation which attempts to satisfy competing purposes of protecting the community, and protecting vulnerable individuals (Healy and Brophy 2002). The Commonwealth has in recent years assumed more of a leadership role in relation to mental health. Through its National Mental Health Plans it aims to monitor state/territory compliance with UN principles on mental health, albeit with questionable effectiveness (Delaney 2003). As Carney says of Australian governments' records in relation to UN principles (2003, p. 24) this is 'an area where Victoria generally heads a somewhat lacklustre federal pack'. It is not surprising that there have been calls for the establishment of a national commission for mental health, akin to HREOC, with powers of investigation and reporting, and responsibility for monitoring the National Mental Health Plans (Mental Health Council of Australia 2003).

There are a number of arenas in which mental health and the law intersect. For example, guardianship has just been mentioned and criminal law provisions were outlined in chapter 8. The most significant piece of legislation for most people with a mental illness, and mental health workers, is the relevant state or territory mental health Act that provides for involuntary detention and treatment of individuals in institutional and community settings. For example:

Mental Health Act 1986 (Vic)
Mental Health Act 1986 (WA)
Mental Health Act 1993 (SA)
Mental Health and Related Services Act 1998 (NT)
Mental Health Act 2000 (Qld).

As with adult guardianship, these mental health Acts incorporate basic human rights principles into their objects. For example, they emphasise best possible care in the least restrictive circumstances and respect for individuals' rights, dignity, and self-respect. But, as has already been seen, these objects may be inadequately realised in practice and not always through breaches of patients' civil liberties. The case of *Presland v Hunter Area Health Service & Anor* [2003] NSWSC 754 (Unreported, Adams J, 19 August 2003) mentioned in previous chapters, provides an illustration of inadequate care through lack of intervention rather than through disrespectful or offensive practice. There the plaintiff argued that he should have been detained under New South Wales legislation. In fact, he was negligently released from hospital and killed someone while mentally ill.

There are jurisdictional variations and inconsistencies in mental health legal regimes but all provide for:

Involuntary detention

This is based only on imminent risk or danger to self and/or others and not on grounds of mental illness *per se*. Large numbers of people have various forms of mental illness, inclusive of depression, and detention will never be a consideration for them. Initial involuntary detention must be brief and both detention and treatment decisions must be founded on comprehensive assessments, preferably by more than one person/doctor. There are jurisdictional variations about the criteria to be met before involuntary detention can take place.

Compulsory treatment

In some jurisdictions like Victoria, the authorised psychiatrist has a significant role in making decisions about and supervising treatment, inclusive of medication, in institutions and the community (Gardner 2000). In contrast in South Australia and Tasmania, involuntary treatment unless urgent, must be authorised by the state tribunal (Carney 2003; Delaney 2003).

A multidisciplinary body/tribunal with determinative and review powers

Delaney (2003) comprehensively outlines the roles and functions of these bodies in Australia. For example, in many jurisdictions, such as Tasmania, Western Australia, the Northern Territory, and New South Wales, they can make orders about treatment. Many of them, but not the Victorian one, can overrule a doctor's decision to use electroconvulsive therapy and consider decisions about voluntary patients. None of them can make orders about restraint or seclusion but the Tasmanian and Western Australian ones do have a monitoring or reporting role in this area. They conduct initial and periodic reviews at different intervals. They have varying approaches to patient access to documents, representation, second opinions, attendance at hearings, and rights of access to judicial review. None of them has any role or authority in relation to resources, approach to service delivery and/or quality in mental health (Rees 2003).

Human service workers' activity in relation to mental health law mirrors that of guardianship. For instance they may sit on mental health tribunals, engage in advocacy, project, or policy roles, and work with clients and families where orders are sought or in place. In mental health direct service work they are likely to experience all of the tensions of guardianship work. There may in fact be additional conflicts as some legal regimes in mental health reflect historical medical dominance and limit the voice of human service workers. Brophy, Campbell et al. (2003) for instance argue that Mental Health Review Boards in Victoria receive insufficient information about patients' social circumstances largely because case managers supervising community treatment orders have no formal role in review or appeal hearings.

Refugees and asylum seekers

Refugee law is currently one of the most contentious areas of federal law in Australia. It is not simply a legal issue but a highly politicised one. Few issues are as emotive and divisive in Australia as refugee policy and the response to asylum seekers, including 'boat people', especially those who bought passage from 'people smugglers' to get to Australia. A raft of changes to Australia's policies and legislation in this area has occurred since the September 11, 2001 attacks. A discussion of these changes is outside the scope of this book, however many helpful and detailed summaries of the law and issues in this area exist elsewhere (e.g. Crock and Saul 2002; Germov 2003; Jupp 2003; Schloenhardt 2003). One consequence of the breadth and rapidity of the changes, as well as the political sentiment that accompanies them, is the tendency to correlate certain concepts and see them as interchangeable. Many people see the terms 'boat people' or 'asylum seekers' as synonymous with the term 'illegal immigrants'. Others see the term 'asylum seekers' as synonymous with the term 'refugees'. Neither of these associations is correct, and these terms have precise and important legal definitions. In reality, people arriving in Australia by boat, perhaps through 'people smugglers' or perhaps not, who then seek protection as refugees are only a small minority of the people who seek this protection in Australia each year (Jupp 2003). Regardless of this, they are among the most vulnerable, and will thus be the focus here. Many asylum seekers may or may not be aware of their legal rights and the obligations Australia has towards them, and many refugees face ongoing legal challenges subsequent to receiving their various protection visas. The emotive nature of these issues at a policy and practical level heightens the need for workers to have a clear focus and mandate, to feel empowered themselves, and if involved in advocacy, to empower their clients. For these reasons, a basic understanding of the law in this area is critical.

This area is one in which human service workers and lawyers often work closely. Many members of both professions provide significant pro bono services to those asylum seekers in detention, and others are involved in processing applications and assessment of individuals for the various classes of visa available. Others are involved in programs with people who have been granted some form of protection visa (Vichie 2003). Regardless of their status, asylum seekers and refugees have very real needs, and human service workers and lawyers alike are involved in significant efforts to meet them.

Practice question and response

Question: But boat people are illegals, aren't they?
Response: 'Illegals' is a colloquial term. The legal status of these people is addressed below. It is very important for human service workers, regardless of their personal and political orientations, to be scrupulously accurate and careful in their use of language in this issue, as many will be taken to have knowledge and authority in the area due to their position as human service workers.

Who are asylum seekers?

An 'asylum seeker' is a person claiming refugee status under the international *Convention Relating to the Status of Refugees 1951* (amended by the 1967 *Protocol Relating to the Status of Refugees*). Australia is a party to the *Refugee Convention*, and thus has obligations under it, among other international conventions affecting asylum seekers. The precise definition of a refugee is provided in Article 1 of the *Refugee Convention* as a person who has a: 'well-founded fear of being persecuted for reasons of race, religion, nationality, membership of a particular social group or political opinion' and who has fled their country of origin for that reason.

The term 'asylum seeker' covers applicants who seek protection under the onshore program for refugee applications (Crock and Saul 2002). It is important to note that this method of seeking protection is permitted under the *Refugee Convention*, along with applying from outside Australia, under the offshore program. Whatever their method of arrival, the right of a non-citizen to apply for a protection visa as a refugee under the *Refugee Convention* is a statutory right contained in the *Migration Act 1958* (Cth), and the Australian Government has consistently maintained that it is meeting its international obligations under the *Refugee Convention*.

It is incorrect to assume either that all onshore asylum seekers arriving in any particular boat are refugees, or that none of them are. Rather, under the *Refugee Convention*, it is not legally possible to determine the refugee status of any applicant arbitrarily. Their applications *must* be processed, under Articles 31-33 of the *Refugee Convention* (Kenny 2003).

Mandatory detention of asylum seekers

Many aspects of Australia's response to asylum seekers have been internationally and nationally criticised (e.g. Gardham and Owens 2001; Flynn and LaForgia 2002; Schloenhardt 2002). However, the most damning criticism has arguably been reserved for the practice of mandatory detention for asylum seekers. The arbitrary detention of all asylum seekers and the indefinite detention of children have been viewed by the United Nations Human Rights Committee as being in breach of Australia's international treaty obligations, and it has also recommended compensation be paid; see *Bakhtiyari v Australia* (2003). The Australian Government is considering the Committee's views and those of HREOC (2004), which reports that Australian detention policy breaches the *UN Convention on the Rights of the Child.*

Domestically, these issues are affected by jurisdictional complexities, and the extent to which the jurisdiction of state and territory governments over people within their state or territory are overridden by the *Migration Act 1958.* Layton (2003) points out each state and territory government may well have jurisdiction over child asylum seekers if those children are at risk, and many (if not all) children in detention centres do arguably meet those criteria.

Jurisdictional issues also apply to Australian courts. In *Minister for Immigration and Multicultural Affairs v B* [2004] HCA 20 (29 April 2004), the High Court held that the Family Court does not have jurisdiction to release children held in immigration detention. Following this decision, a constitutional challenge to the mandatory detention of children was mounted and is yet to be finalised.

Key points for practice

- Whenever an issue of competence, difference, and/or disability arises in Australia there is likely to be at least one applicable legal regime. All human service workers require some sense of the objects and structure of these regimes.
- Informed consent is vital in all human service work. It is particularly critical when the decision-making capacity of the clients or people involved is in doubt or impaired. The law is quite clear that consent must always be properly sought and obtained from individuals or those who have the right to consent on their behalf. The law is equally clear that disability or limited capacity *per se* do not remove a person's rights to make decisions and to be treated with dignity and respect.
- There are both federal and state/territory legal regimes in Australia for dealing with discrimination and harassment. Proficient human service workers are familiar with the shape of both regimes because they may offer different possibilities in the face of different circumstances.
- In all Australian state/territory jurisdictions there is a legal regime for managing substitute adult decision-making. The regime generally has an infrastructure in which there are resources and bodies to assist workers dealing with questions of adult competence to make decisions.
- In all Australian state/territory jurisdictions there is a legal regime that provides for involuntary detention and treatment for mental illness.
- If working or speaking about the area, human service workers have a particular responsibility to ensure they are accurately informed about the law and relevant issues surrounding refugees and asylum seekers.
- There are criticisms of the effectiveness of many of the regimes covered in this chapter. However, most of the main pieces of legislation do articulate fundamental human rights principles in their objects. Human service workers do well to read these objects occasionally. Not only does this process expand their legal literacy but it also serves as an ideological and aspirational refresher.

- When dealing with questions of competence, difference, and/or disability, adept human service workers engage with and utilise the relevant legal regimes in a discriminating and strategic way to achieve their goals. They may join forces with the law on occasions when a powerful formal approach is appropriate. At other times they may determine that less formal interventions may produce better outcomes.

Some useful web sites

Mental health
http://home.vicnet.net.au/~mhlc/
http://mhca.com.au/

Public advocates or guardians
wcc.govt.nz/aboutwcc/public-advocate/
www.publicadvocate.vic.gov.au/CA256A76007E8265/Home?OpenPage
www.justice.qld.gov.au/guardian/pa.htm
www.oca.act.gov.au/index.html
www.justice.tas.gov.au/guar/info_4.htm
www.opa.sa.gov.au/index.htm

Guardianship
www.ijcga.gov.au/
www.lawlink.nsw.gov.au/opg
www.gt.nsw.gov.au/
www.justice.qld.gov.au/guardian/home.htm
www.justice.wa.gov.au/displayPage.asp?StructureID=58321652&ResourceID=783
    27746&division=Public%20Advocate
www.nt.gov.au/health/org_supp/performance_audit/adult_guard/guardianship.shtml
www.vcat.vic.gov.au/vcatguardianshiplist.htm
www.justice.tas.gov.au/guar/index.htm
www.oca.act.gov.au/adults/substitute_decision/sub-dm_index.html

Discrimination, disability, and social justice
www.hreoc.gov.au/index.html
www.hreoc.gov.au/social_justice/
www.hreoc.gov.au/disability_rights/index.html
www.equalopportunity.wa.gov.au/
www.eoc.vic.gov.au/
www.eoc.sa.gov.au/public/
www.lawlink.nsw.gov.au/adb
www.justice.tas.gov.au/adc/adcfrontpage.htm
http://eeotrust.org.nz/

Asylum seekers and refugees

www.mrt.gov.au/
www.abc.net.au/diylaw/e2resources.htm
www.hreoc.gov.au/human_rights/asylum_seekers/index.html
www.refugees.org.au/
www.immi.gov.au/facts/61asylum.htm

11

Housing and **Finance**

Beyond legal responses

Issues of housing, income support, consumer complaints, and debt management are common to much human service work. For many clients they are at the forefront of everyday life and have a significant impact on lifestyle, well-being, and opportunities. Human service workers need to have an understanding of these issues and the ability to provide assistance and referral, as well as a clear concept of their own agency or practice mandate in this area. Perhaps one of the most important things for a human service worker to keep in mind is that a legal response may be a last resort. If it is part of a worker's professional mandate, advocacy and negotiation on behalf of clients faced with these issues may well go a long way to achieving a resolution of them, or at least recasting them into a more manageable form. Similarly, strategic and knowledgeable use of services provided by the Office of Consumer and Business Affairs or the Banking Ombudsman, as well as the appeals process for review of Centrelink decisions, for example, will generally produce good results.

Topics that come under discussion in this area are various and complex. This chapter will address debt and bankruptcy as well as income support, consumer rights, and housing and homelessness, as these areas are fundamental issues for human services. Other issues such as financial advice, gambling, and succession law are not addressed here and others are discussed elsewhere. In particular, child support is discussed in chapter 9. Human service workers may be financial counsellors, specific support workers to a range of client bases, they may work in various government departments or funded bodies, or their roles may intersect with these areas in other ways.

Debt management

A starting point—empowerment and perspective shifting

Human service workers encounter issues of debt management primarily in two ways: either through client interaction or as service providers dealing with a myriad of cash flow, billing, and budgetary strategies. Many people believe that there is little room for manoeuvring when it comes to payment of debts, since in their minds they either owe the money or they don't, and thus the creditor 'holds all the cards'. If they have already asked for more time to pay, or negotiated in some way with their creditor(s) they may have concluded that there is nothing else that can be done. This may lead to a level of disempowerment. Most people have a general knowledge of bankruptcy and what it involves, but may not realise the limits of their own knowledge or see the other options that are open to them. A worker whose mandate does not extend to advocacy regarding debt or other forms of assistance may nonetheless provide a substantial service to their client simply in addressing these sorts of misunderstandings by providing basic information and referral options for them. A client may feel better able to take the steps necessary to deal with outstanding debt if they at least feel as though there are choices that can be made. Thus it is crucial to be alert for issues that clients may not be aware of, and for assumptions they may have made out of feelings of powerlessness.

Financial counsellors and other avenues of assistance

Many people with pressing financial problems seek assistance from a financial counsellor. The Commonwealth Financial Counselling Program provides funding for several financial counselling services in each state or territory, and has done since 1990 (Brading 2003). Many other organisations also provide such services, of course. Financial counselling is a growing human service field in Australia. One reason for its growth is an increase in referral of clients from other human service workers. Financial counsellors work for many different organisations in a variety of capacities. Issues of funding and the desirability of further development in the structuring and funding of financial counselling services are therefore complex, yet no less necessary, as this essential service is often provided voluntarily depending on the service provider (Brading 2003). For workers in other fields it is important to have at least some idea of the dynamics of financial problems, practical assistance that may be given, and where to refer clients for further help.

Fundamental issues surrounding debt

There are several key points to emphasise regarding debt and consumer credit. The first concerns the nature of support available to consumers. A key function of human service workers dealing in this area is information provision. The expense of legal advice often appears prohibitive to people with outstanding debts. Partly due to this perceived need for alternatives to retaining a private lawyer, a number of other sources of professional assistance and support are available to people with debt problems, not least of which are financial counsellors, government regulatory bodies such as Offices of Consumer and Business Affairs, and human service workers themselves. This is not to suggest that such assistance obviates the need for legal advice, but to highlight the increased level of support available to people in financial difficulty. Additionally, many organisations provide free legal advice from qualified lawyers as part of their services. Each state and territory has a variety of community legal centres and some have legal centres providing services in the area of consumer credit and debt. Many people may well be completely unaware of these avenues of support.

The second point to note regarding debt is that due to the expense of taking legal action to satisfy a debt, creditors are generally very open to alternative methods of payment. There is little value for creditors in pursuing a debtor into bankruptcy since this carries no guarantee that the entire debt will be paid at that time; indeed that result is highly unlikely. A creditor would always prefer to be paid, even if that payment were to take much longer than they would like! Similarly many clients would prefer to pay their debts rather than have their financial fate determined for them, especially since financial disadvantage affects every aspect of a person's life. For this reason, workers may have a key role in advocating for a client and assisting them to negotiate a repayment arrangement with creditors, which could be of dramatic practical benefit.

Recovery of debt

It is of course true to say that a person who has incurred a debt is legally required to pay it. There are, however, numerous practical qualifications that may apply in any individual case. It is always necessary for a person who has an outstanding debt to seek specific information regarding the amount that is owed and how that amount is calculated. It may be that too much interest has been added, or that amounts were included erroneously. Checking the accuracy of any demand for payment by a creditor and asking for any extra information that is required is a crucial step. There may be other problems with the creditor's demand for payment also, depending on the nature of the debt. All jurisdictions bar Western Australia have adopted the *Consumer Credit Code*; Western Australia has enacted its own, although with substantially the same provisions. Clients who have incurred debt through the provision of consumer credit may be unaware that the *Consumer Credit Code* allows a consumer to renegotiate credit payment arrangements in certain circumstances if their original financial position changes. However the Code only covers credit provision for terms over 62 days. There have been calls to increase the regulation of the Code to include short-term credit providers also, given that this practice is increasing in Australia (Field 2002).

Harassment

Increasingly, governments are taking steps to protect the rights of debtors in Australia. Under fair trading legislation in each state or territory and the *Trade Practices Act 1974* (Cth) at the federal level, it is illegal for a creditor or person acting on their behalf to use harassment as a method of securing the repayment of a debt. Under s 60 of the *Trade Practices Act 1974* creditors may not use: 'physical force, undue harassment or coercion, in connection with the supply of goods or services to a consumer, or in connection with the payment for goods or services by a consumer'. This remains the case regardless of whether the debt is actually owed', the amount owed, or how overdue repayments are. Threatening to take legal action is not a form of harassment, since a creditor is entitled to do so to recover a debt.

The Fair Trading Acts of most jurisdictions do not define harassment, but they do in Victoria and the Australian Capital Territory. Broadly speaking 'physical force, harassment or coercion' under the Australian Capital Territory and Victorian fair trading legislation includes intimidation or threats of violence to the debtors or their family, but also covers conduct that is designed to embarrass or ridicule a debtor or publicise their debt to other people (especially employers), or which misleads them as to the consequences of nonpayment. Some instances of these are threatening the loss of property on an unsecured debt, or using documents designed to resemble court or official documents. It also includes unreasonable levels of contact with the debtor regarding the debt, such as endless phone calls or phone calls in the early hours of the morning or late at night. Victoria and the Australian Capital Territory also define harassment as refusing to leave a debtor's residence or workplace (Bull 2003). Complaints about harassment by creditors can be made to the Australian Competition and Consumer Commission or the Department of Consumer Affairs or Fair Trading in a given state or territory, and should be encouraged. Ryan (2002) points out that many clients may not realise that some of the less extreme forms of harassment are illegal, but rather see it as a consequence of having a debt, and recommends that workers specifically ask clients about harassing conduct as they may not think that it is relevant. The law has deliberately established parameters such as these to ensure that creditors can be paid without the dignity of debtors being compromised by the process (Bull 2003). Best practice in this area will ensure that a client who has to manage an outstanding debt can at least do so free of harassment.

Many creditors engage debt collectors to recover outstanding debts. Debt collectors are covered by the anti-harassment provisions of fair trading legislation also. Additionally, debt collectors are regulated by other legislation, although this is somewhat diverse given the range of people and agencies involved in debt collection (Australian Competition and Consumer Commission 1999). Debt collection work may be undertaken by a recovery section of a financial institution, private individuals, or independent debt collectors (mercantile agents). All debt collectors are regulated by fair trading and/or consumer credit provisions regarding debt recovery. Additionally, mercantile agents are regulated in each jurisdiction by specific pieces of legislation. Further regulation occurs from debt collection industry bodies themselves, through codes of ethics. The Australian Collectors Association and the Institute of Mercantile Agents both have such codes.

Legal action and bankruptcy

Bankruptcy is governed by federal legislation, namely the *Bankruptcy Act 1966* (Cth). One feature of bankruptcy is that debts incurred prior to the person declaring (or being declared) bankrupt do not have to be paid in full by the bankrupt at a later time. Bankruptcy may thus be seen as an attractive option by a client who can see no reasonable hope of paying off their debt even over time without significant detriment resulting to them. It is important not to make blanket generalised statements regarding bankruptcy. It is not something that should be avoided at all costs for all clients; for some people it may be the best option overall. However, while it has advantages, there are significant disadvantages too, both while the client is a bankrupt, and afterwards. A client's employment and future credit options, for example, may well be affected. The law places restrictions on bankrupts both during bankruptcy and afterwards. Clients need to be aware of these issues in order to make an informed decision. They also need to know that even where legal action has been brought against them due to an unpaid debt, there are a variety of repayment methods that may be ordered by the court, including payment by installments, and that it is always open to them to arrange to pay the debt informally with the creditor even after legal proceedings have begun.

Practice question and response

Question: What about the cause of so many financial problems, namely the shaky financial state of so many Australians because of low government payments, the high cost of child care, limited availability of concessions, casualisation of the workforce and so on? What is the law doing about these issues?

Response: These are very real contributors to the financial difficulties of many people, and the law cannot solve them, as they stem from the political and social sphere, which overarches both law and the human services. However, advocacy from both professions at an individual and systemic level can be powerfully applied to assist in problem solving.

Consumer protection

Legislation and consumer protection

There is a substantial amount of legislation at both a federal and state or territory level governing issues of credit and debt generally. Consumer protection laws, combined with industry self-regulation and consumer 'watchdog' organisations ensure both a high level of accountability and a wide range of options for individuals and agencies or other service providers who have encountered problems as consumers or who have incurred consumer debt. This section will not address financial products and services to consumers but will focus on other goods and services.

A central federal regulatory body for consumer protection of non-financial services and products is the Australian Competition and Consumer Commission (ACCC). It administers the *Trade Practices Act 1974* (Cth). All states and territories have fair trading legislation, which corresponds with the *Trade Practices Act 1974*.

This legislation is administered by state or territory Departments of Consumer Affairs or Fair Trading. The ACCC is also responsible for the *Consumer Credit Code*, which regulates the provision of consumer credit in each jurisdiction.

Each state or territory also has a Sale of Goods Act regulating the provision of merchandise to consumers. Broadly speaking, it focuses on legislative requirements for the quality and condition of goods, including warranties and refunds, whereas the Fair Trading Act in each jurisdiction regards the conduct of traders, both to ensure trade is unrestricted, and also to ensure it is fair to consumers. Thus these Acts include provisions prohibiting misleading and deceptive conduct or advertising etc. The *Trade Practices Act 1974* deals with warranties also.

Human service agencies, workers, and clients may encounter a range of problems as consumers, including the provision of faulty goods, difficulties enforcing warranties, or obtaining refunds. Some human service providers, especially non-government agencies, may encounter the same problems with their own purchases. The central point to note here is that retailers may or may not be correct in the rights and limitations they convey to consumers. For example, certain guarantees regarding goods are implied into every contract of sale. The goods must fit the description given to them, must be suitable for the use they were sold to fulfil, and must be of 'merchantable quality'. Thus whether there is a warranty or not, an item which breaks down soon after purchase is likely to not fit that description and the purchaser can take further action or get a refund accordingly. The key here is to ensure consumers are aware that the validity of blanket statements regarding rights, such as 'we do not allow any refunds', may be questioned (Carvan 1996). The law restricts the limitations that retailers can attach to their liability in certain circumstances. Consumers need to be aware of these limitations, or at least aware that they can raise questions about such issues, and make complaints to the relevant consumer organisations and bodies.

Income support

Income support is a vast and complex area both generally and legally, governed by Commonwealth legislation. Currently, Centrelink has 6.4 million customers (Centrelink 2004). It is clear that most human service workers will at some stage encounter income support in their work, whether through client interaction, policy development and research, or direct employment in Centrelink or in agencies providing emergency financial assistance.

The focus of this section is not on the specific payments or their eligibility criteria, as those are too fluid. A large number of both government and community centre web sites provide detailed up-to-date information on these areas and some of these are listed below. Instead, various aspects of the government system of income support will be discussed, as well as practical suggestions for effective practice within the appeals process for decisions. It is at these grass-roots levels that human service workers can best assist clients, or serve employers. The system of review established for decisions regarding income support will also be highlighted, as it provides a clear example of legal review and appeal processes and their place within the system, as outlined in Part I.

Overview

The Federal Government (Department of Family and Community Services) has primary responsibility for social security. The two main Acts governing this area of its portfolio are the *Social Security Act 1991* (Cth) and the *Social Security (Administration) Act 1999* (Cth). Centrelink is the government agency contracted to provide income support services on behalf of the Department. As can be seen from the statistics above, there are many circumstances and levels of payments received by people from all walks of life.

Trend towards contracting out services

As mentioned in chapter 4, contract law is playing an increasing role in the human services. Related issues are seen in the area of income support, with this area becoming more contractual in nature, as the delivery of services is increasingly contracted out. Downey (2001) argues that this represents a shift in the nature and accountability of service delivery to a 'managerialist culture'. The rise in contracting of services in income support is due to the Federal Government policy of mutual benefit/mutual obligation, seen in part in activity tests and outcome based contract payments (Downey 2001).

Centrelink is itself contracted to the Department of Family and Community Services to deliver its employment and income support services. Job Network is a further example of an outsourced contracted service provider. It delivers employment services for the government to job-seekers registered with Centrelink who are referred to it. Following the 'Australians Working Together' government initiative the Job Network Providers have an increasing role in assessing job seekers regarding their suitability for programs such as work for the dole, as well as referring them to employers. The contracts include incentives, with payments made based on outcomes, and their role is a complex multilayered one. These structures may well have ramifications for human service workers employed within some of these agencies, many of whom in turn may be employed casually or on short-term contracts.

Review and appeal

As previously stressed, appeal of decisions is far less stigmatised in legal culture than in human services. This simply cannot be overstated. Appealing an unfavourable decision is really quite common and at times expected in the legal system. If clients are unhappy with a decision and there seem to be grounds, there is no need to feel it is somehow unusual, wrong, or risky to appeal. The same is true regarding appealing Centrelink decisions.

The area of law that deals with the proper exercise of government power, and thus the appropriateness of government decision-making generally is administrative law, discussed also in Part I. These principles apply to Centrelink and its officers in their decision-making, though the extent to which they apply to outsourced bodies providing services to Centrelink clients is less clear (Bacon 2002). A review process is contained within the system, containing elements of both internal and external review. Much Centrelink paperwork has a section detailing what to do if dissatisfied with a Centrelink decision, but this fact does not mean that clients automatically feel that such a challenge is a realistic option for them. Some clients may be reluctant to challenge Centrelink decisions, not least because some or all of their income is at stake and it may appear akin to 'biting the hand that feeds' them.

Practice question and response

Question: It's all very well to talk about review rights but Centrelink is big and faceless; individuals haven't really got a chance.

Response: It is big, and people may feel intimidated and blocked but they do have legal rights. Exercising them may take tenacity in themselves and their supporters but can have very positive results; see statistics discussed below.

Points to note

*   The appeal/review process is governed, among other things, by time limits. At each stage of the appeal process it is vital that clients stay within these. Some limits will affect whether they can be backpaid if their appeal is successful, and by which date. Others will affect whether they can lodge a further appeal at a higher level at all. The time limits are one of the most crucial requirements to alert clients to. The time limits mentioned in this section are current at time of writing, but are subject to change.
*   There may well be rights regarding ongoing payment during the review process that clients and staff are unaware of. For example, under s 131 of the *Social Security (Administration) Act 1999* (Cth) payments may be able to be continued during the review process, rather than being backpaid later, but a client needs to request this.
*   There is no charge for persons seeking review of Centrelink decisions at any level prior to a court appeal.

Steps in the review process

Discussion with the original decision-maker
A person who wants to appeal a Centrelink decision will usually need to discuss it with the original decision-maker. This is partly as a prerequisite to taking most later steps of appeal, and also as a practical way workers may consider of potentially resolving the issue.

Review by an authorised review officer (ARO)
Time restrictions: within 13 weeks of being notified of the original decision in order to ensure that backpayments will be made. This review can be sought either in person or in writing. It is advisable to seek all reviews in writing. This is an internal form of review, however the ARO must be independent, i.e. not involved in the original decision. They will review the decision either via a personal or

telephone interview. The applicant is entitled to have someone else present at the interview. (Decisions regarding Abstudy or Assistance for Isolated Children are reviewed by an authorised officer whose role is similar to that of an ARO.) Review by the officer is a prerequisite to seeking further review at the Social Security Appeals Tribunal (SSAT). The ARO can consider new information regarding a client's circumstances, correct any errors, and make a new decision.

Appeal to Social Security Appeals Tribunal against the ARO decision

Time restrictions: must be made within three months of the ARO decision.

The SSAT may pay travel and/or accommodation costs for applicants and can provide an interpreter. It has offices in all capital cities and at times will sit in country areas also. The SSAT sits with up to three members of various backgrounds including law and human service work. It is much more informal than a court hearing, and although legal representation is not compulsory, it is advisable since far more appeals by represented appellants are successful than by unrepresented appellants; around 17 to 42 per cent (Raper 1999). Alternatively, the appellant is entitled to have another person present who may also speak on their behalf.

Appeal to the SSAT is a prerequisite of further appeal to the Administrative Appeals Tribunal. See chapter 7 for further discussion of tribunal proceedings generally.

Decisions of an authorised officer regarding Abstudy or Assistance for Isolated Children are not reviewed by the SSAT. Instead they are reviewed by the Minister for Education, Science and Training (Centrelink).

Appeal to the Administrative Appeals Tribunal against the SSAT decision

Time restrictions: must be made within 28 days of the SSAT decision.

This tribunal is more formal. More legal advice is needed for this appeal than for the lower levels of review. Legal representation at the hearing is advised, and some limited legal aid is possibly available for this. Clients are advised to seek the assistance of a lawyer in preparing their case even if the lawyer is not representing them at the hearing.

The AAT will sit as either one or three members. An appeal can be lodged against a decision of the AAT but only on points of law.

Appeal to a Court (Federal then High Court)

Time restrictions: must be made within 28 days of the AAT decision.

Appeals to first the Federal Court, and then from the Federal Court to the High Court, are available from decisions of the AAT but only on questions of law. Legal representation is a practical necessity.

Practice question and response

Question: Many people who want to appeal various types of decisions are seriously unpleasant, rude, pedantic, difficult, and time-consuming: what about them?

Response: This may be so but it is not a legal issue unless they are harassing others. Parliament has given them the same rights as the most polite of people. Thus, relationship and personal style issues are matters of agency and staff management and practice.

Frequency of decision review

As mentioned, most decisions made by Centrelink are not reviewed. In 2001–02, 37,699 people sought review by an ARO, 7647 sought review by the SSAT, and 1261 sought review by the AAT. Between 30 and 33 per cent of the decisions were changed on review at those three levels (Centrelink 2002). These figures suggest a substantial culture of reluctance to seek review even though it may well result in a favourable decision, and highlight the importance of strong worker advocacy and practical advice and assistance encouraged by welfare rights groups generally (Raper 1999).

Complaints

Complaints to Centrelink are obviously not appeals, so if a client wants to appeal a decision, it must be worded clearly so that it does not get dealt with as a complaint, especially as time is of the essence. Complaints about staff conduct or other matters can be made to the local Centrelink manager, its customer relations unit, Federal Members of Parliament, or the Commonwealth Ombudsman, depending on the circumstances.

Workers compensation payments

Workers compensation can affect workers personally, or they may encounter the system through their work responsibilities. A workers compensation settlement amount is taken into account by Centrelink in determining a person's eligibility for income support. This is a very difficult area and one which many people misunderstand. Consequently it can have widespread ramifications on income levels for those concerned. An individual who has received a *settled* workers compensation payment (i.e. their case did not go to trial) should seek legal advice, as this payment can result in their preclusion from eligibility for income support for a substantial amount of time. Ideally legal advice should be obtained prior to accepting a settled payment. Currently the '50 per cent rule' is applied to compensation payments received out of court. Essentially 50 per cent of the compensation payment will be deemed as having been for economic loss, and is used as the basis for calculating a preclusion period from eligibility for income support, usually for months or possibly years.

It is important that workers and/or clients they may be assisting realise that this rule applies regardless of the actual compensation amount for economic loss. Even where it creates an unjust result, that fact alone will not be held to be sufficient to constitute the 'special circumstances' necessary for the decision to be overturned on appeal or review (Booth 2003). In such cases, factors other than the 50 per cent rule will need to be relied on for 'special circumstances' to be found on appeal or review. This will ordinarily be difficult, however, 'clients are not bound by a finding forever' (Lee 2001, p. 21). If review on those grounds is unsuccessful, a client can begin the application process with Centrelink again later, and apply for further review if necessary, since the SSAT makes its decisions based on the most current information (Lee 2001).

Housing and accommodation

Housing affordability and homelessness are fundamental social concerns in contemporary Australia. In addition, several decades of deinstitutionalisation have raised the public profiles of home support and community residential care services. Thus matters of housing and accommodation availability and quality are commonplace in much human service work. The intersection between these matters and the law can be explored from four major angles:

- homelessness in general
- residential tenancies
- residential facilities
- home support services.

There is significant diversity in the legal architecture of each of these areas. Together the areas encapsulate and illustrate the range of legal imperatives, jurisdictional complexity, and variability that characterise so much human service activity. The relevant legislative developments in recent times also reflect evolutionary changes in living arrangements in Australia. For example, caravans or mobile homes, cooperative or community housing arrangements, and premises owned by corporations test traditional legal notions of residence and tenancy. The general legal landscape within each of the four areas is outlined in the following sections.

Homelessness

The law and homelessness interact in human service experience in a number of ways. As Lynch (2002; 2003) explains, the law is part of the problem of homelessness. The law criminalises behaviours in public that may be lawful at home, for instance drinking and fighting. Legislation 'enforced without regard to socio-economic status' is discriminatory, as is the arbitrary enforcement of laws that unduly affect people in public places (Lynch 2003, p. 128). Indigenous people are particularly affected by these impacts of the law. Thus much human service work is with people 'on the streets' who face these legal pressures on a daily basis. Some agencies and workers provide direct service through, for example, emergency accommodation or provision of meals. Some also are active in advocacy activity where rights-based law as described by Lynch (2003) and Goldie (2003) is used to challenge and change current systems.

The law and homelessness coincide for many human service agencies and workers in state and Commonwealth funded programs to alleviate homelessness. For example, the Commonwealth–state Supported Accommodation Assistance Program (SAAP), operating under the *Supported Accommodation Assistance Act 1994* (Cth), targets and funds services for women escaping domestic violence, young people, and single men and women (Department of Family and Community Services 2003). There is also a Commonwealth–state Housing Agreement, Crisis Accommodation Program, and a Commonwealth Rent Assistance scheme. Services established under these initiatives employ many human service workers throughout Australia. The point for current purposes is that the legislative and funding provisions and performance agreements underpinning these services guide, constrain, and sometimes regulate agency operations. Worker employees may be insufficiently aware of the legal backdrop to their agency funding, their salaries, and standards of care expected of them.

Residential tenancies

Housing rentals are regulated in each Australian state and territory by specific legislation, underpinned by contract law that founds the relationships between landlords and tenants. Commonwealth and state discrimination legislation may also apply if prejudice on the grounds of, for example race or marital status, is evident in rental processes. The jurisdictions are similar in that their mixture of legislation, associated regulations, and common law, attempt to balance landlords' and tenants' rights. They do this through constraints on things like bonds, rent, standards of premises, rights of entry, damage and repairs, rent variation, eviction and termination, through education, and through compliance and enforcement measures. They are also similar in their provisions for a tribunal or body to manage and determine disputes between landlords and tenants. Additionally there is commonality in the administration of this tenancy legislation through fair trading and consumer affairs government departments in each jurisdiction.

However, the legislation may differ on the types of accommodation covered or excluded under the legislation and in the details of other rights. There are also jurisdictional differences in the types and pieces of other legislation that interact with the main residential tenancies Acts. Some of these points can be illustrated as follows:

- The *Residential Tenancies Act 1994* (Qld) (under review at the time of writing), covers houses, caravans, units, flats, townhouses, and houseboats and establishes the Residential Tenancies Authority which hears disputes. This Act applies to private and public housing rentals and to rental mobile homes. But short-term holiday rentals, boarders and lodgers, refuges, and retirement villages are not covered, and owner occupiers of mobile homes in parks are covered by the *Mobile Homes Act 1989* (Qld).

- The *Residential Tenancies Act 1987* (NSW) also covers among other things tenancies in moveable dwellings and social housing premises (public housing) and excludes boarders and lodgers, hotels, and holiday premises. The Residential Tribunal adjudicates in a range of fair trading disputes, including tenancy ones arising under the *Residential Tenancies Act*. The *Holiday Parks (Long-term Casual Occupation) Act 2002* (NSW) applies to the long-term occupants and owners of these parks.

- The *Residential Tenancies Act 1987* (WA) also covers some caravan park residential arrangements in interaction with the *Caravan Parks and Camping Grounds Act 1995* (WA), and excludes hotels, boarders and lodgers, and holiday agreements. In Western Australia tenancy disputes, depending on the amounts of money involved, may be heard before the small disputes division of the Local Court.

- The *Residential Tenancies Act 1999* (NT) applies to tenancies entered into after March 2000 in that jurisdiction but the older *Residential Tenancies Act 1979* (NT) covers tenancies agreed prior to that time. The new Northern Territory legislation covers among other things public housing tenancies, houseboats, and caravans as residences. It excludes for example holiday premises, caravans or mobile homes in caravan parks, emergency shelters, and arrangements where no rent is paid. Tenancy disputes fall within the jurisdiction of the Commissioner of Tenancies.

In relation to residential tenancies, human service workers in direct service commonly advocate with and for tenants/clients in their disputes with landlords. It is important for these workers to have a reasonable knowledge of the premises covered and the rights and obligations set out by the main Act and regulations in their jurisdictions. It is also wise to have established solid connections with the relevant administering department for the Act and the tribunal/dispute body staff. However as explained in chapter 7 on courts and tribunals, increasingly human service agencies are themselves landlords, who face disputes with their client tenants. So human service workers may find themselves in tenancy courts or tribunals as applicants or supporters on either side of the tenant/landlord divide in tenancy conflicts. All the comments made in chapter 7 on work in courts will of course apply, whether one is a landlord or tenant applicant.

Many other workers in the human services are now engaged in housing research and policy, general housing/homelessness advocacy, and housing administration and management. In these roles they may be less exposed to tribunal work but perhaps more conversant with legislative change processes and intergovernmental housing funding agreements.

Residential facilities

The state and territory residential tenancy Acts generally exclude certain premises, variously labelled, known as health, educational, disability, refuge, charitable, emergency, or nursing 'homes'. So most of the residential facilities which human service workers may operate, staff, or use for their clients fall outside of the tenancy legislation. Nonetheless these facilities are generally licensed and perhaps regulated in some ways under other regimes, too numerous to detail here. The legal regimes covering these facilities differ in who legislates, about what, for what purpose, and in monitoring and enforcement authorities, powers, and processes.

Increasingly Commonwealth legislation addressing residential facilities is directed among other things at improving service and care standards. The best and most comprehensive example of this is the *Aged Care Act 1997* (Cth) and its complementary legislation, which cover Commonwealth-funded aged care residential facilities. These facilities may be state or privately owned and they offer different levels of care but in all, residents must have been assessed as eligible for residential care. These facilities are required to operate in accordance with principles under the *Aged Care Act 1997* (Cth) (Department of Health and Ageing 2003). The Aged Care Standards and Accreditation Agency, an independent body, determines accreditation, monitors their standards of care and services, supports improvements in them, and reports to the Department of Health and Ageing on their failures to meet standards. Accredited facilities are required to meet certain standards in their management systems, in their provision of health and personal care, in their range and choice of lifestyle options, and in their physical environments. In contrast, retirement villages, which do not receive Commonwealth funding, are regulated, largely on financial matters, by specific state and territory legislation.

Some states and territories in recent times have been attempting to improve quality of care in supported community residential care facilities by legislating to licence and monitor them. For example in South Australia, both profit and not-for-profit facilities that provide residential accommodation together with personal care services are subject to the *Supported Residential Facilities Act 1992* (SA) which is administered by local government. Residents in these facilities may be frail aged, or have mental and/or physical disabilities. This Act does not cover boarding houses, in which standards of facilities and service are inconsistently licensed or regulated across Australia. In Queensland the *Residential Services (Accreditation) Act 2002* and the *Residential Services (Accommodation) Act 2002* are intended to improve quality in the residential services industry. These Acts are administered by the Residential Tenancies Authority, established under the *Residential Tenancies Act 1994* (Qld).

Some other residential facilities are subject, through funding agreements, to regulation by both state and Commonwealth levels of government. Disability facilities often fall into this category, as do for example women's and youth shelters funded under programs such as SAAP. Regulation here may operate through quite a complex web of state and Commonwealth legislation and agreements that attend in greater or lesser degrees to service and care quality, either in the legislation, regulations, or service contracts. Yet another mixed group of facilities, including child welfare, juvenile justice, and correctional facilities, is subject to state or territory legislation, traditionally more concerned with function and authority than with quality and standards of care. Here there is considerable variation across jurisdictions in what facilities may be covered and how.

All residential facilities in all jurisdictions are subject to regulatory regimes of general application, for example in occupational health and safety and in food handling. It may well be that complaint and enforcement provisions under these regimes are more powerful than those under some of the service and care quality regimes outlined above. Human service workers would do well to keep these apparently tangential but possibly effective legal enforcement options in mind when faced with inadequate residential services for their clients.

Statutory licensing and regulation of residential facilities is a complex and vexed subject, and there is debate about the cost and effectiveness of different regimes in improving quality of care. Most human service workers will never know or need to know all the details of the legislation and regulations that bind the facilities in which they work and place clients. But it is important for them to know broadly if there is a statutory framework for these facilities, if it addresses service standards, and who is the administering authority. Responsible workers do need this information so that they can engage with and utilise legal levers in their efforts to ensure or improve their own and confront others' service delivery. It is common for regulatory regimes that address service quality issues to have a developmental rather than punitive approach. Thus human service workers who use facilities covered by these regimes can enter into partnership with facility managers and regulatory authorities to help improve quality of care in residential services with less fear of their closure.

Practice question and response

Question: All this material about standards of care is pretty irrelevant in practice. It is very hard to find a residential placement for most clients and for those with complex needs it is almost impossible. What can or will a worker really do if the facility they finally get is less than adequate?

Response: It is true that places are hard to get and some residential services are not what they should be. But workers do have ethical, professional, and probably legal responsibilities to take action if their clients are not being treated appropriately. The question is more one of what action to take. Activating a relevant legislative regime may be only one of many options, perhaps one of last resort, but also one which can and must be used strategically.

Home support services

Services designed to assist aged and disabled people to remain at home, or those living in community based facilities, are increasingly important. Many have been established under the Home and Community Care Program (HACC) (Department of Health and Ageing 2003). HACC, like SAAP mentioned earlier, is a joint Commonwealth–state and territory scheme which funds targeted services and initiatives. These services are in turn expected to meet specified service standards inclusive of complaint procedures. Human service workers and clients may have some confidence in service standards in agencies funded by HACC, or at least should know the mechanisms for challenging inadequacies in quality of care. For-profit home support services are another matter altogether as they are generally not regulated, at least as to service standards. Both clients and/or workers purchasing services on their behalf must use general consumer awareness strategies in assessing service quality and contracting for services.

Key points for practice

- The human service worker whose mandate extends to involvement in issues of income support can have a very practical and involved role assisting in the resolution of difficulties and the development of a better system. Issues of advocacy and empowerment are critical here.
- Significant issues of power, confidence, and legitimacy surround this area. Workers whose clients are personally encountering the income support system will be most effective if they are both informed and proactive (Raper 1999).
- In relation to homelessness, the law is a two-edged sword. It impacts negatively on people who live largely in public spaces and it can be used as a powerful tool by and for them. Human service workers are likely to be less despondent and more effective if they appreciate this contradiction and understand how to both respond to and actively use law.

- Many residential services and some home support ones operate under legal regimes. Smart human service workers know the contours of these regimes and use them strategically as levers to demand and shape improved service quality for clients.

Some useful web sites

Income support

www.facs.gov.au/sspal/index.htm
www.centrelink.gov.au/internet/internet.nsf/filestores/ih0203b/$file/ih_0210en.pdf
www.welfarerights.org.au

Debt and finance

www.accc.gov.au
www.cclcnsw.org.au/

Homelessness

www.chp.org.au
www.shelter.net.au/
www.afho.org.au/
www.acoss.org.au/
www.facs.gov.au/
www.facs.gov.au/internet/facsinternet.nsf/aboutfacs/programs/house-saap_nav.htm

Residential aged care

www.health.gov.au/index.htm
www.ageing.health.gov.au/legislat/legindex.htm
www.agedcarenetwork.com.au/index1.htm

Residential tenancies

www.rta.qld.gov.au/
www.ocba.sa.gov.au/tenancies/
www.nt.gov.au/justice/graphpages/cba/restenanc/index.shtml

Supported accommodation

www.seniors.asn.au/Aged%20Care%20Services/SupportedResidential.htm
www.dms.dpc.vic.gov.au/sb/2001_SR/S01741.html

12

Practising with Confidence

Reaching equilibrium

Confronted with the weight of material in this book, human service workers may initially experience one of two reactions: paralysis or legalism. That is they may be overwhelmed and frozen in the face of the legal complexity of their work, or they may be stimulated, perhaps even excited into adopting a legalistic style. While each of these extremes is understandable, especially in the short-term, neither is desirable. The mature, 'professional' worker finds a balance between them and appreciates that the legal and human service dimensions of their work must be synthesised. In some situations legal factors may be paramount and a legalistic approach will be fitting. In others, interpersonal and human service intervention factors will prevail and a formalist, legal orientation will be unsuitable. In most circumstances, the appropriate approach is one that accommodates and manages the ebb and flow of different imperatives. It is this balanced perspective that the book endorses and attempts to encourage in the longer term, beyond any extreme initial reactions that it may provoke.

There are no simple or single ways of attaining this balanced perspective in human service work. Experience is certainly important but other things can be done to advance a personal sense of equilibrium. Individuals can set themselves modest professional development goals around the legal aspects of their work. It was suggested in the chapter 1 that a legal dictionary be kept handy and used for looking up unknown legal words when they appear in the course of work. Regularly reading a piece of pertinent legislation has also been recommended. It is a method of familiarising oneself with legal language. In addition it can also often help revitalise the flagging worker, as the objects of many human service–related Acts succinctly and powerfully articulate social justice principles. There are many conferences, public seminars, inservice training programs, and professional association events that canvas the legal elements of human service work. Any worker able to build some of these into their schedules will become more knowledgeable, perhaps more intrigued, and more confident about the legal dimensions of their work. The fostering of contacts within the legal profession and justice administration services has been suggested many times over in this book. There are two additional observations that may help human service workers seeking a balanced perspective. Both accentuate the vital contribution of human service knowledge and skills in complex sociolegal situations.

First, most if not all human service situations with overt legal implications are characterised by powerful human emotions. The law is commonly most apparent in acute and difficult circumstances. There may be anger, distress, fear, and confusion; there may be conflicting needs and unclear objectives; there may be miscommunication. Human service workers are theoretically, through their training and work roles, much better positioned than are lawyers to manage and unravel these human complexities. They can assess feelings and meaning and interpret these contextually. They can help people sift through emotions and events and decide what they really want. In these processes they can explore various outcomes and methods of achieving them. Their eclecticism is an asset. It is true that many lawyers are alert to these things too. Take the words of the lawyer Ford (1985, quoted in Douglas and Jones 1999, p. 214) writing for other lawyers about administrative appeals: '[B]ear in mind that a good solicitor is practical first and legalistic second: friendly negotiation and a little psychology brought to bear on the bureaucracy will solve a hundred times more cases than you will ever win by securing a place for your client in the law reports.' But lawyers are not formally trained in psychology, interpersonal, and intervention skills and their focus will necessarily always be more on legal methods and outcomes.

Human service workers are well placed to reduce the emotional heat in situations before critical decisions are made. Active listening through paraphrasing, reflection, and clarification might well defuse feelings of outrage and negate demand for legal action. Similarly, situations that appear on their face to be relatively innocuous may have undercurrents that suggest legal scrutiny. In these matters of obscure human feelings and dynamics, proficient human service workers can apply to good effect their expertise in assessment, goal setting, and action planning. Thus human service workers do not need to enter relationships in the legal arena as inferior partners. They bring essential skills, knowledge, and methods that are increasingly appreciated, now often appropriated, by the legal system. Awareness of this expertise can bolster human service worker confidence in reciprocal interactions with the law and legal/justice staff. Human service workers who do not understand or who doubt their own knowledge and skills are not in a strong position to connect with the law. Perhaps these individuals are more prone to paralysis in the face of legal questions and could start an unlocking process by auditing their own professional strengths. Those who have human service professional proficiency and know the scope and power of it are well placed to engage and contribute strongly in the legal arena.

The second and related observation concerns the limitations of law in dealing with social problems. It is well known that the law is both imperfect and does not provide 'solutions to the dilemmas of social work [but that it] is in fact integral to those dilemmas' (Braye and Preston-Shoot 1997, p. 49). In the words of Brayne and Broadbent (2002, p. 64) law is a uniquely 'defining mandate' for social work practice but also 'an insufficient mandate to reflect the complexity both of practice and of service users' lives'. It has been noted many times through this book and more extensively in other places, that the law is commonly inelastic in its response to diverse human circumstances and needs. So those human service workers who might incline towards an overly legalistic persona must be cautious. They risk setting an agenda for themselves and others in their work that is unrealistic for a number of reasons. First, access to legal aid is diminishing; second, the experience of legal processes themselves can be a scarring ordeal; and third, the law itself may be often deficient. There are human service situations, many outlined in this book, in which there is little relevant law, where the application of law is unlikely to help, or where the law is confused or conflicting. In other circumstances there may be plenty of applicable law but a legal approach may be inflammatory and damaging to the people involved, their relationships, and their well-being in the longer term.

In summary the human services may have more to bring to a partnership with law than is commonly realised. Any understanding and management of diverse and complicated human situations by the law and the legal system operating unilaterally will be incomplete.

Back to the beginning

It has been asserted throughout this book and visually in figure 2.1 that law is ever-present in human service life. It looms large at times, and in other places and circumstances it has a low profile, but it is always there. In fact the law and the human services are two interrelated components of a larger system as shown in figure 3.1. There must be engagement with the legal system for human services to be planned, organised, staffed, delivered, and evaluated. And engagement does not imply uncritical or passive acceptance. It means learning, using, appropriating, applying, critiquing, sometimes despairing, and sometimes working for change. It is hoped that human service workers who use this book might better see into the opaque and formidable monolith that the law often is for them. As they make out shapes and patterns they may begin to appreciate how they can harness, confine, engage with, or liberate the law across the full span of their decision-making from the minutiae of daily service delivery through to major questions of human rights.

In chapter 1 reference was made to superior human service workers. This elitist phrasing may cause discomfort in the human services but it was and is used deliberately to indicate that they are workers who have the courage to extend and transcend traditional professional and cultural barriers. They are legally literate, they have confidence in their reciprocal relationships with legal and justice systems, and their decision-making incorporates and knits together human service, legal, and other imperatives as necessary. Thus they are workers whose knowledge and skills are rounded. Their practice is richer, more versatile, and more empowered. Their sense of professional satisfaction and their self-esteem is likely to be stronger. These capable workers help build human service agencies that are also attuned to legal imperatives. In turn agencies and their managers have an even greater responsibility to nurture and support their superior workers and to challenge and assist their less advanced ones.

Legally literate human service agencies and workers who make informed and balanced decisions are not created overnight. They evolve over time through conscious processes of exploration, learning, and commitment. It is hoped that this book might stimulate and/or enhance these processes, and in so doing contribute to better human service practice.

Appendix 1—
Finding and Reading Law

This appendix provides a very brief introduction to locating and reading legislation and case law. It is not intended to replace the excellent discussion of these activities in introductory books such as Gifford and Gifford's *How to Understand an Act of Parliament* (Gifford and Gifford 1994) but it may encourage readers to refresh or begin their skill development in working with the law. Several facts must be stated at the outset:

- First, both cases and legislation are available in electronic form and in hard copy, however electronic copies are not official or authorised, and neither are some hard copy versions. It may be important to know the 'official' status of the version accessed, whichever format is used. The status will be declared within the document or report volume itself.
- Second, it is important to check the currency of the version of any law accessed. Official parliamentary web sites have the most up-to-date versions of legislation.
- Third, the structural information provided below relates to hard copy versions of cases and legislation. Electronic versions are necessarily set out slightly differently, for example using hyperlinks and more headings for each individual page within the document.
- Fourth, it is lawyers and ultimately courts who interpret law. Human service readers should read legislation and cases as intelligent laypeople but they will not normally be able to, nor expected to, interpret the legal meaning and implications of legislation and cases.

How to find an Act of Parliament

There are several ways of locating an Act of Parliament. Hard copies of state/territory legislation are generally available in most public and university libraries, or may be purchased through state/territory government bookshops. Electronic copies are principally kept on three types of web sites. The main two are the parliamentary web site of each government and free web sites designed to enable the general public to access legislation and case law, such as Austlii and Scaleplus. Links to these have been provided in many chapters. Finally, some industry web sites have legislation pertinent to that area uploaded on the web site.

How to read an Act of Parliament

Below are outlined some of the main structural features of an Act of Parliament.

Titles

The *short title* of an Act essentially constitutes the name by which it is commonly known, and this is stipulated at the very beginning of the Act itself. Note that the year in which the Act was made forms part of its short title. As seen throughout this book, when written reference is made to an Act (known as a citation), the short title is presented in italics, and the jurisdiction of the Act, either the particular state/territory or Commonwealth, is abbreviated in parentheses at the end of the short title.

The *long title* is set out prior to the sections of each Act and fulfils an introductory function. In part, it reflects the purpose for which the Act was created, for example the long title of the *Racial Hatred Act 1995* (Cth) is 'An Act to prohibit certain conduct involving the hatred of other people on the ground of race, colour or national or ethnic origin, and for related purposes'. Note that long titles are no longer used in Victorian Acts.

Summary of Provisions

The main body of information is provided within an Act of Parliament under sections and subsections. These sections are listed within an index, often called the *summary of provisions*. The first few sections commonly specify important 'administrative' preliminary information such as the appropriate title of the Act itself, and background as to its specific purpose and aims. Some Acts include this administrative information prior to enumerating sections, using those for the body of the Act.

Objects

More information concerning the broader aims of an Act are set out quite specifically as the *object(s) of the Act* with varying levels of detail, for example the *Disability Services Act 1986* (Cth) provides in s 3:

3. (1) The objects of this Act are:

   (a) to replace provisions of the *Handicapped Persons Assistance Act 1974*, and of Part VIII of the *Social Security Act 1947*, with provisions that are more flexible and more responsive to the needs and aspirations of persons with disabilities;

(b) to assist persons with disabilities to receive services necessary to enable them to work towards full participation as members of the community;

(c) to promote services provided to persons with disabilities that:

    (i) assist persons with disabilities to integrate in the community, and complement services available generally to persons in the community;

    (ii) assist persons with disabilities to achieve positive outcomes, such as increased independence, employment opportunities and integration in the community; and

    (iii) are provided in ways that promote in the community a positive image of persons with disabilities and enhance their self-esteem;

(d) to ensure that the outcomes achieved by persons with disabilities by the provision of services for them are taken into account in the granting of financial assistance for the provision of such services;

(e) to encourage innovation in the provision of services for persons with disabilities; and

(f) to assist in achieving positive outcomes, such as increased independence, employment opportunities and integration in the community, for persons with disabilities who are of working age by the provision of comprehensive rehabilitation services.

The section goes on to provide:

(2) In construing the objects and in administering this Act, due regard must be had to:

(a) the limited resources available to provide services and programs under this Act; and

(b) the need to consider equity and merit in accessing those resources.

Sections

The sections of the Act essentially contain the body of law enacted by each particular piece of legislation. A short heading describing the content of each section is listed above it, but the sections themselves are set out simply, in numerical order and in bold print. For example, s 9(1) of the *Racial Discrimination Act 1975* (Cth) is set out as follows:

Racial discrimination to be unlawful

9. (1) It is unlawful for a person to do any act involving a distinction, exclusion, restriction or preference based on race, colour, descent or national or ethnic origin which has the purpose or effect of nullifying or impairing the recognition, enjoyment or exercise, on an equal footing, of any human right or fundamental freedom in the political, economic, social, cultural or any other field of public life.

Parts

Each Act is divided into parts. Their precise nature varies depending on the specific purpose of the Act, however some deal with preliminary matters, others set up any necessary bodies or structures that will be involved in implementing the Act, some deal with enforcement of the Act. Additionally, all Acts have an *interpretation* section setting out the definitions of terminology used within the Act and a *legislative history* at the back, which sets out what amendments have been made to the Act.

How to find cases

Cases can be located either in hard copy or electronically. Hard copies of cases are contained in bound volumes known as *reports* which can be found in most university libraries. Not all cases are included in reports, but only those significant for reasons of precedent. This is what is meant when cases are distinguished as 'reported' or 'unreported'. The reports are variously titled depending on either the jurisdiction or the subject matter of the cases. Each jurisdiction has at least one report, and if more than one, then only one will be designated as the 'official' or 'authorised' version; for example, High Court cases are reported officially in the Commonwealth Law Reports. Additionally, some reports focus on particular types of cases, such as family, intellectual property, motor vehicle, or other law; for example, there are the Australian Torts Reports and the South Australian Industrial Reports.

Understanding case citations

Human service workers who wish to find a case will commonly only know its name, but all cases have both a name and a *citation*. The citation is essentially a reference describing where the case is reported, and finding the citation is the first step to locating a case in hard copy. A *case citator* is a type of index used in libraries to find the citation of a case if it is unknown. Citations contain reference to the report in which the case is found, by title, volume number (if any), and year, and also the specific page at which the case begins. Thus when locating particular cases it is important to first identify the report in which it is contained.

Each report is given an official abbreviation. For example, the Victorian Law Reports are abbreviated to VLR, South Australian State Reports to SASR, Commonwealth Law Reports to CLR. All libraries that hold volumes of reports provide lists of those reports and their corresponding abbreviations, so it is perfectly possible to locate a case despite the fact that the citation itself makes no sense at all to the worker!

Consider the following citation of a famous negligence case: *Rogers v Whitaker* (1992) 175 CLR 479. Clearly the year is 1992. The first number following the year denotes the volume number of the report, here volume 175. Next is the abbreviation of the report itself, the Commonwealth Law Reports. The final number represents the page number of the report at which the case is located.

Finding cases electronically

The main public web site containing full electronic versions of both reported and many unreported cases is run by the Australasian Legal Information Institute, or Austlii. Cases on Austlii are located by searching using the jurisdiction and/or title, not by citation. This can equate to an easier search, especially where the citation is not known, however care must be taken to use correct spelling of names, and to ensure that the correct case is found, given that some may appear to have the same name. Austlii's databases are essentially divided first by jurisdiction, and then by subject matter (i.e. either cases or legislation). Cases can be located alphabetically by title or a search for the case title can be performed.

Reading cases

A case report contains the facts, the judgment[s], and the verdict given in the particular case. It will summarise the important facts of the case, set out the relevant law, and then discuss the arguments made by each party in the case. It will also state and explain the decision. For the most part, reading cases is not something that human service workers spend a great deal of time doing, and it only occurs on a needs or interest basis. However, it is important that human service workers are at least confident enough to find and read a case if the need arises.

All cases contain certain information and follow essentially the same structure whether they are in electronic or hard copy form. To begin with the case name sets out the parties involved. If it is private litigation, both parties' surnames will be used. A criminal case commonly uses either 'The Queen' or 'R' to indicate that the state/territory or Commonwealth is a party to the case, or perhaps 'Police' or 'DPP' (Director of Public Prosecutions). An individual government may of course be a party in its own right. For example, a criminal injuries compensation payment is sought directly from the government (which may or may not recover some or all of the payment from the perpetrator at a later date). The name of the person who began the action (or case) occurs first, followed by the name of the person against whom it was brought, for example, *Kennedy v Richards*, or *R v Richards*. If Richards were to lose the case and then to bring an appeal against the decision, this would begin a new case, and thus it would be called *Richards v R*, or *Richards v Kennedy*.

The case report sets out basic information such as the court or tribunal in which it was heard, the names of any lawyers involved, and importantly, who heard the case. This varies of course depending on the circumstances. It may be one or more tribunal members, judges, a magistrate, and so on. In reported judgments and increasingly in electronic copies, the text then contains a summary of what the case is about and what the verdict was, to make reading the case easier. Following this, the actual judgments in the case are set out. The number of these depends on the nature of the case, and how much agreement there was in reaching the verdict. Where more than one person heard the case and the verdict is not unanimous but by majority, the minority judgments are recorded last.

References

Abbott, P. and C. Wallace (1998). Health visiting, social work, nursing and midwifery: a history. *The Sociology of the Caring Professions*. P. Abbott and L. Meerabeau. London, UCL Press: 20–53.

Albert, R. (2000). *Law and Social Work Practice*. New York, Springer Publishing Company.

Alder, C. and J. Wundersitz (eds) (1994). *Family Conferencing and Juvenile Justice: the Way Forward or Misplaced Optimism?* Canberra, Australian Institute of Criminology.

Alexander, R. (1999). 'Family law in the future.' *Alternative Law Journal* 24(3): 112–16, 126.

Alexander, R. (2002). *Domestic Violence in Australia: the Legal Response*. 3rd edn. Sydney, Federation Press.

Allars, M. (1990). *Introduction to Australian Administrative Law*. Sydney, Butterworths.

Allsop, J. and M. Saks (2003). *Regulating the Health Professions*. London, Sage.

American Psychological Association (1993). Record Keeping Guidelines. www.apa.org/practice/recordkeeping.html. Accessed 18th March 2003.

Ames, N. (1999). 'Social work recording: a new look at an old issue. *Journal of Social Work Education* 35(2): 227–37.

Ardagh, A. (1999). *Administrative Law*. 2nd edn. Sydney, LBC Information Services.

Astor, H. and C. Chinkin (1992). *Dispute Resolution in Australia*. Sydney, Butterworths.

Australian Association of Social Workers (1999). *Code of Ethics*. AASW. Canberra.

Australian Association of Social Workers (2003). Become a Member: Indemnity and insurance. www.aasw.asn.au/becomeamember/aaswmembership/indemnity.htm. Accessed 8th May 2003.

Australian Competition and Consumer Commission (1999). *Undue Harassment and Coercion in Debt Collection*. Australian Competition and Consumer Commission. Canberra. Section 60 Report.

Australian Institute of Criminology (2002). *Australian Crime: Facts and Figures 2002*. Australian Institute of Criminology. Canberra.

Australian Institute of Health and Welfare (2002). *Child Protection Australia 2001–02: First National Results*. Child Welfare Series No. 31.

Australian Institute of Welfare and Community Workers (Undated). *Code of Ethics*. www.aiwcw.org.au/codeOfEthics.html. Accessed 20th March 2003.

Australian Law Reform Commission (1986). *The Recognition of Aboriginal Customary Laws*. AGPS. Canberra. Report No. 31.

Australian Law Reform Commission (1996). *Making Rights Count—Services for People with a Disability*. Australian Government Publishing Service. Canberra. Report No. 79.

Australian Law Reform Commission (1997). *Seen and Heard: Priority for Children in the Legal Process*. Australian Law Reform Commission. Canberra. Report No. 84.

Australian Psychological Society Ltd (2002). *Code of Ethics*. Melbourne.

Australian Society of Rehabilitation Counsellors (Undated). *Code of Ethics*. ASORC.

Bacon, R. (2002). 'Rewriting the social contract? The SSAT, the AAT and the contracting out of employment services.' *Federal Law Review* 30: 39–68.

Bailey, P. and A. Devereux (1998). The operation of anti-discrimination laws in Australia. *Human Rights in Australia*. D. Kinley. Sydney, Federation Press: 292–318.

Bakhtiyari v Australia, Communication No. 1069/2002, UN Doc CCPR/C/79/D/1069/2002 29 October 2003.

Ball, C. and A. McDonald (2002). *Law for Social Workers*. Aldershot, Ashgate.

Barker, R. and D. Branson (2000). *Forensic Social Work: Legal Aspects of Professional Practice*. 2nd edn. New York, Haworth Press.

Baron, A. (2003). 'Helping victims receive compensation.' *Law Society Journal* (June): 50–5.

Bar-On, A. (1995). 'Social workers and case management.' *Asia Pacific Journal of Social Work* 5(1): 63–78.

Barrett, G. (1999). '"Stop it daddy..."' *InPsych* (December): 27–30.

Bates, F., J. B. Blackwood, et al. (1996). *The Australian Social Worker and the Law.* 4th edn. Sydney, Lawbook Information Services.

Blaauw, E., L. Sheridan, et al. (2002). 'Designing anti-stalking legislation on the basis of victims' experiences and psychopathology.' *Psychiatry, Psychology and Law* 9(2): 136–45.

Blagg, H. (1997). 'A just measure of shame? Aboriginal youth and conferencing in Australia.' *The British Journal of Criminology* 27(4): 481–501.

Blencowe, S., C. Sampford, et al. (1998). Introduction. *Justice for People with Disabilities: Legal and Institutional Issues.* M. Hauritz, C. Sampford, and S. Blencowe. Sydney, Federation Press: xv–xxiii.

Blonder, I. (1996). Blowing the whistle. *Codes of Ethics and the Professions.* M. Coady and S. Bloch. Melbourne, Melbourne University Press: 166–90.

Booth, M. (2003). 'Centrelink preclusion periods: interpreting the 50% rule.' *Plaintiff* 55(February): 42–4.

Brading, R. (2003). 'Funding financial counselling.' *New Directions in Bankruptcy* 13(1): 14–15.

Braithwaite, J. (1996). 'Restorative justice and a better future.' *Dalhousie Review* 76(1): 9–32.

Braithwaite, J. (1997). 'Conferencing and plurality: reply to Blagg.' *The British Journal of Criminology* 37(4): 502–6.

Braithwaite, J. (2002). *Restorative justice and responsive regulation.* New York, Oxford University Press.

Brammer, A. (2003). *Social Work Law.* Edinburgh Gate, Pearson Education.

Braye, S. and M. Preston-Shoot (1997). *Practising Social Work Law.* 2nd edn. London, Macmillan.

Braye, S. and M. Preston-Shoot (2001). Social work practice and accountability. *The Law and Social Work: Contemporary Issues for Practice.* L.-A. Cull and J. Roche. Houndmills Basingstoke, Palgrave: 43–53.

Brayne, H. and G. Broadbent (2002). *Legal Materials for Social Workers.* Oxford, Oxford University Press.

Brayne, H. and H. Carr (2003). *Law for Social Workers.* 8th edn. Oxford, Oxford University Press.

Breckenridge, J. (2002). The socio-legal relationship in child sexual assault. *In the Shadow of the Law: The Legal Context of Social Work Practice.* P. Swain. Sydney, Federation Press: 74–89.

Bronitt, S. and B. McSherry (2001). *Principles of Criminal Law*. Sydney, LBC Information Services.

Brophy, L., J. Campbell, et al. (2003). 'Dilemmas in the case manager's role: implementing involuntary treatment in the community.' *Psychiatry, Psychology and Law* 10(1): 154–63.

Brown, T., R. Sheehan, et al. (2001). 'A new case management program involving an inter-organisational collaboration between state and federal socio-legal systems.' *Case Management Society of Australia* 3(2): 3–8.

Bull, K. (2003). 'Regulation of debt collectors.' *Proctor* (January/February): 12–13.

Buys, N. and E. Kendall (1998). 'Stress and burnout among rehabilitation counsellors within the context of insurance-based rehabilitation: an institutional-level analysis.' *Australian Journal of Rehabilitation Counselling* 4(1): 1–12.

Carlton, A.-L. (2002). Occupational regulation of complementary medicine practitioners. *Crime in the Professions*. R. Smith. Aldershot, Ashgate: 185–209.

Carney, T. (2000). Protection, populism and citizenship. *Explorations on Law and Disability in Australia*. M. Jones and L. A. Basser Marks. Sydney, Federation Press: 54–76.

Carney, T. (2003). 'Mental health law in postmodern society: time for a new paradigm.' *Psychiatry, Psychology and Law* 10(1): 12–32.

Carrington, K. and J. Phillips (2003). *Domestic Violence in Australia—An Overview of the Issues*. Department of the Parliamentary Library. E brief www.aph.gov.au/library/intguide/SP/Dom-violence.htm Accessed 18th August 2003.

Carson, D. (1990). *Professionals and the Courts*. Birmingham, Venture.

Carson, P. (2002). 'Centrelink resists subpoenas on basis of privacy.' *Law Society Journal* (October): 30.

Carvan, J. (1996). *Social and Welfare Law*. Sydney, Butterworths.

Carvan, J. (2002). *Understanding the Australian Legal System*. 4th edn. Sydney, Lawbook Co.

CCH Australia Limited (2002). *Australian Master Business Guide*. Sydney, CCH.

Centrelink (2004). *Centrelink Information; A Guide to Payments and Services 2003–2004*.

Centrelink (2002). Centrelink Annual Report 2001–2002. www.centrelink.gov.au/internet/internet.nsf/ar0102/index.htm. Accessed September 14th 2003.

Chappenden, W. J. (1982). *Joske's Law and Procedure at Meetings in Australia*. 7th edn. Sydney, Law Book Company.

Charlesworth, S. (1993). Social workers as experts. *Expert Evidence*. I. Freckleton and H. Selby. Sydney, Law Book Company: 6-2203–6-2354.

Chisholm, R. (1997). 'Court reports.' *InPsych* (April): 9–11.

Clark, G. (2002). 'Not just payback: indigenous customary law.' *Reform* 80: 5–10.

Coady, M. (2002). The role of codes of ethics in preventing professional crime. *Crime in the Professions*. R. Smith. Aldershot, Ashgate: 93–108.

Cole, K. (1996). Introduction. *Administrative Law and Public Administration: Form vs Substance*. K. Cole. Canberra, Australian Institute of Administrative Law Inc.: ix–xvii.

Committee on the Health Care Complaints Commission (2002). *Report on Mandatory Reporting of Medical Negligence*. Parliament of New South Wales. Sydney.

Commonwealth Office of the Status of Women (1995). *Community Attitudes to Violence Against Women*. ANOP Research Services. Sydney.

Commonwealth Office of the Status of Women (2001). *Women in Australia 2001*. Commonwealth of Australia. Canberra.

Commonwealth Treasury (Ipp Report) (2002). Review of the Law of Negligence. http://revofneg.treasury.gov.au/content/Report2/PDF/Law_Neg_Final.pdf. Accessed 1st April 2003.

Connolly, M. (ed.) (2001). *New Zealand Social Work: Context and Practice*. Auckland, Oxford University Press.

Cook, B., F. David, et al. (1999). *Victims' Needs, Victims' Rights: Programs and Policies for Victims of Crime in Australia*. Australian Institute of Criminology. Canberra. Research and Public Policy Series No. 19.

Cook, C., R. Creyke, R. Geddes, and I. Holloway (2001). *Laying Down the Law*. 5th edn. Sydney, Butterworths.

Cooper, J. (1991). 'What is legal competence?' *Modern Law Review* 54(1): 112–21.

Cordon, J. and M. Preston-Shoot (1987). *Contracts in social work*. Vermont, USA, Gower Publishing Company.

Cossins, A. (2002). 'The hearsay rule and delayed complaints of child sexual abuse: the law and the evidence.' *Psychiatry, Psychology and Law* 9(2): 163–76.

Creighton, B. and A. Stewart (2000). *Labour Law: An Introduction*. 3rd edn. Sydney, Federation Press.

Criminal Justice Commission (1995). *Protecting Public Sector Whistleblowers—A Statutory Responsibility*. Brisbane. Issue Paper Series (2) 1.

Crock, M. and B. Saul (2002). *Future Seekers: Refugees and the Law in Australia*. Sydney, Federation Press.

Cull, L.-A. and J. Roche (eds) (2001). *The Law and Social Work: Contemporary Issues for Practice*. Houndmills Basingstoke, Palgrave.

Daly, K. and H. Hayes (2001). *Restorative Justice and Conferencing in Australia*. Australian Institute of Criminology. Canberra. Trends and Issues in Criminal Justice No. 186.

Daniel, A. (1998). *Scapegoats for a Profession*. Amsterdam, Harwood.

Davidson, G. (2002). Dealing with subpoenas: advice for APS members.' *InPsych* (October): 31–5.

Davis, L. (1998). Rights replacing needs. *Justice for People with Disabilities: Legal and Institutional Issues*. M. Hauritz, C. Sampford, and S. Blencowe. Sydney, Federation Press: 15–27.

De Maria, W. (1996). 'The welfare whistleblower: in praise of troublesome people.' *Australian Social Work* 49(3): 15–24.

Delaney, S. (2003). 'An optimally rights recognising Mental Health Tribunal— What can be learned from Australian jurisdictions.' *Psychiatry, Psychology and Law* 10(1): 71–84.

Department of Family and Community Services (2003). SAAP—the Supported Accommodation Assistance program. www.facs.gov.au/internet/facsinternet.nsf/aboutfacs/programs/house-saap_nav.htm. Accessed 19th November 2003.

Department of Health and Ageing (2003). Home and Community Care. www.hacc.health.gov.au/abouthacc.htm. Accessed 19th November 2003.

Department of Health and Ageing (2003). Residential Care. www.ageing.health.gov.au/rescare/index.htm. Accessed 19th November 2003.

Department of Human Services (2003). *Proposal to Develop a Single Registration Act for Specified Health Practitioners*. Department of Human Services. Adelaide. Discussion Paper.

Department of Justice (2002). *Report of the Evaluation of the First Six Months of the Operation of the Restraining Orders Act 1997*. Ministry of Justice. Perth.

Devereux, J. (2002). *Australian Medical Law*. 2nd edn. Sydney, Cavendish Publishing.

Douglas, R. and M. Jones (1999). *Administrative Law: Commentary and Materials*. 3rd edn. Sydney, Federation Press.

Downey, C. (2001). 'Shifting models of accountability: the consequences for administrative law in the rise of contractualism in Social Security.' *AIAL Forum* 30(September): 28–37.

Dyer, C. (2003). 'Judges rule that children can sue for wrongful diagnosis of abuse.' *British Medical Journal* 327(9th August): 305.

Eastwood, C. (2003). *The Experiences of Child Complainants of Sexual Abuse in the Criminal Justice System.* Australian Institute of Criminology. Canberra. Trends and Issues in Crime and Criminal Justice No. 250.

Family and Community Services (Undated). *Reporting Child Abuse and Neglect: Mandated Notification Guidelines.* Adelaide.

Family Law Council (2002). *Family Law and Child Protection: Final Report.* Family Law Council. Canberra.

Field, C. (2002). 'Pay day lending: an exploitative market practice.' *Alternative Law Journal* 27(1): 36–41.

Flynn, M. and R. LaForgia (2002). 'Australia's Pacific solution to asylum seekers.' *LawAsia Journal*: 31–43.

Forbes, J. R. S. (2002). *Justice in Tribunals.* Sydney, Federation Press.

Forster, C. (2002). 'The failure of criminal injuries compensation schemes for victims of intra-familial abuse: the example of Queensland.' *Torts Law Journal* 10(2): 143–66.

Franklin, J., D. Gibson, et al. (1996). 'Trends in the demand for psychology graduates.' *Australian Psychologist* 31(2): 138–43.

Freiberg, A. (2002). 'Drug courts.' *Alternative Law Journal* 27(6): 282–6.

Gale, F., N. Naffine, et al. (eds) (1993). *Juvenile Justice: Debating the Issues.* Sydney, Allen & Unwin.

Gardham, J. and R. Owens (2001). 'The border protection legislative package.' *Law Society Bulletin (SA)* 23(11): 30–2.

Gardner, J. (2000). Mental illness—freedom and treatment. *Explorations on Law and Disability in Australia.* M. Jones and L. A. Basser Marks. Sydney, Federation Press. Vol. 17: 120–46.

Gelsthorpe, L. and N. Padfield (2003). Introduction. *Exercising Discretion: Decision-Making in the Criminal Justice System and Beyond.* L. Gelsthorpe and N. Padfield. Cullompton: Devon, Willan Publishing: 1–28.

General Social Care Council (2003). Standards: The Social Care Register. www.gscc.org.uk/care_register.htm. Accessed 25th May 2003.

Germov, R. (2003). *Refugee Law in Australia.* Melbourne, Oxford University Press.

Gibson, A. and D. Fraser (1999). *Commercial Law*. 3rd edn. Melbourne, Addison Wesley Longman.

Gibson, A. and I. Kelsen (1993). *Essentials of Australian Business Law*. 4th edn. Melbourne, Longman Cheshire.

Gifford, D. J. and K. H. Gifford (1994). *How to Understand an Act of Parliament*. 8th edn. Sydney, Law Book Company.

Goldie, C. (2003). 'Rights versus welfare.' *Alternative Law Journal* 28(3): 132–5.

Graycar, R. and J. Morgan (2002). *The Hidden Gender of Law*. Sydney, Federation Press.

Gursansky, D., J. Harvey, et al. (2003). *Case Management: Policy, Practice and Professional Business*. Sydney, Allen & Unwin; New York, Columbia University Press.

Gursansky, D. and R. Kennedy (1998). 'Discourses of case management: a labour market program analysis.' *The Australian Journal of Career Development* 7(2): 17–21.

Guthrie, R. (2002). 'Illegal contracts: impropriety, immigrants and impairment in employment law.' *Alternative Law Journal* 27(3): 116–20, 132.

Hacker, S. (1999). 'Prescription vs. litigation: doctors and lawyers—pervasive paradigms and clashing cultures.' *Psychiatry, Psychology and Law* 6(1): 5–11.

Harries, M. and M. Clare (2002). *Mandatory Reporting of Child Abuse: Evidence and Options*. University of WA. Perth.

Hawkins, J. W., N. W. Veeder, et al. (1998). *Nurse Social Worker Collaboration in Managed Care: a Model of Community Case Management*. New York, Springer Publishing Company.

Healy, B. and L. Brophy (2002). Law, psychiatry and social work. *In the Shadow of the Law: The Legal Context of Social Work Practice*. P. Swain. Sydney, Federation Press: 230–43.

Hodgkinson, T. and L. Scarman (1990). *Expert Evidence: Law and Practice*. London, Sweet & Maxwell.

Hogg, R. and D. Brown (1998). *Rethinking Law and Order*. Sydney, Pluto Press.

Holloway, K. and A. Grounds (2003). Discretion and the release of mentally disordered offenders. *Exercising Discretion: Decision-making in the Criminal Justice System and Beyond*. L. Gelsthorpe and N. Padfield. Cullompton: Devon, Willan Publishing: 139–63.

Howells, K. and A. Day (1999). *The Rehabilitation of Offenders: International Perspectives Applied to Australian Correctional Systems*. Australian Institute of Criminology. Canberra. Trends and Issues in Crime and Criminal Justice No. 112.

Hulls, R. (2002). 'Koori courts.' *Alternative Law Journal* 27(4): 188.

Human Rights and Equal Opportunity Commission (2004). *National Inquiry into Children in Immigration Detention Report—A Last Resort?* Sydney.

Hunt, G. and D. Campbell (1998). Social workers speak out. *Whistleblowing in the Social Services*. G. Hunt. London, Arnold: 147–64.

Jackson, R., J. Powell et al. (eds) (1992). *Professional Negligence*. 3rd edn. London, Sweet & Maxwell.

Jackson, M. (2001). *Hughes on Data Protection in Australia*. 2nd edn. Sydney, Lawbook Co.

Jebb, B. (2003). E-mail Policies—Weighing up the Legal Risks. www.cch.com.au/fe_news.asp?document_id=43470&topic_code=9category. Accessed 31st October 2003.

Johns, P. (2003). 'Crimes compensation: three approaches to a common purpose.' *Plaintiff* 58(August): 20–4.

Johnstone, R. (1997). *Occupational Health and Safety Law and Policy*. Sydney, LBC Information Services.

Jones, M. and L. A. Basser Marks (eds) (2000). Law in Context. *Explorations on Law and Disability in Australia*. Sydney, Federation Press.

Jones, M. and L. A. Basser Marks (2000). Valuing people through law—whatever happened to Marion? *Explorations on Law and Disability in Australia*. M. Jones and L. A. Basser Marks. Sydney, Federation Press: 147–80.

Jupp, J. (2003). 'There has to be a better way: a long term refugee strategy.' *ARENA* 65(June/July): 1–12.

Kagle, J. (1991). *Social Work Records*. 2nd edn. Belmont CA, Wadsworth.

Kane, M., M. K. Houston-Vega, et al. (2002). 'Documentation in managed care: challenges for social work education.' *Journal of Teaching in Social Work* 22(1/2): 199–212.

Katter, N. (1999). *Duty of Care in Australia*. Sydney, LBC Information Services.

Kelly, G. (1998). 'Editorial: patient data, confidentiality and electronics.' *British Medical Journal* 316(7th March): 718–19.

Kennedy, R. and J. Harvey (2001). 'Advertised jobs in the human services: advice to prospective employees.' *Australian Journal of Career Development* 10(2): 28–31.

Kenny, M. (2003). 'Terrorism & exclusion under the refugee convention.' *Reform* 82(Autumn): 37–42, 71.

King, M. (2003). 'Applying therapeutic jurisprudence from the bench: challenges and opportunities.' *Alternative Law Journal* 28(4): 172–5.

King, R., P. Yellowlees, et al. (2002). 'Psychologists as mental health case managers.' *Australian Psychologist* 37(2): 118–22.

Lang, A. (1998). *Horsley's Meetings—Procedure, Law and Practice*. 4th edn. Sydney, Butterworths.

Law Reform Commission (2002). Discussion Paper 45 (2002)—Apprehended Violence Orders: Part 15A of the Crimes Act. www.lawlink.nsw.gov.au/lrc.nsf/pages/dp45chp1. Accessed 22nd March 2003.

Layton, R. (2003). *Our Best Investment: A State Plan to Protect and Advance the Interests of Children*. South Australian Department of Human Services. Adelaide. Child Protection Review.

Lee, G. (2001). 'Compensation preclusion periods—the effect of the GST and other recent developments.' *Proctor* (November): 20–1.

Legal Services Commission of South Australia (1999). *The Law Handbook*. 4th edn. Adelaide, Legal Services Commission of South Australia.

Limerick, M. (2002). 'Indigenous community justice groups: the Queensland experience.' *Reform* 80: 15–21.

Lipsky, M. (1980). *Street-Level Bureaucracy: Dilemmas of the individual in public services*. New York, Russell Sage Foundation.

Loevinger, L. (1992). 'Science and legal rules of evidence. A review of Galileo's Revenge: Junk Science in the Court Room by Peter Huber.' *Jurimetrics Journal* 32(Spring): 487–502.

Lymbery, M. (1998). 'Care management and professional autonomy: the impact of community care legislation on social work with older people.' *The British Journal of Social Work* 28(6): 863–78.

Lynch, P. (2002). 'Begging for change: homelessness and the law.' *Melbourne University Law Review* 26: 690–706.

Lynch, P. (2003). 'From "cause" to "solution": using the law to respond to homelessness.' *Alternative Law Journal* 28(3): 127–31.

Mack, K. and S. Anleu (1998). 'Reform of pre-trial criminal procedure: guilty pleas.' *Criminal Law Journal* 22(5): 263–76.

Makkai, T. and K. Veraar (2003). *Final Report on the South East Queensland Drug Court*. Australian Institute of Criminology. Canberra. Technical and Background Paper Series No. 6.

Mann, S. (2003). 'Tort law reform.' *Alternative Law Journal* 28(5): 216–24.

Martin, M. (2000). *Meaningful work: rethinking professional ethics.* New York, Oxford University Press.

McBride, N. and M. Tunnecliffe (2001). *Risky Practices: a Counsellor's Guide to Risk Management in Private Practice.* Palmyra WA, Bayside Books.

McCullough, S. (2002). 'Aged care: a Victorian perspective on complaints handling and the enforcement of consumer rights.' *Alternative Law Journal* 27(2): 57–67.

McDonald, M. and P. Slaytor (2002). Legal and ethical dilemmas in post adoption practice. *In the Shadow of the Law: The Legal Context of Social Work Practice.* P. Swain. Sydney, Federation Press: 109–19.

McGillivray, J. and B. Waterman (2003). 'Knowledge and attitudes of lawyers regarding offenders with intellectual disability.' *Psychiatry, Psychology and Law* 10(1): 244–53.

McGlone, D. (2003). 'Drug courts—a departure from adversarial justice.' *Alternative Law Journal* 28(3): 136–40.

McMahon, M. (1992). 'Dangerousness, confidentiality and the duty to report.' *Australian Psychologist* 27(1): 12–16.

McMahon, M. (1997). 'Criminalising professional misconduct: legislative regulation of psychotherapist–patient sex.' *Psychiatry, Psychology and Law* 4(2): 177–93.

McMahon, M. (1998). 'Confidentiality and disclosure of crime related information.' *InPsych* (February): 12–13.

McMillan, J. and N. Williams (1998). Administrative law and human rights. *Human Rights in Australian Law.* D. Kinley. Sydney, Federation Press: 63–90.

McRae, H., G. Nettheim, et al. (2003). *Indigenous Legal issues: Commentary and Materials.* 3rd edn. Sydney, Thomson Lawbook Co.

McSherry, B. (2001). 'Confidentiality of psychiatric and psychological communications: the public interest exception.' *Psychiatry, Psychology and Law* 8(1): 12–22.

Mendelsohn, O. and L. Maher (eds) (1994). Law in Context. *Courts, Tribunals and New Approaches to Justice.* Melbourne, La Trobe University Press.

Mental Health Council of Australia (2003). '*Out of Hospital, Out of Mind'.* Mental Health Council of Australia. Canberra.

Milne, J. (1995). 'An analysis of the law of confidentiality with special reference to the counselling of minors.' *Australian Psychologist* 30(3): 169–74.

O'Brien, D. (1991). The impact of administrative review on Commonwealth public administration. *Administrative Law*. M. Harris and V. Waye. Sydney, Federation Press: 101–19.

O'Connor, I., P. Smyth, et al. (2000). Introduction: the challenge of change. *Contemporary Perspectives on Social Work and the Human Services: Challenges and Change*. I. O'Connor, P. Smyth, and J. Warburton. Sydney, Longman: 1–10.

Office of the Federal Privacy Commissioner (2003). Complaint Case Notes and Complaint Determinations. www.privacy.gov.au/act/casenotes. Accessed 6th December 2003.

Office of the Privacy Commissioner (2001). Guidelines on Privacy in the Health Sector. www.privacy.gov.au/publications/hg_01.html. Accessed 30th March 2003.

Ogilvie, E. (2000). *Stalking: Policing and Prosecuting Practices in Three Australian Jurisdictions*. Australian Institute of Criminology. Canberra. Trends and Issues in Criminal Justice No. 176.

O'Neill, A. (1996). The rules of evidence and administrative law. *Administrative Law and Public Administration: Form vs Substance*. K. Cole. Canberra, Australian Institute of Administrative Law Inc.: 290–312.

Parkinson, P. (2003). *Family Law Council: family law and child protection*. Child Sexual Abuse: Justice Response or Alternative Resolution? Adelaide, Australian Institute of Criminology.

Partlett, N. (1985). *Professional Negligence*. Sydney, Law Book Company.

Paterson, M. (1998). 'New rights of access to and amendment of medical records: an analysis of the relevant policy issues relating to proposed changes affecting private sector health consumers.' *Psychiatry, Psychology and Law* 5(2): 215–30.

Pearce, A. and P. Easteal (1999). 'The "domestic" in stalking: policing domestic stalking in the Australian Capital Territory.' *Alternative Law Journal* 24(4): 165–9.

Pearson, M. (1997). *The Journalist's Guide to Media Law*. Sydney, Allen & Unwin.

Preston-Shoot, M., G. Roberts, et al. (1998a). 'Social work law: from interaction to integration.' *Journal of Social Welfare and Family Law* 20(1): 65–80.

Preston-Shoot, M., G. Roberts, et al. (1998b). 'Working together in social work law.' *Journal of Social Welfare and Family Law* 20(2): 137–50.

Public Service and Merit Protection Commission (2000). *No. 1 Managing Breaches of the APS Code of Conduct*. Canberra, Commonwealth of Australia.

Puregger, M. (1998). *The Australian Guide to Chairing Meetings.* Revised Brisbane, University of Queensland Press.

Raper, M. (ed.) (1999). *The Independent Social Security Handbook.* 3rd edn. Sydney, Welfare Rights Centre.

Rees, N. (2003). 'International human rights obligations and mental health review tribunals.' *Psychiatry, Psychology and Law* 10(1): 33–43.

Renton, N. (2001). *Guide for Meetings and Organisations.* 7th edn. Sydney, Lawbook Co.

Reynolds, C. (1995). *Public Health Law in Australia.* Sydney, Federation Press.

Roberts, J. (1991). *The Committee Members' Handbook.* Melbourne, The Business Library.

Rodger, B. (1995). 'Equal treatment among professions? Public policy and social workers' liability.' *Professional Negligence* 11(4): 114–20.

Ronalds, C. (1998). *Discrimination Law and Practice.* Sydney, Federation Press.

Rose, A. (1998). ALRC review of the *Disability Services Act 1986* (Cth). *Justice for People With Disabilities: Legal and Institutional Issues.* M. Hauritz, C. Sampford, and S. Blencowe. Sydney, Federation Press: 85–108.

Rosenman, L. (2000). Turning threats into challenges: a positive perspective on the future. *Contemporary Perspectives on Social Work and the Human Services: Challenges and Change.* I. O'Connor, P. Smyth, and J. Warburton. Sydney, Longman: 190–7.

Ryan, M. (2002). Social work practice and debt. *In the Shadow of the Law: The Legal Context of Social Work Practice.* P. Swain. Sydney, Federation Press: 219–29.

Saltzman, A. and D. Furman (1999). *Law in Social Work Practice.* 2nd edn. Belmont, Wadsworth.

Sampford, C. and S. C. Blencowe (2002). Raising the standards: an integrated approach to promoting professional values and avoiding professional criminality. *Crime in the Professions.* R. Smith. Aldershot, Ashgate: 251–67.

Sarre, R. and D. Wilson (1998). *Edited Proceedings of Roundtable on Sentencing and Indigenous Peoples.* Australian Institute of Criminology. Canberra. Research and Public Policy Series No. 16.

Schloenhardt, A. (2002). 'Deterrence, detention and denial: asylum seekers in Australia.' *University of Queensland Law Journal* 22(1): 54–73.

Schloenhardt, A. (2003). *Migrant Smuggling: Illegal Migration and Organised Crime in Australia and the Asia Pacific Region.* Boston/Leiden, Martinus Nijhoff Publishers.

Setterlund, D., C. Tilse, et al.(1999). *Substitute decision making and older people*. Australian Institute of Criminology. Canberra. Trends and Issues in Criminal Justice No. 139.

Shapiro, M. (2000). Professions in the post-industrial labour market. *Contemporary Perspectives on Social Work and the Human Services: Challenges and Change*. I. O'Connor, P. Smyth, and J. Warburton. Sydney, Longman: 102–15.

Sheehan, R. (2003). 'The marginalisation of children by the legal process.' *Australian Social Work* 56(1): 28–39.

Sinclair, A. (1996). Codes in the workplace: organisational versus professional codes. *Codes of Ethics and the Professions*. M. Coady and S. Bloch. Melbourne, Melbourne University Press: 88–108.

Smith, D. (1995). 'Standards of practice for case management.' *The Journal of Care Management* 1(3): 6–16.

Smith, R. (2002). Crime in the professions: an introduction. *Crime in the Professions*. R. Smith. Aldershot, Ashgate: 3-26.

Staller, K. and S. Kirk (1998). 'Knowledge utilization in social work and legal practice.' *Journal of Sociology and Social Welfare* XXV(3): 91–113.

Stevens, B. (2003). 'In the witness box: preparing for court and giving evidence.' *InPsych* (April): 22–4.

Stewart, D. and A. Knott (2002). *Schools, Courts and the Law*. Sydney, Pearson Education Australia.

Stoesz, D. (2002). 'From social work to human services.' *Journal of Sociology and Social Welfare* XX1X(4): 19–37.

Stone, J. (2002). Evaluating the ethical and legal content of professional codes of ethics. *Regulating the Health Professions*. J. Allsop and M. Saks. London, Sage: 62–75.

Strang, H. and J. Braithwaite (eds) (2002). *Restorative Justice and Family Violence*. Cambridge, Cambridge University Press.

Sutherland, P. and A. Anforth (2001). *Social Security and Family Assistance Law*. Sydney, Federation Press and Welfare Rights and Legal Centre.

Swain, P. (1998). 'What is "belief on reasonable grounds"?' *Alternative Law Journal* 23(5): 230–3.

Swain, P. (2002a). Advocacy, administrative law and social work practice. *In the Shadow of the Law: The Legal Context of Social Work Practice*. 2nd edn. Sydney, Federation Press: 50–60.

Swain, P. (2002b). Confidentiality, record keeping and social work practice. *In the Shadow of the Law: the Legal Context of Social Work Practice*. 2nd edn. Sydney, Federation Press: 28–49.

Swain, P. (ed.) (2002c). *In the Shadow of the Law: The Legal Context of Social Work Practice*. 2nd edn. Sydney, Federation Press.

Symons, M. (2002). 'Privacy Act legislation: I've read the theory, now what about the practice?' *InPsych* (February): 10–11.

Thompson, J. (1989). *Social Workers and the Law*. Sydney, Redfern Legal Centre Publishing.

Thornton, M. (1990). *The Liberal Promise: Anti-Discrimination Legislation in Australia*. Melbourne, Oxford University Press.

Tucker, G. (1992). *Information Privacy Law in Australia*. Melbourne, Longman Professional.

Turner, J. (1997). 'Jake's progress in the Family Court.' *Law Institute Journal* (September): 40–5.

Urbis Keys Young (2002). *Research into Good Practice Models to Facilitate Access to the Civil and Criminal Justice System by People Experiencing Domestic and Family Violence*. Office of the Status of Women. Canberra. Final Report.

van Wormer, K. (1992). 'No wonder social workers feel uncomfortable in court.' *Child and Adolescent Social Work Journal* 9(2): 115–29.

Vernon, S. (1998). Legal aspects of whistleblowing in the social services. *Whistleblowing in the Social Services*. G. Hunt. London, Arnold: 222–39.

Vichie, S. (2003). 'Seeking protection in a world of conflict.' *Australian Journal of Social Issues* 38(2): 145–8.

Vigod, S., C. Bell, et al. (2003). 'Privacy of patients' information in hospital lifts: an observational study.' *British Medical Journal* 327(1st November): 1024–5.

Vogelsang, J. (2001). *The Witness Stand—A Guide for Clinical Social Workers in the Courtroom*. New York, Haworth Social Work Practice Press.

Walmsley, S., A. Abadee, et al. (2002). *Professional Liability in Australia*. Sydney, Thomson Lawbook Co.

Walmsley, S., A. Abadee, et al. (2002). *Professional Liability in Australia: Publisher Update 16th Dec 2002*. Sydney, Thomson Lawbook Co.

Walsh, F. (1995). *The Meetings Manual*. Canberra, AGPS.

Wardlaw, G. (1984). The psychologist in court: some guidelines on the presentation of psychological evidence. *Issues in Psychological Practice*. M. Nixon. Melbourne, Longman: 133–43.

Waters, N. (2001). *The new Australian privacy landscape*. UNSW Continuing Legal Education Seminar, Sydney.

Weber, L. (2003). Decisions to detain asylum seekers—routine, duty or individual choice? *Exercising Discretion: Decision-making in the Criminal Justice System and Beyond*. L. Gelsthorpe and N. Padfield. Cullompton: Devon, Willan Publishing: 164–85.

Weinbach, R. (2003). *The Social Worker as Manager: A Practical Guide to Success*. 4th edn. Boston, Pearson Education.

Wexler, D. and B. Winick (eds) (1996). *Law in a Therapeutic Key*. Durham, Carolina Academic Press.

Willison, D., K. Keshavjee, et al. (2003). 'Patients' consent preferences for research uses of information in electronic medical records: interview and survey data.' *British Medical Journal* 326(7385): 373.

Wilson, B. (2002). Health providers, complaints and unprofessional behaviour in a changing environment. *Crime in the Professions*. R. Smith. Aldershot, Ashgate: 123–38.

Wilson, R. (1997). Bringing them Home—National Enquiry into the Separation of Aboriginal and Torres Strait Islander Children from their Families. Human Rights and Equal Opportunity Commission. Sydney.

Winick, B. (2003). 'Outpatient commitment: a therapeutic jurisprudence analysis.' *Psychology, Public Policy and Law* 9(1/2): 107–44.

Winick, B. and D. Wexler (eds) (2003). *Judging in a Therapeutic Key*. Durham, Carolina Academic Press.

Young, M., J. Byles, et al. (2000). *The Effectiveness of Legal Protection in the Prevention of Domestic Violence in the Lives of Young Australian Women*. Australian Institute of Criminology. Canberra. Trends and Issues in Criminal Justice No. 148.

Zifcak, S. (2002). Towards a reconciliation of legal and social work practice. *In the Shadow of the Law: the Legal Context of Social Work Practice*. P. Swain. Sydney, Federation Press: 256–65.

Zins, C. (2001). 'Defining human services.' *Journal of Sociology and Social Welfare* XXV111(1): 3–21.

Index